Ahead of the Pack:

Balancing Your Way to Personal Success in College

Ahead of the Pack:

Balancing Your Way to Personal Success in College

JOSH RICHARDSON

THOMSON

DELMAR LEARNING

Australia   Canada   Mexico   Singapore   Spain   United Kingdom   United States

THOMSON
DELMAR LEARNING

Ahead of the Pack: Balancing Your Way to Personal Success in College
Josh Richardson

Vice President, Career Education:
Dawn Gerrain

Director of Editorial:
Sherry Gomoll

Acquisitions Editor:
Martine Edwards

Developmental Editor:
Kristen Shenfield

Editorial Assistant:
Jennifer Anderson

Director of Production:
Wendy A. Troeger

Production Coordinator:
Nina Tucciarelli

Composition:
Larry O'Brien

Illustrator:
Ryan Klemek

Director of Marketing:
Wendy Mapstone

Marketing Specialist:
Gerard McAvey

For permission to use material from this text or product, submit a request online at http://www.thomsonrights.com. Any additional questions about permissions can be submitted by e-mail to thomsonrights@thomson.com.

Library of Congress Cataloging-in-Publication Data

Richardson, Josh.
  Ahead of the pack : balancing your way to personal success in college / Josh Richardson.
      p. cm.
  Includes bibliographical references and index.
  ISBN 1-4018-8274-9
  1. College student orientation. I. Title.
  LB2343.3.R53 2005
  378.1'98--dc22
                                    2004025242

NOTICE TO THE READER

Publisher does not warrant or guarantee any of the products described herein or perform any independent analysis in connection with any of the product information contained herein. Publisher does not assume, and expressly disclaims, any obligation to obtain and include information other than that provided to it by the manufacturer.

The reader is expressly warned to consider and adopt all safety precautions that might be indicated by the activities herein and to avoid all potential hazards. By following the instructions contained herein, the reader willingly assumes all risks in connection with such instructions.

The Publisher makes no representation or warranties of any kind, including but not limited to, the warranties of fitness for particular purpose or merchantability, nor are any such representations implied with respect to the material set forth herein, and the publisher takes no responsibility with respect to such material. The publisher shall not be liable for any special, consequential, or exemplary damages resulting, in whole or part, from the readers' use of, or reliance upon, this material.

Contents

Introduction

Leaving for college is an exciting time in life, full of eagerness and anticipation. After all, you are beginning a great new chapter in the book titled YOU! Along with all the fun of college comes the responsibility that comes with being an adult. Although college is a great teacher (with enough mistakes to learn from, too), it's better and easier if you, the student, can learn without having to crash and burn first.

Many students have found it possible to have fun, perform well, and grow as a person while in college, and that's my wish for every one of you. In *Ahead of the Pack: Balancing Your Way to Personal Success in College*, my goal is to give you a comprehensive glimpse of what's ahead so that you can prepare for, rather than repair your own college experience.

Ahead of the Pack contains loads of student experience and tried-and-true advice. That, combined with the sharp observations of the Advisor—perhaps the best college advisor you will ever know—will help you develop as a student and a person.

Ahead of the Pack will help you understand college from the inside. After that, it's your job to begin balancing your way to college success. I hope that you learn as much from reading this book as I did from writing it, and that you will use the tools inside to lead with the right foot!

FEATURES OF THIS BOOK

The Advisor

The Advisor is the voice of experience. Condensed from interviews with college advisors, corporate managers, and college professors to name a few, the Advisor's input is well-heeled in experience and appears throughout the book.

Student Quotes

Hundreds of students were interviewed and surveyed in completing this book, specifically to gain a broad range of opinions on the same subjects. The quotes are included so that you may identify with the perspectives of college students from all backgrounds and all walks of life.

Student Profiles

The Student Profiles are meant to illustrate the book's message with real students' stories—and make you think. Questions are included in many of the profiles, and I encourage you to answer them.

Motivational Quotes

Appearing at the beginning of each chapter, the Motivational Quotes are meant to begin the chapter on the right foot. Hopefully, you find them mildly entertaining, too.

Figures and Worksheets

The worksheets are designed to help you, the reader, take action steps throughout the text. There is no progress without action, so be sure to complete the worksheets as you see them. Extras of certain worksheets may be found in Appendix C.

Online Companion

An online companion is available to accompany the text. It includes worksheets from the text for ease of printing and re-use. To access the companion, go to http://www.CareerSuccess.Delmar.com, click on Online Companions in the navigation bar, and search by author (Richardson) or title (*Ahead of the Pack*).

ACKNOWLEDGEMENTS

My thanks to everyone who helped with this book. I would like to personally thank Dr. Robert Oman, for your encouragement, advice, and generous gift of your time; this book would not have been possible without your help. I am grateful to Arlene Robinson, for your editing genius; to Martine Edwards, for believing in the project; to Shelley Esposito for your patience, steadiness, and advice; to everyone I interviewed or surveyed, for your time; and to my family and friends—you have had to deal with this book almost as much as me!

The Deal with College

"What's important is finding out what works for you."
—Henry Moore

THE "COLLEGE EXPERIENCE": WHAT WILL IT MEAN TO *YOU*?

College is stuck right in the middle of the prime years of your whole life, and you have seen a million movies telling how much fun it is. No wonder everyone thinks of it as the be-all, end-all good time it appears to be. There are the "Spring Break" stories and *Animal House* movies—that certain idea of what college should be like. And then there is what college is really like.

College is more of a stage in life than just a place, and many others have been through it before. I am guessing that you have heard all kinds of stories from friends and relatives about what college life is like, or what it is really about. These folks are convinced

"There's a lifestyle that's been promoted by movies that just isn't real. A lot of people keep pushing at that. There is a lot more satisfaction in writing a good paper, seeing your column get published in the school newspaper, or any other accomplishment; more than a one minute keg stand. No one counts their beer afterwards."
—Senior, Mass Communications Major

1

> "Life begins in college, not just after!"
>
> —Junior, Economics Major

Did You Know About These College Students?

Before they were famous actors, actresses, governors, athletes, rock stars, and businessmen, these celebrities were just another one of you college students.

- **Tommy Lee Jones**—A Harvard student who was roommates with Al Gore.
- **Arnold Schwarzenegger**—Studied business at Wisconsin University.
- **Kevin Costner**—Studied marketing and finance at California State University at Fullerton.
- **Jerry Greenfield**—The other half of Ben & Jerry's attended Oberlin College as a premed major.
- **Mick Jagger**—The Rolling Stones front man attended the London School of Economics.
- **Rick de Oliveira**—A producer of *The Real World* and *Road Rules* on MTV graduated from the University of South Florida.
- **Brooke Shields**—Princeton grad with a degree in French Literature.
- **Jack Welch**—Legendary CEO of General Electric was a grad of both the University of Massachusetts at Amherst and the University of Illinois at Champaign.
- **Donald Trump**—Billionaire real estate mogul and famous personality, studied business at the University of Pennsylvania.

their experience was the only right way (or wrong way) to do college. "Go to community college first," "Grades are more critical than any other element," "Networking is more important than anything else," "Save your money and live at home." Sound familiar? Sure, it's advice coming from every angle. If you live life on campus just like they say you should, you will be sure to make it out a success.

Well, so they say. But everyone's experience is different, and every campus is different. The basics of college success—not just getting by—are the same everywhere. College is about balance. There are many aspects of life that will fall into the mix, but balancing them all is the key. We are going to try to get past the differences that exist from place to place and person to person. Sure, if you attend a community college, you might not have Fraternity Row. If you attend a small liberal arts school, you might not be attending those 70,000-crowd football games. But that's all gravy, as they say. We are going to get down to the meat.

The best college experience is figuring out what college will mean to you. No book, teacher, or guru can figure out your wants, desires, and expectations and put them into action. That is your job. The basics in this book teach you how to make the most out of college. The doing part is up to you.

In the meantime, I want to get you thinking about college from a different angle—in fact, from a variety of angles! Instead of looking at college from just one perspective, use the perceptions of others who came before you and succeeded. Pay close attention to the Student Quotes and Profiles, see what others have done, and learn from their experiences. Many students became part of this book for that very reason, to present many takes on the same journey—college.

WHAT IS COLLEGE WORTH?

What is college worth these days? It had better be a lot. After all, it is quite expensive. Taking on thousands of dollars in loans or spending your relative's money for a diploma is beginning to sound a bit dated. And then there are the stories of Internet millionaires who dropped out of or never attended college. These two thoughts can make anyone take a second look at sacrificing four years and many, many paychecks.

The stories we read about are a little skewed, though, and the price of college has gotten a bad rap because of it. We somehow miss the success stories—the millions of people whom college has helped, whether in searching for a job, teaching an approach to problem solving, or building confidence. We hear that Bill Gates dropped out of college, but we do not hear that movie director

Spike Lee majored in mass communications. Sure, Michael Dell, the founder of Dell Computers left college without graduating, but Warren Buffett, arguably the most successful investor ever, did graduate. This does not prove that college is worthwhile, but these examples show that a university can offer a great training ground for any career, whether it is making movies or trading stocks.

Three Distinct Advantages

My suggestion is to start thinking about college differently, while remembering the well-known benefits too. You can gain three distinct advantages by earning a diploma, namely: credentials to succeed, time to learn skills, and confidence to get ahead.

Credentials to Succeed

Even if you do not go for advanced degrees (B.A., B.S., Masters, Ph.D.), the fact is that many employers today will not consider an applicant who does not have advanced certification or a college degree. Possessing a level of credentials is as necessary now as having a high school degree was 20 years ago.

THE ADVISOR SAYS:

For the best jobs, it may not be required to have a college degree/certification, but landing an interview, let alone a job offer without one can be almost impossible.

In addition to just obtaining a degree, performing at a high level in school can add to your résumé. Being a Dean's List member or honor society inductee will certainly help you no matter which path you choose in school.

Unless you have stumbled onto the cure for the common cold (or the infamous hangover), there is a good chance that a college degree will widen your career options; and adding more honors to your name will boost your salability even more.

Time to Learn Skills

THE ADVISOR SAYS:

Some students are very eager to start on the rest of their life, and college is just getting in the way of the real world. That's an unfortunate attitude to have, because college is a lot more than the course work to get your diploma. College helps develop a personal philosophy of life in addition to practical skills for the workforce.

College teaches students how to solve problems. There are many people working today, far out of college, who claim that they do not

---

More Credentials

Try having one of these on your degree—never hurts when job hunting or applying to grad school. Although the numbers can differ a bit from school to school, they tend to fall in these ranges:

- **Cum laude:** Graduating with honors—usually given to students with a cumulative GPA of 3.500 to 3.749
- **Magna cum laude:** Graduating with high honors—usually given to students with a cumulative GPA of 3.750 to 3.899
- **Summa cum laude:** Graduating with highest honors—for all of the rock stars out there, given to students graduating with a whopping 3.900 to 4.000

use any of the materials or knowledge they learned in college. I am willing to bet that these people are sorely mistaken. But when they are right, it is usually because of one of two things:

1. These people lived passively in college—they did not engage in the learning experience. If you sit idle in college and do not work or think, you waste more than half of the reason for attending. Oh, you may receive the credentials, but you will have left behind the time to learn skills and the confidence to get ahead.

2. Some people fail to realize the value behind learning a way of thinking. This is another benefit college will give to you. Beyond the math, science, and humanities, universities teach an approach to thinking.

STUDENT PROFILE—Ed B. on College Learning

College taught me how to think. Everyone there knew that regurgitating formulas was a sure way to perform poorly in any class, and rehashing someone else's thoughts was far from a real learning experience. We knew that learning an approach, where we thought critically about the question or problem, was the true path to learning. In chemistry, we learned how to evaluate problems based on the facts and from there to use our critical thinking skills. Although professionally I do not use the facts I learned in chemistry, I certainly use the critical thinking skills I was taught.

Though the two (chemistry and business) may seem to hold nothing in common on the surface, the similarities lie in my approaches to the problems. The time at my new job has been exciting and challenging, and learning, the way I did at college, has enabled me to think in the right direction. Success comes from your ability to solve problems and work analytically, not necessarily using every formula you ever memorized.

➤ *Do you agree or disagree with Ed that learning in college is deeper than just the facts, and why?*

People can use their degrees in different ways. Some use the book knowledge they learned in school; others may find the social engagements at college more useful. For example, a structural engineer will definitely use the formulas and applications taught in physics classes to design a bridge. On the other hand, a finance major might end up being a salesperson or manager and use very little of the book knowledge gained in college. However, the attention to detail required for a finance degree and the social experience a person gains in clubs, fraternities/sororities, or in student government are always extremely useful in the job market.

So college, regardless of anything else, gives students an opportunity to develop a way of thinking: to solve problems and approach situations. An overlooked benefit? Sure. But one that many millions of college graduates have used to take them to the top of their professions.

Confidence to Get Ahead

To gain the most benefit out of college, you must put forth a solid effort. Just as the benefits of the Time to Learn Skills in college depend on the effort put forth, so does the confidence level. The four years at school do not necessarily build confidence, but working hard to understand the concepts you are taught will. In this respect, it is no different from any other time in your life. When you do well in school, you begin to feel smart and confident and feel that you can handle any curveballs life throws. This might be considered a fringe benefit, but gaining confidence will most certainly pay off later in any avenue of work or study you choose.

Luckily, college provides ample opportunities to assume leadership roles in social situations as well. Leading an organization (club, fraternity/sorority, student government, etc.) can help to build a comfort level with making decisions, public speaking, and overall self-assurance in your abilities. College is far from one-dimensional, and the resources available can be of great assistance for increasing your confidence and comfort with leading and getting ahead.

> "It's not that I couldn't have done it, but walking in the door, knowing that I was resourceful at solving problems and experienced in working through financials, gave me the *confidence* to do well in my internship and make a better impression on my boss *and* clients."
>
> —Senior, Finance Major

SUCCESS REQUIRES SOME QUESTIONING

Finding your own college success is going to take some questioning—starting with yourself. Just remember that *many* roads lead to success, not just one! There is a lot to college life. Not just grades, or parties, or any one thing, a healthy college life is a balance of many different activities. Studying leads to academic success; social interaction provides a break and a chance to make friendships; exercising and eating healthier foods increases your energy level, appearance, confidence, and overall health. All of these activities, together, lead to a fun, fulfilling, and productive life on campus, but first you have to ask some questions.

Take a minute and write down your expectations for college—what you think you can reasonably expect. Then, write down your desires for college—what may not be possible, but sure would be nice. This is to help you find out where you stand, and knowing where you stand can help you find out where you want to go. And knowing where you want to go will help you travel in the right direction! So, take a minute and fill out Worksheet 1. No matter if it sounds grand, less-than-amazing, or downright dumb, just list it. (You will see the benefits later, I promise.)

WORKSHEET 1-1

The Difference Between Expectations and Desires

Expect is what you think will happen.
Desire is what you want to happen.

No matter how small, or insignificant, write what you *expect* and *desire*.*

1. What do you **expect** to get out of college this semester?

2. This year?

3. By graduation?

4. What do you **desire** to get out of college this semester?

5. This year?

6. By graduation?

---

* Hold on to this sheet. In Chapter 5, "*Maximizing Your Time and Energy*," we come back to these answers.

Now that you have an idea of your destination, you can begin learning the tools to help get you there. When you are finished, I know that you will understand the tools for achieving all you expect in your college life. From the grades to healthy eating, from a workout plan to a budgeting plan, get ready to become a campus expert.

GRADES, PLAYTIME, AND THE FRESHMAN 15: COLLEGE Q & A

Students usually have some basic questions about the college experience. Unfortunately, the answers are not all that easy to find. Here is what many students, including me, found out.

Q: Is college fun?

A: College is definitely fun. There are many organizations, clubs, and social events to keep you busy for multiple lifetimes. But to enjoy the most exciting four years of your life, you have to want to have fun. Remember, you are an adult. No one is going to force you to get involved. You will often have to seek out the opportunity to have fun. The work is there too, but fun is an enormous part of college. I highly recommend that you try some.

Q: Is college a giant party?

A: Only if you want it to be. Let's say that you are in that minority who only wants to get a college degree and a good job afterward. For you, college can still be a great time. Or, if all you want is an extended spring break, you will get what you pay for. But just because college has its share of good times, the phrase "one big party" probably is not the best way to describe it, or think of it.

Q: Is college full of work?

A: Yes and no (and you thought you were confused before!). To make great grades will definitely take work—let's be honest. The key to making the work livable is to pick a major that interests you. The more the work interests you, the less effort it seems to take. The bulk of your courses are your major, so they are your choice.

Q: Can I still have a life if I want to do well in school?

A: Even if you take hard classes or get stuck with a large workload for an entire semester, no one will even blink if you take your work seriously. But to do well in classes, you do not have to wear a pocket protector and speak only about mathematical theory. It's all right to dress and act like a normal person. Remember: This is not high school anymore. The whole "dumb is cool" thing is way over. The better you learn to manage your time, the easier it will be to juggle everything that you want to do. There will still be time left for fun stuff.

Q: Is there any way around the Freshman 15?

A: Unlike the Bermuda Triangle—weird, unexplained, and mysterious—fitness is mostly just common sense. You do not have to be the college version of Richard Simmons; after all, spending hours exercising and eating rice cakes is out. All you have to do is be consistent and reasonable. If you work out every day that you plan and eat like a normal human being—not a starving refugee left in a Baskin Robbins—you can look and feel like a million bucks. You can throw the Freshman 15 myth out with the *Animal House* myth; it is all about staying focused on your goals and doing what you plan to do.

WHY YOU ARE THERE . . . REALLY

It would be fun to say that you are at college just to have a good time. On the other hand, it would be a total drag to say that you are there just to learn about literature, economics, and science. The truth is, all of these are a part of being a college student. Some more than others, but each reason for being in college has its own purpose and needs careful attention.

In no particular order, here are some of the reasons you are becoming a college graduate:

- To learn more about the real world, and become a better person
- To gain knowledge personally, academically, and socially
- To get out of the pile and stand out
- To discover your potential

In other words, college is the preparation for a broader world. It is where you can learn how to succeed, put forth the change, and make a difference. Every student perceives the experience a little bit differently, but there is a way for everyone to have a great college experience and not stumble out of it the way too many grads do—burned out and lacking any true direction. You can make it through college, graduate, and be able to look back—and ahead—with pride and purpose.

"Initially I thought college would be about meeting people and rigorous academic activity; when I left though, I realized how much I had grown as a person."

—Graduate, Business Management Major

Through the following chapters, I (and many other students) will tell you all about college, how to handle being there, and what to look out for to push your success to new heights. You do not need to be David Blaine to use the tools in this book. You only need to be a person with a desire to see results and a willingness to give the ideas a try. This book will help you gain that balance you need to succeed.

Now that college has some meaning, and you have a better idea of the truth about real college life, let's dig in!

Knowing What Matters

All Work, No Play...

"The best and safest thing is to keep a balance in your life, acknowledge the great powers around us and in us. If you can do that, and live that way, you are really a wise man."
—Euripides

FINDING THE BALANCE

Keeping your eye on the important stuff in college can be tricky. I guarantee that you will ask yourself many times over, "What matters?" After all, if you do not know what matters first, then it is a little difficult to get focused.

Ask many people today what college is all about, and you are bound to hear many conflicting answers. There are the partiers, who believe that college is the last chance to have a blowout every night. Ask the members of academia, and you may walk out thinking college is only an intellectual experience.

> "There's a balance there. People tend to stay too focused on the academics, too focused on the socialization, or too focused on fitness. It's tough to gain balance, but it is possible."
>
> —Senior, Psychology Major

Personal Success

Personal success means defining success in your own terms. Success to one student is not necessarily success to another. Every person has different talents, abilities, and strong points. Balancing your own life with your interests is the only way to find true success. Living someone else's dream will never do it.

> "If you have completed the plan you decided on, you have been a complete success."
>
> —Junior, Philosophy Major

> "You may be in trouble in job hunting if you haven't done at least fairly well. There will be stories where that isn't true, but in general, you'll get a return on your investment for doing well."
>
> —Graduate, Chemistry Major

Sure, both camps have success in mind when they discuss a college education's goals. They just define success differently. To a certain degree, both are right. What matters is the perspective, and to take a little bit from both sides. Obviously, your time at school is a time to learn. We know that. But this is also a time to meet people and develop interpersonal skills.

Moreover, college is a time to begin understanding yourself. Personal success (emphasis on "personal") is best achieved through a balanced approach to life, and college is life for a number of years.

A straight-A student who never gets out of the classroom is likely unhappy. Neither is a party animal who never studies. And it is likely that neither student is paying much attention to staying healthy. How about the students in between? That can vary, but in general, students who let either the partying or classroom take over their life are not likely to be happy.

So, happiness is best realized through a mix of performing well in school, letting loose here and there, as well as staying healthy and in shape. Every aspect of college life can benefit you, so try to find the right balance of all of them.

GPA AND ACADEMICS *MATTER!*

I know what you are thinking: "No, No, No . . . not a lecture on grades and school!" Well, this isn't anything like a lecture, but it is definitely about school and grades. So why academics? What's the big deal?

Three Reasons

Schoolwork is a big deal.

1. It teaches an approach to learning and problem solving.

   Critical thinking is important in today's workplace, where, eventually, we all use our knowledge. No matter how much trouble you had with studying before, you can develop these skills if you work on them. College, more than any time before, is the time for refining these important skills.

2. It provides a safety net, no matter which path you eventually choose (job, advanced degree, or anything else).

3. It gives an opportunity to shine and impress yourself and others.

   If you have been a great student so far, you know how good it feels to get a great report card. Well, I did not when I arrived at college. In fact, I had not been a great student by any stretch of the imagination. I am not sure whether I thought that working for high grades was too time-consuming or just impossible, but I blew it off. Yet when I did decide to work hard at school and began receiving those high marks, it became inspiring. I impressed myself and everyone who knew me. No, I amazed myself and everyone who knew me. However, the most important point for you will be impressing yourself. Take it from one who has been there: Realizing what you are capable of is motivating and inspiring.

STUDENT PROFILE—Jeff S. and Indecision

It is very common for people to switch their path in college. For me, medical school was the goal when starting college, but, part way through, that changed. I became unsure of my choice, wondering whether that was the place for me. I always worked hard through college and received great grades in all my classes, but I was not sure whether medical school made sense for me.

I was unable to make up my mind, but in the mean time, I had to find a focus. I directed my energy toward my grades, figuring that perfect grades could never hurt me whether I decided on medical school, another graduate school, or a job search. Eventually I began to look at graduate school, and my grades helped me get my foot in the door. My professors took me seriously and were helpful in assisting me through the mentoring process, mainly because they knew I was a hard worker.

I know that a good academic performance will not overcome every obstacle, but it certainly made my undecided life easier—and much less stressful.

➤ *Do you think Jeff handled his uncertainty in the correct way? Why or why not?*

➤ *What would you do if you felt uncertain like Jeff?*

Academics have a lot more value than just how the grades look on your transcript. After you get in the groove of studying hard for classes and turning in research papers on time, you will begin to see the underlying value—you will have developed a first-class work ethic that will go with you in anything you do.

Ahead, I give you more information about schoolwork, tests, and professors. If you use these correctly, your college experience can be successful.

PEOPLE, PEOPLE, AND PEOPLE

You Need It Now

Your relationships are the single most important part of life in general. College is no different. Relating to people is one of the most important skills you can refine, or perhaps learn as a human. That is why the social atmosphere is probably the most exciting thing about college life. You might think that the people I mentioned previously were students who looked at college as just an intellectual experience. On the contrary. For them, too, college was an extremely social experience, and they agree with me that to create a successful college life, it is important to cultivate relationships.

But, it is not as easy for some of us as it is for others. For many, college is the first time away from home. There may not be parents, brothers or sisters, or even old friends to hang around with. The teachers you were used to have been replaced with a group of strangers whom you rarely ever see or talk to. To fill that void, students have to create some new friends and strike out to get to know the other people in college life. Easily said, but making friends (especially if you are away at school) can be tough.

If you feel uncomfortable in social settings or have some trouble making friends, it may be easier to fix than you think. Just take a moment and consider this: What type of traits do you enjoy in people?

- People who are welcoming
- Individuals accepting of your personality
- Kind people
- Friends who laugh at your jokes
- People who invite you to do things

The list could go on forever, but the point stands: Treat others how you would like to be treated, and you will gain friends. It is that simple!

You Need It Later

When you are thinking about people and social life in college, do not forget the importance of networking. More often than you think, landing a terrific job or gaining admission to a grad school program can come down to one thing: the people you know. In jobs, networking gives you an edge over other applicants. That's because many job openings are filled through acquaintances of current employees. So it's a simple deduction; the more employees you know at different companies, the better chance you have landing a job there, or at least having the chance to interview.

"To be successful, know that there's an academic life and personal life. It's all about doing well in school but also meeting people, interacting with people, and learning from them."
—Senior, Education Major

"My grandmother passed away during school and my friends were really there for me. Without them, I do not know how I would have handled it."
—Senior Psychology Major

"Initially I focused on learning everything, memorizing everything—the facts, but talking to my peers ended up being half of my education, at least."
—Graduate, History Major

"You'll get a good education wherever you go; the name doesn't matter, it's what you make of it and learning from other people."
—Senior, Criminology Major

Network—a widespread group of people who stay in contact informally to assist each other when needed

Networking is one of the easiest ways to enhance your chances of finding a job, or continuing on for further education—basically it helps anything where an application is in order! Networking is what most of us enjoy: making friends and finding common ground with other people. As far as where to network, that is up to you. Commonly, school clubs, societies, and organizations have numerous opportunities; just ask around.

THE ADVISOR SAYS:

It is just a fact that if you know someone who works for the company, you have a much better chance at getting an interview, and hence a better shot at the job.

Communication: The Skills

Diving into the college social life is fun and will improve your communication skills. The types of jobs that require little or no personal interaction are becoming fewer and farther between. So, whether you plan to start your own business or work for someone else, the ability to communicate effectively is crucial to your success. Following are some simple starters to communicating more effectively.

Essential Communication Skills: The List

- Be a listener. It is impossible to communicate if you cannot listen. Beyond listening—sometimes called "active listening" —it is important to ask questions and be involved with the conversation.

- Be succinct. Nothing is more frustrating than listening to people walk circles around their point. Extend others the courtesy of expressing your points amply, but succinctly.

- Practice. Communication skills take practice to learn and master. Being involved around campus will give you the opportunity to become better at listening and getting your point across.

"Communicate with people over the phone. Using just instant messaging or the computer can make person-to-person interaction strange. Plus, if you can type 50 words per minute and talk 120, why type?"

—Junior, Computer Science Major

THE ADVISOR SAYS:

If you have plans to move up in the corporate world, or any world for that matter, you must be able to get your point across quickly and effectively. Great communication skills are key.

How They Will Help

Much to the chagrin of many, the Old Boy Network—getting special treatment because of who you are and who you know—still exists. It exists in all lines of work, so it is not only business grads who need to know how to network. A chemistry major who wants to attend graduate school can improve her chances by meeting professors at conferences, or even around her school. Never underestimate the power of comments like "Let me make a couple of phone calls and see what I can do." Professors are important to network with because they hold some degree of power, and may even provide an important key to an advanced degree or graduate school—letters of recommendation.

The alumni association is another gold mine for networking. Although not everyone will be thrilled that you both attended the same school, it can be an easy way to get your foot in the door for an interview or some face time.

Keep Working on 'Em

If you cannot work a room like Bill Clinton yet, don't fret. Some people have more of a knack for communication skills than others. Yet everyone can improve. Like anything, creating terrific interpersonal skills requires practice: one more reason to get out there and get to know some people. Plus, there are an endless number of books, workshops, and general help available on this subject. Learn these skills, because they can help in more ways than one.

YOUR BODY

What goes with you to class? home for the holidays? on late-night library runs? Friday night parties? even the shower?

Your body!

Clothes might make the (wo)man, but the body is the most powerful engine in your college garage. The way I like to think of my body is as a close friend. Just like close friends can do, your body can make you happy, sad, excited, or depressed. But unlike a close friend, if your body is making you miserable, it is impossible to dump it and get another.

Making your health a priority is of utmost importance throughout college—not only because college is a time where life-long habits begin, but because of the immediate benefits a healthy body will bring you.

Watch Yourself Feel Better

We all take showers every day (I hope!), and there are mirrors in every bathroom. We walk to class and pass windows, or use glass doors. Guess whom we see staring back at ourselves? You guessed it. Seeing our image is unavoidable. How we look is a constant reminder to ourselves—for good or for bad. So, improving your body can add to your confidence every single day, multiple times per day. The body is the most tangible symbol of our work, and of the goals we have set. So here's the opportunity, every day, to give one more boost of energy and confidence to your life.

Looks Aren't Everything

Now that I have said that, I am going to say something else that sounds like a contradiction. Looks aren't everything. Sure, they are part of the whole picture. But you have to understand that some of us may have metabolic problems that prevent a superlean physique or a rock-hard image. Here's what I mean.

Jake was a hard working, committed guy. He loved to run, swim, and bike. He even did some triathlons. There was one thing different about him and the other athletes though; Jake was dozens of pounds overweight, and no matter what he did, he could not lose it. He was a champion triathlete; he ate healthy; and he had lived healthy for years. But people who saw him on the street most likely could not tell the difference between him and the typical couch potato. What they did not see was his ability to throw on running shoes at a moment's notice and go for a 12-mile run, a long bike ride, or a swim that would drown most people! Yes, even though he was technically overweight, Jake was quite fit and was congratulated after every race by many people (probably those that he had beaten!). Jake could not help his inability to lose the weight, and he definitely proves that people are built differently.

The point here is that judging others, or yourself for that matter, solely based on looks is a dangerous way to live and will lead to an unhappy existence.

Unlike grades, a game-winning catch, or landing a great college acceptance, keeping in shape gives a feeling—not necessarily a look that never quits. It is the most visible result of effort, and the benefits to other areas of your college life can be endless.

Eating and Exercising Disorders

Because we know that our bodies (and our perceptions of them) can be a powerful force in our lives, it is important to realize when exercising and eating healthy are getting out of control. Disorders relating to eating and exercising are, sadly, far too common in society (and college campuses) today. As mentioned previously, looks aren't everything! The benefits of exercise are the satisfaction, discipline, and fresh feeling you can gain; not weighing X number of pounds and solely how thin or muscular you look. For some warning signs relating to these disorders, turn to Chapter 12.

"Working out can make you feel proud of your physical accomplishments. It can also inspire other people. After running a half marathon, I inspired another person at my job to run a race herself. You can encourage others through leading by example."

— Senior, Biomedical Sciences Major

Your Body as a Stepping-Stone

Whether you agree with his politics or not, bodybuilder-turned-actor, turned-businessman and philanthropist, now governor, Arnold Schwarzenegger is a testament to fitness and its underlying power. Arnold has often talked about the discipline and determination that bodybuilding taught him. He has spoken about how the mental benefits from exercise transferred to other areas of life, including the number of projects he has accomplished. The discipline he learned as a bodybuilder easily transferred to business, philanthropy, and campaigning. So whenever you think of not going to the gym or putting on your shoes and going for a walk or run, listen to Arnold's strong accent in the back of your head saying, "Just do it!"

Arnold's life story shows that discipline is not exclusive to just one part of a person's life. More often than not, a disciplined person in one respect will show a similar resolve in any area to which he applies himself. Using fitness to exercise your mind and willpower is a tried-and-true way of boosting your performance in life, and it works no differently in college. Applying that dedication to schoolwork, making new friends, or finding creative outlets can make the difference between reaching your desires and not even coming close.

I am not making this stuff up. The corporate world has begun to include this type of training for employees. LGE Performance Systems is a consulting agency that works with professional athletes, corporations, and individuals to incorporate the mental training techniques of high performance athletes into the business world. Just as these principles can be applied to sports and business, so can they work for college life.

Sound nutrition falls directly in line with exercise. Eating a healthy array of foods helps keep your energy level high and your mind sharp.

Later, in Chapter 11, you can piece together your own exercise plan using our advice and suggestions. To be safe, it is best to get a checkup with your doctor at the campus health center before starting any kind of workout plan. Your doctor can give you important advice, tailored to your personal expectations and concerns.

Exercise is considered a real component of overall well-being. The benefits begin immediately, and the long-term advantages are even better. Even if you have never exercised before, you can lay the groundwork for a healthy life in college. If you do, your life now, and later, will be easier and more fun. Affecting exercise and most everything else in your life still comes down to attitude.

"Let exercise work for you in a variety of ways. Let it broaden your perspective and widen your outlook all while making you a better person. Commit to a daily regimen of energizing your body. It will make the college experience less stressful, more pleasurable, and more productive. Staying in great shape will give you a mental edge."

—Senior, Biology Major

ATTITUDE *IS* EVERYTHING

Does attitude determine circumstances, or do circumstances determine attitude? After all, what came first, the chicken or the egg? Many times, attitude is a compilation of the other events in your life, but at the same time, the greatest people in history have lived by deciding how they will feel. It's true: Your attitude about the future affects where and how far you go.

The difference is living actively or passively.

A passive attitude puts your circumstances in control. In college, there are rough periods and tough times personally, academically, and socially when nothing seems to go right. An active person decides how great they will feel. Unless you actively decide that you will get through the rough times and focus on the future, the passive, depressing circumstances will take over. Take a stance and live actively! It's important in college and for the rest of your life: Your attitude is the basis for everything else that happens to you—and most important, you do have control. So exercise it!

Keep It Positive

Attitude is everything. Attitude determines outlook, and outlook determines results.

Three Techniques

To gain a positive attitude in the face of tough circumstances, try these techniques:

1. **Be optimistic.** With the great outcome as your focus, your motivation will stay higher, and your performance will be enhanced.

2. **Expect to experience disappointments along the way.** We all experience setbacks. Knowing that this will happen can help dampen the blow when your plan does not work out perfectly.

3. **Review your goals, and your progress toward those goals, often.** Chapter 5 is all about goal setting and attaining those dreams, so there will be plenty of direction for you. Reviewing your journey will keep you tuned in to the progress of your efforts—that even on large goals, you are moving. Feeling that you are going nowhere can turn your feelings negative very quickly.

Your time in college can have a real impact on your life ahead, so take on college with a positive attitude. Learn as much as you can in every way, and keep faith in yourself.

KEEP THE BALANCE

Everything I have said to this point applies to staying healthy. Sure, in an extreme situation, working out may take a backseat to studying. So will too many social engagements. This does not change the fact that a balance of these elements is the framework for a successful experience on campus. This balanced framework will lay the foundation for everything that happens to you in college, and after college.

Remember, college can be a very short time—1 year, 2 years, 4 years (depending on your particular program). Everything you do today, though, will affect where you start tomorrow. Do college the balanced way, and you will be prepared for tough spots and hard circumstances down the line.

- Make friends with students, professors, and people outside of college. This will keep your life fulfilling and fun while beginning a network for the years to come.

- Study your hardest in school. Learning all you can will always be a feather in your cap and benefit you in direct and indirect ways.

- Stay healthy. As we discussed, your body goes with you everywhere. It can be a great helper or a great hinderer in your quest for personal success in college.

- Finally, get and keep an upbeat attitude. This outlook will greatly determine each of the other elements in the mix.

Adjusting

"Just when I think I have learned the way to live, life changes."
—Hugh Prather

NEW SURROUNDINGS

College, like any other new place, can seem intimidating. Even so, settling in to college is the first step toward a successful college career. Because you are going to be there for a while, it is a good idea to make campus feel like home. To begin with the right foot forward, it is important to make your surroundings comfortable.

First Impression: Orientation

The purpose of this extravaganza is to introduce the new students to all the amenities of the institution or university. This includes campus resources, campus layout, and helpful hints about almost anything.

"Pay attention during orientation instead of looking for a date. They give tons of useful information and will get you prepared for the start of classes."

—Senior, Computer Science Major

Many times, there will be a mix of administrators, older students, and others from the university to give information or answer questions. Do not be bashful. If you want to know the school's policy on something or have a general question about the school, this is the time to ask. The students who help are usually the most outgoing and will give you an earful about your question. Orientation is also a great time to meet new friends. All the students there are new, one just as clueless as the next, and ready to meet some companions.

Diversity

Diversity is a hot topic on campuses nationwide, and for good reason. Meeting and associating with people from different backgrounds broadens perspective and adds to the education at college. As another student told me, much of your education will come from your peers—and the more diversified, the more there is to learn.

Expect to

- learn about different beliefs, religions, and values.
- see differences in the small things (speaking, dressing, eating).
- witness an eclectic group of life experiences.

I was lucky to attend a university with large student diversity. In fact, one of my roommates for 2 years was Indian. Through discussing points of view and listening to his stories, I learned a great deal about the Indian culture. I gained perspective into the large adjustment of moving to a new country, from learning the language to assimilating into the schools. It was not always intellectual learning, though; I always enjoyed trying his food and he mine. So, from the large experiences to the everyday chores—like eating— I was able to learn.

Here are some tips on dealing with diversity:

- Be unassuming. Learn from differences rather than judge them.
- Share your experiences. People come from different places, so each person has something to share. Let others learn from you, as you learn from them.
- Be inclusive. Invite people to hang out and get to know students who are different from you.

Where to Go: Where the Heck Is Everything?

One of the most stressful times on a college campus can be finding your first classes. (Orientation is thorough, but there is no hand-holding on the way to your first class.) Colleges are notorious for putting buildings in strange places, on other parts of the campus, or just renaming places without updating the map. Classrooms tend to be numbered rather strangely, too. Finding classrooms can feel like an Easter egg hunt sometimes, especially if they are located in one of those random, tucked-away buildings. Why wouldn't 201 be next to 202? That sounds logical. But 202 may be around the bend, kitty-corner, and down two flights of stairs.

Finding classes does not have to be boring though. One student explained how, at the start of her freshman year, a large group of people from her dorm found their classes together. They scoured the campus for each building while making the outing a social event. Starting to meet hall mates, if you live on campus, can begin to build your social network from the moment you arrive. Smart, huh?

Do not take for granted that you know where your classes are until you have been there in person. Campuses are infamous for following absolutely no pattern (that anybody can figure out, anyway). They are also prone to change rooms on the first day of class.

Getting Around

If you attend a large institution, transportation can be an issue. To be a successful college student, you have to get to class. If a class is far, far away, walking may be a little bit tedious, or even a problem if your schedule is cutting it close. Driving, or for many, riding the bus (some schools do not allow all students to have cars) could become a necessity—many campuses nowadays have bus systems. Of course, there are also bikes. Bikes are great for exercise and quick commuting across campus, and they are cheap (obviously depending on the bike you purchase)! So, before classes, grab a couple of maps and figure out your route.

To make sure you get to class successfully your first day:

- Do a dry run before classes begin.

- If you are driving, purchase the correct sticker, and find the parking lots available to students. (You might be slapped with a hefty ticket if you forget the sticker or park in the wrong place.)

- If you are biking, locate the closest rack to lock your bike. And yes, lock your bike from the start. Many students learn this the hard way—by losing their bikes to theft.

- If you are bussing, find your route and try it out.

Following some or all of these tips will keep the first week's stress level to a minimum.

THE DORMS—YOUR SANCTUARY

If you live on campus, moving into the dorms is your first taste of college. It's a simple procedure: Your parents help move your stuff in, your mom cries, they leave, and wham! You are living the college life!

I remember arriving. Guys playing guitars and video games . . . some already with a case of beer . . . bongo drums at 2:00 A.M., waking up to the party next door, and laughing hysterically at the practical jokes that got pulled.

The dorms are the best introduction for the next years to come. Dorm life is a socially rich environment where you will get the chance to interact with and meet a wide variety of people. The simple fact that colleges take students from outside your neighborhood, and even outside your country, broadens the range of backgrounds and experiences you will encounter.

Getting Settled and Comfortable

To jump-start your successful college career, make your room comfortable. Would you have a better day waking up in a concrete jail cell or in a five-star hotel in Maui? That's a little extreme, but being ready to tackle the day can definitely be affected by your surroundings. A bed and a computer desk may be all that you have inside your room. Still, there is no need to drop thousands of dollars renovating your dorm room. Making it nice might only cost you a few bucks. Search out those poster sales on campus and pick up some wall art. While you're at it, grab a cheap rug at Wal-Mart. Make sure you have comfortable sheets. A plush pillow will be important.

If your college has especially small dorm rooms, consider bunk beds or a loft (one of those wooden bunks with room underneath for a desk, chest of drawers, etc.). These will leave more floor space and will add a cool look to the room for a relatively small price. Some other cheap décor items include:

- cool desk lamp.
- tapestry.
- pictures (of friends, family, pets, etc.).
- bulletin board.
- calendar.
- mirror.
- curtains.

Roommates

"Part of living together was trying to figure out how to get along on a level a little bit higher than high school."
—Junior, English Major

Just when you think the room is perfect and you are happy with everything, in walks the roommate. Roommates can be a blessing, or a major problem. If you are one of the lucky students with a great roommate, you will have a much lower stress-life than your unlucky counterparts. If you are living with someone you do not like, 150 square feet can seem even smaller.

It's Our House, Not Yours!

The biggest lesson to learn with a roommate is that the space belongs to both of you. Granted, it can be a cramped way of life, but it is still important to think in terms of "we" instead of "me."

So, just because you don't mind the pile of dirty laundry on the floor or the two-week-old bowl of mac n' cheese does not mean that your new live-in friend feels the same way. Clean up after yourself—if not for yourself, out of respect for your roommate. Hopefully, she will be doing the same thing.

Getting Along

First on the list with any roommate is honesty. Learning what each other truly likes and dislikes can save many arguments and headaches down the road. Not disclosing the truth can spur a building animosity between you. That buildup, if it continues, usually ends in some sort of volcanic eruption. Unlike Mount Saint Helens though, it can be prevented.

If you are lucky, the school's roommate matching service will have resolved most of the main issues. Unfortunately, this matching service is not perfect. On top of its imperfections, your roomie may have put down some incorrect information. If Mommy and Daddy were peering over his shoulder, he may have skipped over some vital areas. Perhaps he did not want his parents to know that he parties until all hours, smokes, and so on. You might be expecting a librarian-to-be and get a *Girls Gone Wild* star. Though not the norm, it does happen.

Back to the more likely scenario: Your roomie told the truth on her application. Because you most likely agree on some of the larger issues, tread carefully on small things. A straw that broke the camel's back, so make sure to address the little issues right away.

- Be honest and lay out your issues. It's a good practice. Both of you can sit down for a talk, or discuss things more informally. Whatever works. After all, this roommate thing is not over your first year; it goes on through college and sometimes further!

- If you feel tension or a building resentment toward your roommate, address it earlier rather than later.

- Be respectful of their possessions. Unless you already have her okay, do not help yourself to her Pop Tarts or borrow a coat without asking.

> "The benefits are being around someone completely new, and the roommate situation in general is your place to first develop your social life and social skills."
> —Junior, Anthropology Major

> "Buy a vacuum; it makes your place nicer for everyone who lives there. Hardly any students have them; they are cheap and will make a big difference in keeping your place clean."
> —Senior, Computer Science Major

> "Stay open-minded. The worst thing is fixing opinions about the person when you first meet, give everyone a chance."
> —Graduate, English Major

> "Approach the situation with the knowledge that you may not end up best friends."
> —Junior, Italian Major

> "Everyone's friends until you start sharing things."
> —Senior, Business Major

> "One of my roommates had a girlfriend who stayed over constantly. It put me in an awkward situation—I was 'sexiled' (not able to get in my room) when they were together. Be careful about abusing the privilege you have; treat your roommate with respect."
>
> —Graduate, Accounting Major

- Be tolerant. Schools' matching services have been known to pair a cattle rancher's daughter with a vegetarian—it's important to accept each other's differences.[1] College is a time to be mature, and maturity means seeing life from a different perspective. You do not have to give up what you believe in, or change your own behavior. However, a successful student learns that his own opinion is not always right.

When the Friction Is Too Much

Roommates may not always work out. If you have been honest and have tried to talk things out, and the relationship just is not working, talk to the housing office. They have the power to move people around if needed. If the friction is because of some illegal activity such as drug use or excessive alcohol use, do not hesitate to let the office know. This is no longer considered tattling. Your college career is at stake. But even if the problem is less serious, giving concrete reasons better than, "We just do not get along" may help your case. Before you go this route, make sure that you:

- Give your roommate more than one chance.
- Be objective about the problem. (Does this person have real issues that you cannot handle, or are you the one who is impossible to live with?)
- Be honest. Once again, telling your roommate your feelings regarding her behavior might curb the situation.

LIVING OFF-CAMPUS

This can be a tough situation, especially for a freshman who is looking forward to living in the dorm, but sometimes it is the only option if you attend a community college or attend as a commuter. For the traditional students, college enrollments are up. Some schools are so overcrowded that their dorms simply cannot handle the number of new students. Students stuck in this situation can feel that they are missing the college experience and feel left out.

As discussed before, meeting new people and developing new friends are crucial to having a balanced and successful college career. Living off-campus gives you all the more reason to get involved in as many activities as you can, like clubs and sports (more about this in Chapter 9). And you might still have access to the college's facilities, which likely include a workout facility, a swimming pool, and/or a running/walking track.

Where to Meet People

Even so, meeting people will be a bit more of a challenge. Whether you live in an apartment or commute from your parents' house, you may have to go the extra mile to meet new friends. First and foremost, stick around school if your schedule permits. Many commuters do just that, come for class and leave right away! I have heard the term "residential commuter" referring to students who live off-campus but spend time at school whenever possible. Coincidently, the more time you spend at your school, the more people you will meet. Instead of

- studying at home, head to the school library.
- grabbing food on the way home, stick around school and grab a bite.
- going home for a quick nap, relax on a couch in the student center or grab a spot on the lawn.

Above all, do not think that living off-campus ruins your chance at a normal college life. It just means that you may have to be more creative. Here are some sure bets for meeting people at college:

- Before and after class
- Any club or organized group
- Fraternities and sororities
- Intramural athletics (If you played any sport in high school, more than likely it is offered as an intramural sport at your college.)
- Any religious/church-oriented groups
- Ethnic/cultural clubs

STUDENT PROFILE—Chris P. on Living Off-Campus as a Freshman

When I arrived at college—a large state school—I knew I was living off-campus. This was a little bit depressing since I knew I would miss out on dorm life. It didn't get any better for the first month, so I decided to begin looking at fraternities. I went to a couple of recruiting events and found the guys to be down-to-earth and pretty fun in one fraternity. I rushed, pledged, and ended-up joining. Almost instantly my social life became full and fun; there were always parties, barbecues, and other stuff to do. I met a huge number of new people and made a whole new group of friends. Without deciding to come on-campus and actually get involved, there is a lot about college I would have missed out on so far. It saved my social life and probably my entire college experience.

➤ *What are some other ways Chris could have developed his social network?*

➤ *Would Chris's decision to join a Greek Organization work for everyone looking to meet people? Why or why not?*

"I lived on campus one more semester than most people. I had all of the amenities like cooking and convenience and had plenty of friends' places to go on the weekends. You'll miss the amenities, this way it worked well for me."

—Graduate, Graphic Design Major

"Move in with people that you can trust as a friend, or people you can have a business relationship with."

—Senior, Finance Major

"Things got bad with my roommate and me. By sitting down, we came up with a plan that left us both satisfied and improved our relationship."

—Senior, Psychology Major

The first weeks and months of classes will keep you busy, so you might not have time to put out the extra effort you will need to meet new friends. But don't give up. Though it is always easiest to begin these activities early, plenty of students start them later. Never think it's too late to get involved.

Moving Off-Campus

This differs from school to school. At some schools, living on campus is a perfectly fine option from freshman to senior year. At others, many students move off-campus starting in their sophomore year. If you are going to move off-campus, there are some important items to consider.

The New Challenge

The roommate laws still apply, but there are more elements to consider. Moving off-campus means that many things are no longer taken care of for you. If you had your bathrooms cleaned, you won't anymore. If you had your trash taken out, you won't anymore. And if you enjoy cooking, the dishes tend to keep piling up. Dirty dishes are an infamous problem-causing issue. Students who have made it work suggest making a list or schedule at the start (look in the Appendix for your own).

Keep Your Digs Running Smoothly

If you believe that the cleaning, dishwashing, and trash removal will just magically happen between roommates, stop kidding yourself. In addition to the mess that builds up, so do angry feelings.

Roommates can quickly begin playing the blame game. "I always take out the trash; Andrea's only done it twice since we moved in." Such statements arise more often than you think. A list keeps everything done, and keeps track of "who done it" as well! Keep a list to

- keep the residence running smoothly.
- track who does what.
- keep hard feelings from causing problems between you and your roommates.

Getting comfortable and adjusted at college can be a challenge for even the best of students. From navigating your way around campus to outfitting your crib, it is important from the get-go to feel at home. Learning to deal with roommates, make concessions, and compromise with people are all parts of a healthy college life—and one that I hope you will discover.

WORKSHEET 3-1

Roommate Chore Sheet

Add names, and rotate every week.

	Trash	Dishes	Common Area	Bathrooms	Vacuuming	Mopping
Week 1						
Week 2						
Week 3						
Week 4						

CHAPTER 4

Challenges of Non-traditional Students

"Progress always involves risks. You can't steal second base and keep your foot on first."
—Frederick B. Wilcox

The old definition of nontraditional students described them as students age 25 and over. Now, being a nontraditional student is defined by much more than just age. Nontraditional students come from all walks of life: employees wanting to move up at work, laid off workers, single parents, divorced individuals, even commuters —basically anyone who does not fall into the category of the traditional four-year college student. Nontraditional students attend trade school, professional school, graduate school, community college, four-year colleges and universities, and online institutions. Basically anywhere an education is offered you can most likely find a nontraditional student. The questions surrounding returning to school, being a successful student, and running the rest of your life can be scary for all students, including nontraditional students. They do not have to be, however. Let's dig in and find answers for meeting the challenges of nontraditional students.

THE DECISION TO GO BACK: NO ONE ELSE THINKS IT'S A GOOD IDEA!

Adult students are in a unique situation. They have the traditional responsibilities of living on their own and, at the same time, are attempting to complete a degree. It is not uncommon for others—including friends, family, and significant others—to think that returning to school is an unwise decision. After all, many nontraditional students are working in jobs that pay the bills, and the thought of going to work for nothing does not seem like the best use of time. Plus, it can be comfortable in the status quo of earning decent money and getting by. Many students who have returned to college say that actually deciding to return to school was the hardest part. Because no one lives in a vacuum, it is important to realize that other people can influence your decisions and that their support may make or break the deal to go back to school. This can be especially true if you have a significant other, children, or a job that you must keep. Going back to school in this type of situation is a team effort, requiring the cooperation of others. Before you can convince those around you to cooperate, you have to present them with your idea.

FINDING INFORMATION AND CREATING A PLAN

Broaching the subject of returning to school can be challenging, whether you are approaching your mate, your boss, or a family member. As always, starting with a plan is the first step. It is very important to have a plan in place before knocking someone off his or her feet saying, "I've decided to go to college, and that's that." So, before you sit down, gather some information from the local community college, university, or wherever you plan to attend and information on yourself and your goals. Through learning about the school and learning your own reasons for wanting to attend, your plan will have more than just information; it will have some meaning behind it. Some important information to obtain is reflected in these questions:

- How long will the degree take? Do you plan on a certificate, two-year degree, or a four-year degree? Will you be able to attend full-time or part-time?

- In what field of study are you interested, and does the school offer a program? Might you have an idea of where this degree will lead? What will you do with it once you graduate?

- How will this degree benefit everyone in the long run? Will this degree help make a better life for your family, children, or significant other? Will it help you realize your dreams and ambitions at work?

- How will you pay for the education? Is there financial aid or grants and scholarships available? How much will the schooling cost?

Some of these questions you can answer yourself; for the others try reviewing the school's Web site, phoning the school, or meeting with an admissions officer.

Receiving Support from Significant Others

When thinking of making the leap into college as a nontraditional student, hopefully those closest to you will be very supportive. This will make the decision much easier to follow through with. Supportive or unsupportive, your significant other will most likely have some questions about the practicality of heading back to school—so plan on talking about it. Using the information you obtained through talking with the school and answering the questions just posed would be a good start. Be prepared to discuss questions from the practical side and fears perhaps unspoken, which arise from the emotional side. Common practical topics include:

- How are you going to handle work and school?
- Will we have any time together, or will you be too busy?
- You are working now, how will we replace that lost income?
- Are you willing to sacrifice and cut back on hobbies/outside interests to make this work?

Common emotional topics include:

- Will I be left behind when you graduate?
- Will I be inadequate if I do not have an advanced education?
- Will you meet someone who is more interesting than I am?

"My girlfriend had doubts whether it was a good idea to return [to school]. She had questions about the practicality of it, where our relationship was headed, and mainly how I was going to pull the whole thing off."
—Sophomore, Business Major

Of course, not every couple will have every one of these questions, but some are likely to appear. Try to have practical answers already solved (think about it before you discuss it) and be reassuring and understanding on the emotional side. View college as a team effort with you and your significant other, and explain it that way. Explaining yourself in a reassuring and inclusive manner will make your case easier to handle. If you can get past your significant other, that's one thing; you still have to face . . . the boss!

Receiving Support from Bosses and Employers

Juggling work responsibilities with school responsibilities is a large concern for students returning to college part-time (or full-time). Can my job work around my school schedule? Will my employer work with me? It can be unsettling, thinking of approaching a boss with a request to work around your new school schedule. As with anything else, having that well thought-out plan is vital. There are numerous stories of employees receiving the full support of their employer (some employers have even supported their workers by paying for their degree). When approaching your supervisor about returning to college, some of the following information will be helpful:

- Time line
- Sample schedule
- A firm commitment to both the company and school
- Future plans to stay a part of the organization (If this applies. Do not claim this if you plan on working somewhere else.)

Supervisors and employers are people too. If you are very satisfied and aim to stay at the same company both through and after college, tell them. Lay out the benefits that you will bring as a college graduate to the table. Showing your boss that you would like to help the company with your education is an extra incentive for her to work with you. If your employer is unwilling or unable to accommodate your new schedule, try other options. Getting another job may be the answer, or living off of loans and attending school full-time might work. Be creative and think outside of the box. Do not let one crummy boss or employer ruin your dreams of college success!

> "I really wanted to get a few promotions and work my way up the ladder. But, quickly found out if this was my goal, then I needed further education. I'm through the first couple of years, which have been hard but rewarding and can already see the benefits materializing."
>
> —Junior, Business Management Major

STUDENT PROFILE—Phil B. on School, Work, and Family

I always knew that college was meant for me. My goal has been to earn my bachelor's degree and continue on to law school, but getting married and having a couple of children delayed my ambitions for a while. Two years ago I started taking classes at my local university majoring in political science, beginning the long road to becoming a lawyer. During this time I have continued to work almost full-time at the distribution business I have been employed with for years. Since they were unable to accommodate a traditional school schedule—daytime classes—I have been enrolled in night courses. I can't say that the journey thus far has been easy, but it has been doable. Any spare time is spent with my kids and my wife, so it's basically work and family. So far, my grades have stayed high and my plans to attend night law school seem to be coming true. My kids see a little bit less of me than either of us would like, but I know that all of us will be happy in the future that I am making these sacrifices now. The journey has been rewarding and exciting to this point and hopefully will continue to be. The clock is ticking; I'm just trying to fit my dreams into the allotted time!

> "It was different going to work every day knowing that I had something else going for me—I'm going to college!"
>
> Freshman, Med Tech Major

Three Rules for College Planning

No matter who you need to discuss your college plans with, always:

1. Know your reasons. Articulate your motivations for wanting to go to college. As you will see, knowing your reasons for attending college—the Why—will help you on the days when you feel that school is just too much to handle.

2. Be willing to compromise. Perhaps it will be too stressful to finish a bachelor's degree in four years. That's okay! Be willing to compromise to keep your domestic and work life running smoothly. The time will pass regardless. If you keep plugging away, you will reach your goal eventually.

3. Be willing to commit. Commitment is a vital part of the discussion. Let others know that you are serious and committed to improving yourself with the degree—they will be more likely to be supportive. Also, commit to yourself! This degree will take your work, your brainpower, and your commitment. Without a real commitment, it is easy for everything to unravel. Make a commitment!

BACK IN THE SADDLE: ADJUSTING TO CLASSES AND STUDYING

As a nontraditional student, taking a seat in the classroom again may feel a bit strange. Being out of a school environment for a time will mean that there are adjustments for getting back in the swing of classes, studying, and everything else that goes with earning a degree.

Am I Cut Out for This?

Once you are preparing to start, some insecurities and questions may arise. Most of these questions revolve around the same theme: Am I cut out for this? From questions about college monetarily paying off, handling the academic workload, to more personal concerns such as sticking out in class, there are real concerns accompanying a return to school. Rest easy though. Being a nontraditional student has never been more common—in fact, well over half of all college students in the United States are nontraditional! Plus, there is a real payoff both personally and professionally for returning for a degree. As one student put it, the thought of attending college is more traumatic than actually being there. She said that prior to classes starting she was "so worried" about being the odd one out, asking stupid questions that the rest of the traditional students knew the answers to, and being out of touch with all of her classmates. When she actually got there, she was pleasantly surprised when there were a number of other non-traditional students in her classes, and that the traditional students considered her no different than any other student. So, don't worry about college; just get ready to learn, you are up to the challenge!

The Who's Who and What's What of Campus

If you previously attended a college or degree-granting program, you are likely familiar with the ins and outs of campus life, but may need some brushing up. If this is your first time at college, it is important to start learning who's who and what resources will make your college life easier.

Advisors

As with traditional college students, advisors are the first players to get on your team. They can help you sort through your goals, time line, class selection, and general advice about the school. Whether you are assigned an advisor or must pick one yourself, make an appointment as soon as possible!

Classes

Adjusting to classes is another crucial step in the journey of college success. If you are used to functioning as an employee, sitting through a one- or two-hour lecture may take time to get used to. Never fear, if the lecture goes much longer than 45 minutes, ample breaks are given—time to stretch, relax, and recoup. Classes are the front lines of learning as well. Usually, classes are the first place course material is discussed and the best place to ask questions. Professors commonly give valuable hints in class that you are unlikely to know about unless you have attended. Further, some professors enact mandatory attendance policies or suggested attendance policies—like giving random pop quizzes that count toward the final grade. If you miss class, you miss that portion of your grade. Learn to handle and get the most out of classes—they are the center of the college experience!

Professors

Be mindful of your professors. It is important from day one to understand their value to your education. Professors are experts at what they teach, so meeting them during office hours for outside help can add depth to your education. Plus, many professors especially enjoy nontraditional students for their more motivated and

"I thought I would stand out and look awkward in class, but slowly I realized the younger students don't care and treat me just like everyone else."
—Sophomore, Sociology Major

serious approach to school. If you want to make the most out of your educational experience, make the most out of the college resources (advisors, financial aid office, career center, to name a few), classes, and professors. By taking advantage of what your institution has to offer, you will most certainly stay ahead of the pack.

For more helpful hints on advisors, classes, and professors, turn to Chapter 6.

Your Advantages and Disadvantages

It is important to realize up front that there are both advantages and disadvantages to being a nontraditional student. It can be easy to focus on your lack of experience (or recent experience) with studying and test-taking, but it is important to remind yourself of the positives you bring to the table.

Advantages

The Real-World Edge: Work Experience

> "I found in class discussions that I brought a different and welcomed point of view. I think it was because of my ability to see the practical side of learning that made my comments different."
>
> —Graduate, Accounting Major

Many nontraditional students have worked and continue to work while earning their degree. Maybe that is not the traditional way to do college, but it certainly can be useful experience, and you are in good company. For example, some of the best business schools in the country require years of work experience before applying to their program. They do this for one reason: Students who have worked in real jobs for a number of years bring a very insightful and real perspective to the classroom. Though we are not necessarily talking about attending business school in this book, you can see similar benefits in whatever type of degree or certification you are pursuing. You, your professor, and the other students will all benefit from your different and more mature take on classroom assignments and discussions.

Life Experience

Beyond just work experience, nontraditional students have more life experience than traditional college students as a general rule. Whether you have been responsible for a family, been a single parent, or are returning to school after living on your own for a number of years, you have seen more than the average student coming straight from high school. Living through more circumstances gives you more wisdom and will help you see the big picture much better through your time in school. Professors appreciate students who can see the value of the material they are teaching beyond the next test, and you as a nontraditional student are better equipped to see this.

Self-knowledge

Probably the most underrated advantage that nontraditional students have coming into college is their self-knowledge. By self-knowledge I mean understanding your strengths, weaknesses, how you work best, a clearer picture of what you want out of life, and where you want to be. The more of life that you see and the more mature you become, the dust settles a little bit more and you are better able to see and understand yourself. From a better understanding comes the opportunity to focus, plan, and work toward a meaningful goal, second-guessing yourself less as time goes on. On a whole, nontraditional students outperform traditional students in college, perhaps because of better knowing themselves. After all, performance is directly linked with knowing where you want to end up—exactly the reason nontraditional students have an advantage!

> "I knew exactly what I wanted out of school from the start—that gave me a leg up over the younger students. While I was concentrating on studying, they were trying to figure out what to major in."
>
> —Graduate, English Major

Disadvantages

Rusty Study Skills

There is no sense in denying it: Getting back to the books will be a challenge. Whether you are brushing up on old study skills or starting from scratch, there's going to be some adjusting. Plus balancing your studies, work, and everything else that people have in life is not an easy task, but certainly a doable one.

Time Away from the Books

Many schools have courses and/or workshops to help develop better study skills. If you are worried about this aspect of going to school, by all means sign up for a course. It is often said that many students returning to school after working for a number of years do well with group studying. Let's face it, at work you are more likely to troubleshoot a problem with a coworker than to research the problem in a textbook somewhere. People-to-people interaction and teamwork are two skills to which nontraditional students seem unusually well-adapted, likely because of their life and work experiences. If these are areas of strength for you, take advantage of them and organize a study group or team-oriented reviews. Whether you are signing up for a study skills course or taking part in a group study session, there is plenty of help and opportunity for nontraditional students to get acclimated to the academic demands of college—so take advantage!

> "The thought of studying for hours freaked me out. I had never done that before. I started slow, met with my professors, and gave it my best shot; by the end of the semester I had received an 'A' in all three classes. If I can do it, anyone can!"
>
> —Graduate, Associate Degree in Manufacturing Technology

Responsibilities Beyond School

There is more to life than going to class and worrying about grades. There are jobs, significant others, children, and numerous other important going-ons outside of class. To sum it up, there will be more constraints on your time perhaps than other students'. These extra responsibilities can definitely be fit into your life, you will just have to be willing to plan and manage your time. In Chapter 5, time management is discussed, and there are worksheets to help you schedule your time. I highly recommend taking the brief time to fill these sheets out. You will see immediately how much more efficient you spend your time and how much more (than you think) you can get done.

MAKING THE TRANSITION A SUCCESS

Making the transition from "working you" to "college you" successfully will require some planning, effort, and lastly great execution! Writing down your goals and plans is an important step in starting a successful college life, but to truly make those plans into reality, you have to follow through, which means putting in the work and dealing with the stresses on a consistent basis.

Work and Stress Come with Juggling College and *Life*

Struggles with the stress of life versus college haunts almost every student, traditional and nontraditional. After you have planned though, you only have two items left to deal with: the work and the stress!

Work

- **The grunt factor.** The grunt factor is the part of the equation that comes down to having the guts to put in the work to get something done! Let's face it, to get things done and handle a busy life there is a grunt factor involved. It's not complicated— sometimes you just have to suck it up and do it!

- **Consistency is king.** Working your brains out just the night before a big test will not do the trick. To truly learn the information, keep your stress levels to a minimum, and live a healthy life, you must work consistently. Cramming for 14 hours the day before a test not only leaves you looking and feeling like a zombie, but without the same mastery of the material than if you had worked over a longer period of time. You could have easily studied 30 minutes per day for 2 weeks instead, had an in-depth and more well-thought-out take on the material as well as a more balanced life! To keep everything in your life (including school) running smoothly, shoot for consistency.

- **Take a break.** Breaks are an essential part of any successful student's routine. Studying every day, all of the time is an unreasonable (and unbalanced) way to complete any degree program. One terrific characteristic of college is the flexible schedule. If you want to organize your week so that you study four days per week and take three off, or study six days and take one day off, it's up to you! There is no schedule that dictates when and where you study, just tests to determine if you did, in fact, put in the time.

- **Work is a friend, not a foe.** Work is not an enemy; it is a tool that enables you to achieve your goals. Though at times it is unpleasant, the satisfaction you will reap after putting in hard work toward reaching your objectives is the best feeling. Putting in the extra work is the difference between getting by and succeeding in college life.

Stress

- **Lack of time is temporary.** Feel like you are not spending enough time with the family, significant other, or kids? Many nontraditional students cite these issues as the most difficult and the most stressful to deal with. Remember our earlier discussion about knowing your reasons? If any of your reasons cite improvement of life for your family (which many do), focus on that. If you have kids or a significant other or both, you know that earning your degree will benefit them in a number of ways, from a more secure financial background to a positive example of achievement that you have set. Every undertaking has some degree of sacrifice associated with it. Focus on earning your degree and giving those close to you the remainder of your time. The sacrifice is temporary, and only to better everyone's life in the long run!

> "Kids learn by example. Because I am working and going to school, my kids see that and look up to that. Showing them that they can achieve their goals through working is a positive example to set."
>
> —Freshman, Associate Degree in Information Technology

- **Play keep up, not catch up.** Much of the stress associated with college comes from tests and deadlines. Tests and papers require preparation, and it can be easy to procrastinate. The single largest factor in lowering the stress and successfully completing your college degree will come from playing keep up, not catch up. Feeling unprepared because you were not studying and working on a consistent basis can be prevented by sticking with, or ahead of, the class when it comes to knowing the material. Stay ahead and watch your stress level plummet!

- **Find support.** There are multiple places to find support as a nontraditional student. Obviously, there are family members and friends, but not everyone receives the support of those close to them. Many schools have nontraditional student groups that can serve as support for students experiencing many of the same stresses during college. Search around your school. These groups can help with everything from general encouragement to child care services—this is one more benefit of getting involved at your school.

Managing the Rest of Your Life

There has been a lot of talk about handling the challenges of school, but what about the rest of your life? You need to handle money, transportation issues, and domestic issues while going to school as well. Let's have a look!

Money and Income

The biggest concern of managing both college and home life is money. Luckily, many community colleges and other local programs can be less expensive. There are many options with money and income. Here are a few:

- Choosing to attend part-time to enable you to keep a day job
- Meeting with the Financial Aid office to assist in finding loans or budgeting
- Searching for scholarship and grant opportunities
- Having your partner or spouse cover the living expenses while you attend school

The bottom line is that your life must go on, school or not. For more detailed information on handling money at college, budgeting, and budgeting worksheets, turn to Chapter 8.

Transportation

Perhaps you are married or partnered and can only afford one car, or maybe you cannot afford a car at all. How will you get to campus? If you attend school in a metropolitan area, the subway/metro or the bus system may connect you. A large number of people do not live in areas where public transportation is possible, though. If this is the case, you do have a few options:

- Carpool
- Family/Friends
- Bicycle
- Walk
- Moped/Scooter

If you cannot find transportation and tried everywhere, you may still be in luck! Most colleges and community colleges offer courses on-line. So, if transportation is a problem for the semester, and you have access to a computer, sit right at home and do the work! If you have access to a computer but are not comfortable with the technology, contact your school about free classes that teach using computers—most schools offer them.

Domestic Issues

Being a parent, especially a single parent, can be a tough addition to an already working student. The truth is that many men and women attend college every year while being great parents at the same time. If you have children and are planning to attend college, it may seem a bit challenging to find quiet time to study. That quiet study time that many students have at home can easily be replaced with parenting responsibilities.

Another challenge faced by student-parents is the uncertainty of their schedule. If your child comes down with a sickness and cannot go to school, you may have to miss class to stay home with your child. One nontraditional student returned to college when his son was in first grade. Due to some behavioral issues, his son was unable to ride the bus to school anymore, and guess who had to drive the boy to school? That's right, his dad. This was not an ideal setup because the boy's father had to miss an economics class to be able to drop the child off. Because of the time conflict, the father had to drop the class. Though he took the class the following semester, he realized that being a parent and a student has its own unique challenges. So, as far as schedules, be ready to be flexible if you are attempting to parent and attend school. Because flexibility is so crucial to success as a student-parent, take a minute on a sheet of paper and brainstorm what you can do to create more time. Whether it is deleting some hobbies while you finish your degree or cooking only once every three nights and freezing the rest for the next couple of nights, come up with anything that you can do to save time and energy. The more options you have, the better off you will be.

> "Handling my kids was the most difficult part of going back to college. I had to remind myself everyday that getting a degree was in all of our best interests, and they would thank me for it later."
> —Graduate, Education Major

Unless you are taking on-line courses, you will have to find child care for times when you need to be at school. Obviously, having a relative or significant other watch the children is ideal. If this is not an option, you will have to find either a child care center or a babysitter. Luckily, many colleges and community colleges either have child care available or have contracts with organizations that do. Either way, the care is most often cheaper than finding a place yourself, and it is convenient—either on or near campus! Also, many states have child care grants for parents trying to attend

"I hosted study groups at my house; that way I didn't need to pay for a (baby)sitter, or arrange anything special. He either slept or watched movies while we went over class material; it worked well."

—Sophomore, Nursing Major

college, which can cover a significant portion of the costs associated with attending college as a parent. To determine if your institution offers child care services, talk to the Student Services Center; and to ask about child care grants, a great starting place is the Financial Aid Office.

Lastly, most institutions have nontraditional-student support groups. These groups usually consist of parent-students there to share what ideas and strategies have helped them manage everything from parenting while in school to managing the demands of work while attempting to study and juggle a family. Some groups have created a child care service, where parents take turns watching children thereby creating time for studying and class while not having to pay cash. If you are having a tough time finding the resources for child care, this is one more option to explore.

Reducing the Stress: Making Time for Everything

In your plan at the beginning of the chapter, you laid out some ideas to make time for those people important to you. Reiterating the theme of this book, many students consider balance as the key to leading a successful life in college. To keep yourself on track, constantly track and plan your time to make sure you are using it wisely. Use the three-step process from Chapter 5 to do it:

1. Find where your time goes.
2. Organize it.
3. Be efficient and carry out the plan.

Leaving zero time for those closest to you only increases their dissatisfaction (and in turn, yours) of the whole experience. The purpose of returning to college and completing your program is to better your life. After all, how much will a college degree mean if there is no one around with whom to share your life? Use your time management skills and make time for those who are important to you—you will never be sorry!

STAYING MOTIVATED

Success as a student is all about the long haul. It is not your performance on one test that determines your success or failure, but the series of accomplishments over the course of your program. That is exactly why you should not only be motivated but, more important, stay motivated.

The two most common reasons for students losing ground on their goals are

1. taking on more than is possible.
2. forgetting why they returned to school in the first place.

Take On Only What You Can Handle

Set high goals while at the same time considering all of the responsibilities in your life. To set goals without consideration of the other factors in your life can prove to be a frustrating and deflating experience. On the other hand, setting manageable goals and meeting or exceeding those goals will boost your motivation level and confidence in your abilities. Take on classes and responsibilities that you can handle. And if you are not sure, start out slow. Learn your limit by staying under rather than over!

> "If you have any doubts about how you'll handle college, start small. It's not impossible to do well, but it can be a big adjustment."
>
> —Junior, Physical Therapy Major

Rushing May Be a Bad Idea

As the old adage goes, "Patience is a virtue, obtain it." Patience is crucial in college and perhaps even more for nontraditional students. A significant number of nontraditional students return to college at an older age than their traditional counterparts. It can be easy to fall into the trap of rushing to finish because you feel behind the eight ball from the start and feel that you need to earn a degree in the quickest possible time frame. To get the most out of your college experience and finish in the best possible manner, be careful not to rush. Most anything that is rushed turns out less than ideal. Whether it is making a relationship work, boiling spaghetti, or attempting to lose weight, rushing the process usually has less than ideal results—and college is no different.

Pay Attention to Signs of Burnout

Now that you are taking on only what you can handle and being patient with the process, burnout should not happen, right? I hate to say it, but we are all susceptible to burnout, and the more responsibilities you are trying to juggle, the higher your susceptibility. By paying attention to the signs of burnout, you can take steps to prevent it from taking over. Do you have

- an indifferent attitude toward your original goals?
- a desire to only get by, not perform your absolute best?
- a feeling that your life is crumbling around you and there is nothing you can do?

If so, you may be feeling burnout! But that's okay. Almost every student feels this at one time or another; one more reason to go back to the beginning and find comfort in your reasons.

Finding Comfort in Your Reasons

Previously we discussed knowing the why for heading back to college. It is vitally important to write these whys down and keep them somewhere readable because the tough times are when we forget. If you have written your reasons down, it is a way to kick-start that motivation again and truly see what your sacrifice has been about. You certainly will not be in the mood to write this stuff down when you are fighting to tread water in your college classes. That is why you must do it as soon as possible. Reading your reasoning can be a powerful thing. It could be the heat that gets your blood boiling again! Seeing in your handwriting "I want to make a better life for my family by earning a college degree so I can get a better job. This will give us more financial support and security and a better overall life" is powerful. Some people put reminders everywhere (my preferred technique). Whether your kids are your motivation, your written goals, or both, lay them out so you can see them! So set yourself up for future success by taking the time to write down your whys now! Reminding yourself of the why on a periodic basis can give enough relief and purpose to fan a second wind. Find comfort in your reasons for returning; whether it is for you, your family, or another important reason, let your reasons fuel your fire.

Maximizing Your Time and Energy

"Happy people plan actions, they don't plan results."
—Dennis Wholey

It is a fact of campus life: College demands a lot. To keep up with the high-energy life school can require, it is necessary to extract the most out of the time and energy you have. However, if you are willing to put in some old-fashioned work, learn how to push your limits a little, and manage your time well, you will stay on top.

The ideas in this chapter work not just for college, but any time in your life. Even if you know one or more of the following tips, this is probably the first time you have had to put them to use. And, if you do not know them, learn them!

GOALS: PUSHING THE ENVELOPE

Goal setting: Stop thinking of it as something your teachers and parents always told you was important, and start thinking of it as setting the path for getting where you want and what you want. Goals are the framework for exceeding your expectations and achieving your desires, so pay attention, then you can return to the first worksheet and set your goals.

The Three Characteristics

All goals are

- unmistakable.
- measurable.
- possible.

My Story

One semester, I signed up for a physics class. My goal was to receive an A, no less, in the class.

Very difficult? Sure. Unrealistic? Nope. I received the A, and here is how I did it. I wrote this goal on a sheet of paper and taped it to the inside of my physics notebook. This way, it was a constant reminder of the contract I made with myself. There was no way I could get out of it—I looked at it every time I went to class or did homework.

After a few months of toughing it out, I got the A, not because I wrote it down, but because I took it seriously enough to write it down, tape it to my notebook, and do the work.

- You have to be unmistakable in what you want. For example, if you want to lose weight, there is a lot of room for fudging. But if you want to lose 10 pounds, you either do it or you don't. In the physics class, I either made an A or I didn't; it was as simple as that. It was unmistakable.

- You need to be able to measure your goal. After all, what good is committing to something if you are unable to measure success or failure? If you set goals you are unable to measure, you will never know whether you reached or fell short of your goal. What is doing well in school? What is great shape? Your goals should be specific, so that you can see your success.

  For example, if you decide to keep schoolwork a priority in the coming semester, you will not have any way of knowing that you did, in fact, make schoolwork more important than parties, playing pool, or just hanging out. You have to add more description so that you can measure it. "Keep school a priority by maintaining a 3.0 or better GPA" is measurable.

- What you want has to be possible. Many people set themselves up for failure by setting outrageous goals. Let's face it, it is unreasonable to expect to receive a 4.0 while working 40 hours per week, training for a marathon, and running the student government. But students set these outrageous expectations for themselves all the time!

Understand me: I strongly believe that everyone should strive to push their limits and be the best they can be. But this does not mean disappointing yourself because you expected far too much. So start small, then build. Set small goals and achieve those slowly, and with experience you will begin to understand how much you can handle. Go ahead and set goals for the semester, the year, and by graduation based on your answers to the first worksheet. Write them out so that they are unmistakable, measurable, and possible. (See Worksheet 5-1.)

Be Realistic

It is all right to test your limits— a little bit. But remember, the goal is to get things done, not crash and burn in the middle of eight classes! So, before you set your goals for the semester, meet with an advisor and/or professor to discuss your schedule. Definitely consider their advice—at least the first time.

Today and Tomorrow

Baby Steps

It is easy to start out happy, upbeat, and invincible, but it is difficult to maintain that attitude. Motivation likes to crumble over the course of anything hard, and that can make you feel lost in all you have to do.

There are goals for today and goals for tomorrow. Set some for the near future, and some for the far future. The short-term projects keep you on the right track to achieve the big goal you have in mind. Have you ever heard of the term "baby steps"? Short-term goals can be thought of in just that way. They will keep you motivated toward your bigger, long-term goal and make the whole ordeal seem more possible.

Dave Matthews was an overnight success, right? Not so fast. He and his band made a name for themselves through their rigorous touring schedule, and even produced and financed their own first album.[14] Only after all this were they signed to a big record label. Their fame was not a giant leap; it was a series of small successes that culminated with a huge win.

The idea of being a big shot can be fun, but getting there usually takes a long time. Working hard every day and enjoying the road are necessary to achieve your dreams.

STUDENT PROFILE—Carrie G. on Mind-set

I take a certain mind-set on everything I do, from schoolwork to résumé writing. I view the work I need to do just like getting into shape. Just like molding a body into better shape takes a little bit of time every day at the gym, so does any other goal. By this comparison, studying for tests (or whatever I am doing) is like working

WORKSHEET 5-1

Goals: Getting Where You Desire!

Turn back to Chapter 1 and look at your desires. Set your goals based on these. Go ahead and aim high, it will push you further!

Semester:

Goal:

Unmistakable Characteristics:

How Will You Measure Progress?

Make sure you aim high toward a goal that stretches you but is possible.

Year:

Goal:

Unmistakable Characteristics:

How Will You Measure Progress?

Make sure you aim high toward a goal that stretches you but is possible.

Graduation:

Goal:

Unmistakable Characteristics:

How Will You Measure Progress?

Make sure you aim high toward a goal that stretches you but is possible.

out. I view the work as "little workouts." By putting in a small amount of effort everyday, there are no sleepless nights or anxieties over finishing on time.

➤ *Everyone's mind works differently. What mind-set do you take to accomplish tasks?*

My Story

At the start, writing this book was the coolest thing since sliced bread. But it definitely did not stay that way. Sitting down at a blank computer screen and having a million thoughts racing through my head was intimidating. I could only do it by doing a little bit at a time, word by word. I set goals for the month, week, and semester about how much I would get done. Eventually, it really became something, and here we are!

While you are setting up your baby steps, do not forget your big goals. The big goals are for far-off, but they give meaning to what you are doing now. It can be easy to look at all the studying, time in the gym, or good-tasting food you pass up and wonder, "What am I doing?" Simply put, you can look at the bigger goal and remember the lofty idea of what you really want.

> "I keep long-term goals in the back of my head. Short-term goals are my focus. You have to reach for the clouds before you can reach the stars."
>
> —Senior, Biomedical Science Major

STUDENT PROFILE—Mike T. on Running a Marathon

The discipline I have learned from running marathons translates to other areas of my life and the ability to carry out a goal. In training for a marathon, first I build a mileage base so that I can handle the long distances. At the same time, if I am going for a time goal, I'll do shorter runs with speed work—everything has its purpose. Therefore, I am not wasting time, energy, and effort. I am staying focused. Starting with a plan and working everyday toward it provide a framework for my efforts. This way nothing ends up being a haphazard attempt without any plan in advance to forsee the outcome.

People say that it is just too hard to run a marathon. That is exactly what makes it worthwhile. I ate breakfast this morning, that was not difficult or challenging, so I did not really get any satisfaction out of it. If everyone was running marathons and it was not hard, it would not be worth doing. This parallels everything else; everything really worth doing is difficult, but possible with a plan, focus, and determination. The difficulty is part of the satisfaction.

➤ *What is the hardest thing you have ever done? How did you do it?*

➤ *What difficult goal do you have for the future? Briefly describe how you plan to undertake attaining it.*

The Big Goals

New Year's Eve can be an exciting time to plan what you want to get done by the next one, and write down your goals. Or, you might prefer to do your planning in the summer before fall semester. After you identify major, long-term goals, then decide what small steps you will need to get there.

Making Progress and Heading Off Problems

Through college (and life), there are many people and ideas that will help you in your journey. There will also be obstacles that appear to hinder your progress. Following are some of both to find and to look out for.

Your Goals and Other People

Other people can help or hinder you in your quest for success. It is important to realize the power of other people at the outset. And by all means, do not dismiss that power or think that it will not matter. Most people claim that other people's opinions of them do not matter—and nothing could be further from the truth. The overwhelming majority of humans care, usually quite a bit, about what others think of them. This can be a damaging way to think, but sometimes you can turn this into a positive and use it for motivation.

Tell People about Your Plans

Once you write down your goals, do not be shy about them. There is an element of accountability when others know what you plan to do. Some of the most successful people I have known make no mystery of their future plans or how they will go about achieving them. Whether it means prominently displaying your goals where people can see them or being upfront about your ideas when asked about them, make your goals known! You are much more likely to follow through with your reputation at stake.

Use the Encouragers, Forget the Discouragers

As if most of you do not already know this, many people will mock your plans, and the grander your ideas, the more crazy they will try to make you feel. Though it is not necessarily on purpose, these people exude negative energy. This might not be obvious to you, though. Many people do not consciously want to keep others from doing great things; their actions just naturally expose themselves in that way.

If you have ever heard the story of Rudy, it explains this phenomenon. Rudy was a poor kid from Illinois who wanted, worse than anything, to become part of the Notre Dame football team. Because he was not extraordinarily big, athletic, or strong, almost no one thought that in a lifetime Rudy would make the team, or that he could even get into the school. Through sheer effort and determination over a number of years, Rudy was accepted to Notre Dame, made the football team, and even played in a game! He is now a highly respected motivational speaker and counselor.

Rudy did not fulfill his dream because he listened to everyone else. He achieved it by doing exactly the opposite. So, if someone claims that you can't do what you have set out to do, remember our definition of personal success. Personal success is success to you, and you only. The people telling you that it's impossible may not be able to do it, but that does not mean that *you* can't.

In contrast, you will find other people who believe in everything you plan to do. Surrounding yourself with these people will be one of the most powerful enablers in your life at college.

The more you succeed at your goals, the more you will understand one thing: Many people never take your first endeavor seriously. The toughest hump to overcome is the first one. Take a million dollars from a millionaire, and he/she will make it back much easier than someone who has never had any money. Another example: Take an average lacrosse player and an out-of-practice but excellent player. For the first few minutes, the average player may get the better of the more experienced teammate. But after warming up, the experienced player will come to life and perform better than anyone on the field. Get through your first hump—your warmup—and see what you are capable of. It may surprise you and everyone else!

> **C-A-N'-T stands for Can, And Need To!**

Two Factors That Will Slow, if not Halt Your Progress

- Fear
- Laziness

Fear is a natural emotion that we all feel, and it will hold us all back if we indulge it.

Why don't many people change? Why don't they put themselves up for a challenge if it can mean a great result?

Many people avoid taking the first step to success: making the decision to change. If you look closely, the most prevalent reason is fear. Fear is the emotion that overrides just about everything else; it is the hardest feeling to ignore or conquer. Fear keeps us from realizing our potential. When it takes over, we do not even give ourselves the chance to prove it wrong!

What you have to understand and remember is that, most of the time, what you are trying to do is not that terrifying.

We have all experienced this: I know I have heard guys in the gym say, "I am definitely not maxing out (on the bench press). I do not want to know how weak I am." And I know that women have certainly heard others say, "I am not getting anywhere near that scale. I do not want to know how much I weigh. It will depress me." Nobody wants to walk away—from the gym, the scale, or anywhere—feeling disappointed.

The first and hardest choice to make is to face your fear. Only then can you organize a plan and put in the work to overcome the fear.

Laziness is the more obvious of the two obstacles. It is simple: If you put in the work, sometimes that goal will not pan out; if you do not put in the work, that goal will never pan out! If you are ever unsure of the outcome, do not give up. If you are a quitter and never complete the work, there is a 100 percent guarantee that none of your ideas will come to fruition. Work hard toward that first undertaking, whether it involves grades, fitness, friends, a business idea, or anything else. Once you complete the goal, your confidence and others' belief in you will skyrocket.

Building your confidence while ignoring the naysayers and achieving your goals will be the first, hardest, and most important step to fulfilling your goals and dreams. So use the encouragers and forget the discouragers.

TIME, TIME, TIME: WHERE DID THE DAY GO?

Have you ever asked yourself this question? Sure! Time tends to get up and walk away while we watch TV or talk on the phone. We hardly even notice.

Did you know there are 24 hours in a day? Of course! So put it to use! It might not seem like it, but there is more than enough time in the day to get what you need done, and what you want done.

Let's face it, many college classes require about six hours of studying and homework per week. The average full load of classes is four to five on average, and you spend about 12 hours in class per week. A solid workout schedule takes about six hours per week, so taking a full load of classes and working toward the cover of *Muscle and Fitness*, we are talking 42 hours per week. Considering there are 168 hours in a week, I think we can find 42!

If you cannot, consider that you had better get a handle on the whole 40-hours-per-week thing if you ever plan on working.

Look at how and where you spend your time. If it is hard to go by memory, make a journal and keep track of it as you go for a week. Once you discover where your time is going, you can sit down and reorganize it, putting it toward what you want to achieve. Fill out the Time Tracker worksheet and find where you spend your time.

After two days of recording your activity:

Q: Did you find any time-consuming activities that you could trim? If so, which activities and how will you be more efficient?

Q: Did you find any ways you could use spaces of time more wisely (like studying in between classes instead of getting on the Internet)? If so, when and how will you be more efficient?

WORKSHEET 5-2

Time Tracker

For two days, write down where you spend time. This will allow you to find what you are doing right and what you are doing wrong. Turn to Appendix C for blank Time Trackers.

Date: _____

Date: _____

7 AM	7 AM
7:30	7:30
8	8
8:30	8:30
9	9
9:30	9:30
10	10
10:30	10:30
11	11
11:30	11:30
12 PM	12 PM
12:30	12:30
1	1
1:30	1:30
2	2
2:30	2:30
3	3
3:30	3:30
4	4
4:30	4:30
5	5
5:30	5:30
6	6
6:30	6:30
7	7
7:30	7:30
8	8
8:30	8:30
9	9
9:30	9:30
10	10
10:30	10:30
11	11
11:30	11:30
12 AM	12 AM
12:30	12:30
1	1
1:30	1:30
2	2

Thinking Ahead

Planning gives you a written out idea of what needs to be done each day. After finishing what needs to be done, you get to do what you want. Planning is easy, painless, and generally simple. Yet nobody does it except for you (you will be doing it after reading this, I'm sure!).

Just take ten or fifteen minutes, either at night before bed, or in the morning before anything else (maybe during breakfast), and decide what needs to be done and the time when you will get it done. Worksheet 5-3 is an example of the sheet I use.

Putting Things Together

Efficiency is a necessity when you have a busy schedule. If you are not well organized, you can find yourself falling behind very quickly. You are juggling all kinds of responsibilities like classes, work, fitness, and a social life, so you must use time in a way that makes everything as easy as possible. In other words, learn how to multitask.

If you open your eyes and think about it, being efficient on a college campus can be easy. Check this out:

- Students go to class on campus.
- Many students have housing on campus.
- Many students eat on campus.
- Many students exercise on campus.
- Many students' friends are on campus.
- Students can work on campus.
- Students have recreational opportunities, right on campus.

Well, if you happened to notice, there is a common denominator running through the list: "On Campus!"

Before, you might have lived far away from your school. Maybe your friends all lived in different neighborhoods, and the gym you worked out at was several miles away. Going to all those places took up a lot of time. But now, everything is in one place. College has actually made it easier for you to be efficient!

Even if all items on the list are not convenient for you, there are certainly some things you can piece together:

- If you have a class close to the gym, bring your workout clothes and exercise before or after class.
- Anxious to speak with a friend? Call on your way to and from classes.
- Time between classes? Perfect time to work on your research paper.

It's surprising—learning to become more efficient will free up a huge amount of time. Being disorganized and constantly playing

WORKSHEET 5-3

Planning Worksheet

Now you know where your time is going. Next is planning how to best use your time. Fill out this sheet to plan your day, either in the morning or the night before. Turn to Appendix C for more blank Planning Worksheets.

Date: _____

7 AM	5 PM
7:30	5:30
8	6
8:30	6:30
9	7
9:30	7:30
10	8
10:30	8:30
11	9
11:30	9:30
12 PM	10
12:30	10:30
1	11
1:30	11:30
2	12 AM
2:30	12:30
3	1
3:30	1:30
4	2
4:30	2:30

During very busy times during the semester, if I wanted to watch some TV and chill out, I would click on my favorite show and watch it while I rode the exercise bike.

"Use the down time. On Saturday mornings when everyone else was sleeping or laying around, I studied for two to three hours and made serious progress on my schoolwork."

—Graduate, Computer Science Major

Maybe you cannot hang out with your friends because of a giant project that is due. So why not take them to the gym with you to work out? Not only will your workout be more fun, but having your friends nearby might even give you extra motivation to work out better and harder.

catchup just eats away at our limited time and energy. Use the convenience schools have provided, and plan your day in an efficient manner.

Concentrating

Not only should you be a great goal-setter and planner, you also need focus. When you are focused, you harness your mental and physical abilities to get a particular job done.

Some things do not take much focus: walking on the treadmill, an easy jog, or social interactions with friends. But others can take every bit of your attention and willpower. Even if you have a medical condition that makes it harder for you to concentrate, like attention deficit disorder, if you can target your energy when—and where—you need to, you will get better results. If you do have ADD or AD/HD, it is even more crucial to have an organized schedule for your time. Continue to schedule your time, and, if need be, work with a partner or counselor to help you stay on track. Behavioral therapy, emotional counseling, and practical support are all options for those suffering from ADHD.[15]

Next we discuss an area where increasing your focus will give you better results.

At School

Forgive me for sounding like your parents here, but when you work on something specific, give all your attention to it. Splitting your attention between two or three (or more) things is the first enemy to getting a job done. And trust me, it will show. Studying in the library is not the time to think about that car you really want or Britney Spears jumping out of your birthday cake. A small amount of concentration is going to give only small results, so when it is time to work, buckle down and work.

Staying on track is a little harder when you are with others. When you go to the library, try to avoid sitting with your best friend. If you do sit with your friend, you are not likely to finish much. Find your own niche to concentrate on your English paper or homework problem. If you do study with a group, stay on task and do schoolwork. Save the jokes and gossip for before and after the studying. If you talk about it with your friends and/or study group in advance, they will probably appreciate it, because they probably have to work to keep their focus, too.

THE ADVISOR SAYS:

Although group study is a great tool, it can be detrimental if you are not careful. The group should have at least one task-oriented person to make sure everyone stays focused.

Putting Time Management into Practice Requires Work

Planning and managing your time is useless unless you are going to put it into practice. To make your schedule and get everything done, you will have to roll up your sleeves and get your hands dirty every day. This may seem unpleasant, but as my grandfather says, "It's never easy and seldom fun, but it sure does feel good when it's over and done."

Remember in Chapter 2 we said that attitude is everything? Here again is an application of that. Whatever work needs to be done, it is important to think of it as enjoyable. Everyone has to do the work, but life can be much less stressful if you have a positive outlook and attitude about your job. Reviewing your goals—and your progress toward those goals, often—is important for enjoying the ride. Reviewing your journey will keep you tuned in to the progress of your efforts—that even on large goals, you are moving. Feeling that you are going somewhere may be just what you need to keep going!

Have fun with your college life and everything that you get to learn. This will determine your success in achieving your goals, but also your quality of life along the way. Success is not a destination, it is a journey, and enjoyment is part of it.

In addition to enjoying yourself, you have to make a commitment.

> "Juggling sports and classes, I had meetings, practice, weight room, and plays to learn. It was a lot more than I had expected. Putting that much time into athletics and then adding classes to the mix, then try to be social—it can seem overwhelming, but it is possible with planning and hard work."
>
> —Graduate, Media Communications Major

Meet Bill Dickenson

Bill Dickenson was quite an intense guy. He was the director of a main branch for one of the largest investment firms in the country. Bill did not have an MBA, a Ph.D., or any degree for that matter. His education stopped at the eighth grade. From starting in the mailroom as a kid, Bill had worked his way to his position, grinding out the daily routine without any excuses. The most amazing story about Bill, though, was not his title at work, his "overcome all the odds" corporate story, or anything to do with work. It was his coaching intensity with a local Little League team in his hometown. Bill took every thing and every commitment very seriously. When his son started playing Little League, the coach suddenly quit, and it was Bill who took the reigns. All the players wanted to win the league championship more than anything in the world, so Bill was going to deliver.

His first day of coaching, Bill rounded up all the parents and players to lay out his plan for the season. His plan to win? The team would practice seven days per week for two hours per day. Missing one practice meant sitting out for the next game—no excuses. Missing more than one practice meant you were off the team. Being fair, Bill basically told everyone, "If you do not like this policy, leave now, because it will not be changed."

No one left. From that day forward, the team practiced as hard as possible, and Bill continued to coach for seven years. His team not only won the championship that year, but every one of the seven years that he coached.

Bill's team won because of their commitment to the schedule set forth and hard work put into each practice. Scheduling was important, but so was the commitment. To put your time-management skills into practice and really count for something, it is necessary to keep that commitment and follow through.

Keeping that commitment means fending off something else, too.

The Evil Procrastination

I know, I know. Now you have all this knowledge on how to manage your time, and you know how to fend off people who do not want you to succeed. But there is yet another enemy I want to warn you about. It is something all of us fight against every day—procrastination.

Tomorrow Is Not an Excuse

- The alarm goes off. You hit snooze. Time to leave for class. "We're not really going over anything important," you think.
- Time to go to the gym. You are tired. "I'll just skip today and go tomorrow," you think.
- That research paper? "I don't need to start yet, I have the whole weekend!"

There are so many small jobs that you can put off. But if you look down the road, it hardly makes sense. If you put one job off, and then another, they are all going to crowd together to become a big, collective pain. Even worse, putting them off can hold you back from getting where you want!

Procrastination, boiled down, is thinking in the moment. Think about the alarm clock example. Is it really worth it to be late to class or work to sleep in for 10 more minutes? Is it worth missing an important lecture for just being lazy?

How about getting/staying in shape? Is that worth tossing out the window for a little bit of that chocolate-cherry-cream-whipped-caramel-glazed-M&M-sprinkled sundae (even if it does sound pretty good)?

NO!

Right now, you might be asking, "Just one missed class or late paper can derail all my efforts?" Sounds ridiculous, huh? Although each one of these issues—alone—may not create much of a problem, the cumulative effect can be potent. Ridiculous it may sound. But it does not change the fact that all these small decisions are what make the difference between success and failure.

Good grades are not the sole reason to fight against procrastination, though. There was a study on college students that showed at the end of the semester, procrastinators experienced higher levels of stress and even illness in comparison to their peers—and lower grades on top of it![16]

Stressed, sick, and a low GPA—does that sound like where you want to be?

Some tips for crushing procrastination:

- Review your goals every day.

- Follow your schedule. Using the worksheet from earlier in this chapter, stick to your schedule. Consult your plan for the day throughout the day.

- Have a place to work. It is important to find a place where you can focus on schoolwork. Some people can work at home; others need a less tempting environment like the library. Find what works for you.

- Give some incentives. If you head to the library, let yourself take a short break every hour or so. Take a few minutes to talk on the phone or surf the Net—this will give you a reward to look forward to.

Beating procrastination is a crucial step toward your college success, and away from getting stressed out, even sick.

Never Let Yourself off the Hook

If you commit to a goal and a certain time line, never let yourself off the hook. There is always a reason or some room to make excuses, but there is no place for it in a successful college life. Excuses are the quitter's way of not really quitting—so they think. It is important to take your goals and plans seriously. However you decide to reward yourself for staying committed (or punish yourself for not), follow through on it. The easiest way to fail on your current goals is to make an excuse and let yourself get away with it. Devise a system where you are rewarded for your accomplishments and punished—not for your failures if you tried—for not trying. This is a direct challenge from me to you to follow through and never quit. It is obvious, but a tough goal might not be accomplished if you try it, but it definitely will not be accomplished if you do not try.

Just Get Started!

The hardest part is going to the gym, starting the paper, or getting out of bed. Instead of putting yourself through all the anxiety, just start! The best treatment for a stalled project is to get off your butt and get to work. Yep, it's that simple!

"To make time for everything, set your priorities —that's it!"

—Junior, Math Major

WHEN THE GOING GETS TOUGH—
HANDLING SETBACKS

"If you have a setback and need to get back on track, adjust. You may have to cut back on one thing or another, but always keep some of everything."

—Senior, International
Affairs Major

Now for the tough situations. So what happens when you get a bad grade on a test, if you miss a couple days working out, if your girlfriend/boyfriend breaks up with you? What happens when the momentum suddenly halts? Can you recover? Can you pick back up and still reach the goals you have set for yourself?

Sure you can.

Setbacks are a part of life. In fact, the greatest leaders and most highly regarded people are those who made it through setbacks and rose up in the face of adversity. If you have set realistic goals and have the right attitude, you can make it through these situations; it is only a matter of mentally preparing yourself for them before they smack you upside the head. The way you deal with tough situations is actually the time to shine.

How do you prepare for interruptions in your perfectly planned-out life? The key is, plan for them. Factor them into your daily plans. First, do not assume everything is going to follow the blueprint you have laid out. There are going to be little inconveniences and rearrangements in your plan. But if you have planned on some adversity, if you have thought about it beforehand, what's the big deal when you hit a little roadblock?

- Live for the future, and do not get caught up in yesterday. There is nothing you can do if your schedule crumbles occasionally. Some circumstances are beyond your control. No matter how badly you want to go back, you cannot. So let it go. Learn what you can from the experience and move on.

- Whatever you do, do not let a mistake convince you to give up. If you miss one class, that does not mean the semester is a wash. If you eat one bad meal, that does not mean the rest of the day is over. Get right back on track and do not wait until tomorrow. Keep moving ahead, toward your goals, and remember that small setbacks will happen. So be prepared to handle them in a mature fashion.

- Remember: You are not the only one who ever had something go wrong in life. Keep (or lift) your head up, look around, and know you can, and will, get past this—and you will be a better, stronger person for it.

Staying in the Game

Keep these tips in mind when college gets tough.

The original motivational tool is positive thinking, and it is still the best. At least once (maybe even a number of times), you will walk away from a test or class disappointed with your grade. But if you can look at the upside—what you can learn from it— that bit of knowledge will help you the next time.

A friend of mine did poorly on one of our upper-level biology classes and was not happy about it. But, after thinking about it, he decided that his study time was not enough: that maybe if he studied a little more for the next one, he could still earn an A in the class. And it worked. He looked on the positive side—what he could still do—instead of focusing on the low grade.

Ever heard the saying, "When it rains, it pours?" Well, that can certainly be true. Positive and negative outcomes tend to snowball. They build momentum and get bigger and bigger, many times in whichever direction you push them.

My best workouts come when I am in the best shape. In other words, the times when I need to work out the least, I actually work out the hardest. The same can be said for attitude. When you build confidence to a certain level, it tends to build on itself. It may even seem like everything you touch turns to gold. On the other side, when you are down, everything seems to go wrong.

In college, keeping the snowball rolling the positive way is a challenge. But it is much harder to stop the snowball when it is going the wrong way. So strike first to keep that snowball rolling uphill.

Stoking Your Motivation

To keep you riding on the Success Express, use these three pointers:

- Remember WHY.
- Use personal motivators.
- Keep your good friends around.

Remember WHY

If you do not have a relatively deep reason for achieving a difficult goal, it may be hard to cross the finish line. Chances are, if you have taken the time to write your goal down and plan how you will achieve it, you have a good idea of why you are attempting it. It is important to write this WHY down and keep it handy. When the road gets tough (and it will), you will need to read your deep-seated reason for wanting this. When you have three tests in one week, a paper due, and a 15-minute presentation coming up, it can be easy to get bogged down and forget the real reason. When you refer back to your original motivation, though (such as gaining admission to law school because you have always wanted to be a lawyer), it will give you a fresh perspective to see the situation. Never underestimate the power of reason in achieving your goals.

Use Personal Motivators

For some people, it is a certain song; for others a picture, a quote, or something else. For one reason or another, we all have items that strike a chord with us and motivate us to get a move on. Use this phenomenon to your advantage. Feeling down? Put on that favorite song and get fired up again! Read that certain quote and let things brighten up a bit. Only you can know which of these works best for you. I only ask you to use it!

Keep Good Friends Around

As we discussed earlier, keep those people around that encourage you. Ask them, or let them give you a pep talk now and then. Another, outside perspective can really open your eyes again. Whatever you do, do not let others' insecurities get to you. They are self-destructing and damaging. Focus on the positive outcome and listen to your positive peers!

THIS STUFF IS REALLY USEFUL!

You may be thinking that this stuff is not really necessary to keep ahead in college. All the planning, motivational techniques, and encouragement—they may all seem a bit over the top. It is true, though. This is not meaningless information to fill blank pages; it is real, tried-and-true advice from those who have experienced success in college. Many of the top students and those who really come out ahead actually do these things.

Many students will find it easy to criticize this way of thinking, but they have not tried it. Others will contend that it is impossible for students to live this way and do all these things and still enjoy themselves. Once again, not the case! The techniques here are the basis for a great and productive time at college. Furthermore, learning to use these skills will lay a foundation for tremendous success for the rest of your life. After all, college is only four years; there will be many more to come that demand the same (if not more) effort.

Forget any doubts you have or the baseless ranting of people who never succeeded. Listen to your gut feeling that pushed you to be the best, and feed it with these ideas. You will never be sorry, and will be sure to stay ahead of the pack.

Classes, Professors, Majors, and Resources

"Failure to prepare is preparing to fail."
—Mike Murdock

SCHEDULING: YOUR FIRST ENCOUNTER WITH COLLEGE CLASSES

Most colleges require you to register for your own classes right from the start, and making sense out of all the numbers and prefixes can seem like translating the Dead Sea Scrolls. So the first appointment to make for college is with an academic advisor.

61

Advisors Are There for You

THE ADVISOR SAYS:

The students who are most successful and finish in a timely manner see their advisors every term.

Your advisor will more than likely be assigned to you, and in most colleges, your advisor will be on staff in your major's department. The advisor is there for you, and the most efficient way to get on track is to use the advisor to help guide you through the swamp of schedules and class choices.

Just in case you think it is too much trouble to contact your advisor, or that you can go it alone, think twice. Even if you are able to get information on which classes you need in another way (like the college's Web site), advisors have the inside scoop. Classes can be cancelled, or the available classes may be full. No matter how often a Web page is updated, that kind of information will be hard to find out. And if you do not find out in time, you could end up having to take more summer classes—even extend your graduation date! So do the smart thing: Meet your advisor early and often.

Advisor Problems?

Starting with an advisor who is not the perfect fit happens. Colleges do their best, but some of the legwork—to find the best advisor for you—is left to you. It usually is not a problem to switch advisors. If your college assigns advisors, just approach the head of academic advising for the department. Chances are, if the bad advisor really is doing a poor job, you will not be the first to complain. Be sure to speak up and not be shy about your displeasure. You are paying good money to attend college; make sure to get your money's worth.

For colleges that do not appoint advisors, the dirty work is left to you. If this is the case at your school, do some informal research. Ask other students about their advisors. Chances are, you will find the best advisor by asking just a few people. If you do not know anybody and cannot find the information through the grapevine, do the old trial-and-error method—set an appointment and see what happens. You may burn through a few before you find the perfect fit, but the time you spend will be worth it.

My Story

As a transfer student wanting to switch majors, I needed to find an advisor, *stat*. I did not know a soul, so I went to the office to make an appointment with . . . anyone. Lo and behold, my first session was a dud. My advisor seemed to know little more than I did about what classes to take (and I didn't know anything). So, I kept going.

Luckily, on my second try, I struck gold. My new advisor was extremely intelligent, organized, and in the know. Not only did she help me switch majors and set up my new courses, she gave me advice on professor selection, course load information, and tips to make my college career more successful. She was able to share stories (without names, of course) of other successful students, and the interesting things they had done to achieve their goals. This was both helpful and motivating.

My advisor guided me through the rest of my time at college, helping me hurdle obstacles and overcome problems. To make everything to do with college classes easier and add another name to your mounting network, find a terrific advisor.

The campus has many resources available; academic advisors are just one. Use them like coaches to help you plan your academic strategy and stay on top of the most recent developments. Advisors are also a great resource when applying to another college or any type of graduate school. So visit their office and ask them questions—it's their job!

Transfer Students

Transfer students need be especially vigilant about finding an advisor. Beginning at a new school thinking you know this whole college thing can be an unpleasant surprise when it comes to light that those 30 credits you thought you had do not count. So, one of the absolute first things to do when you get on campus is find your advisor using the steps just discussed. Your advisor can help you sort through what counts and what does not count and where it all fits with your new school's requirements.

Make a Reasonable Schedule

Getting used to college can be tough for a lot of folks. A huge class load is the best way to ruin your semester and your sanity. Many students receive their lowest GPA the first semester in school, so taking a smaller number of credits early can have less of an impact while you get adjusted. Bottom line: Be reasonable when making your class schedule; do not overload yourself, especially in the first semester.

THE ADVISOR SAYS:

The biggest mistake students make is overloading themselves with too many credit hours. Trying to rush through the process because of what tradition says, or what your family says. Take five or six courses, try to add on a job, and it just becomes a catastrophe.

"Be careful starting with a full-time load the first semester in college. I started at ¾ time, so I learned the environment and study skills. Then after, I would up it bit by bit. When you have reached your threshhold, stay below it. For me an average of 14 to 15 credits and working on the side is about my limit. It's like wading into a pool of ice water—you want to do it kind of slow."

—Senior, Science Major

THE ADVISOR SAYS: | *A most common mistake: Students take an easy senior year in high school and come completely unprepared for college classes. Work hard at the end of high school, it will help once you get to college.*

Learn the Lingo

Every college has its own terminology and coding systems to identify classes and potential schedules. Understanding that PHY 2053 is physics with calculus, and that PHY 2043 is physics without calculus can make or break (literally) a semester schedule. If you do not believe it, just ask me! Learning the abbreviations can eliminate much of the hassle of finding your class schedule for the next semester, and can prevent mishaps.

Also, pay careful attention to when classes are offered. You may have a perfectly planned schedule; for example, you planned to take Principles of Marketing next fall. Then you find out that Marketing is only offered in the spring! Sure, your advisor will help with this kind of thing, but that's just the thing—they will help. If you are going to be the boss of your college life, you have to keep your eyes and ears open to everything. Only relying on an advisor is an unwise way to approach the academic side of college. Knowing when classes are offered (and not offered) can save you some major scheduling headaches.

The Reasonable versus Unreasonable Schedule

THE ADVISOR SAYS: | *When [students] start off in college, they think they know what they can handle based on what they handled in high school. It is usually not a fair correlation.*

Deciding what you can and cannot handle can be a tough call, especially if you work and have other responsibilities. The best advice to live by under these circumstances is "Schedule conservatively." Racking up an impressive schedule is harmful if those classes end up as C's, D's, F's, and Withdrawals.

Who determines what is reasonable and what is not? At first, rely on an experienced advisor. True, the advisors may be wrong—you may have been able to handle more than was suggested. But it is better to find that out and still have good grades, than to find out that you were wrong and have a big dent in your transcripts. After a semester or two, you will be able to make the call yourself.

Once again, transfer students need not be cocky on this issue, either. Different schools can differ in difficulty level. A course load that might have been simple at one school could be next to impossible at another. Check with your advisor.

About Withdrawals

THE ADVISOR SAYS:

Usually a withdrawal is better than a D or F. Policies at each institution vary widely. Speaking to faculty often will let students know how or if they can set themselves straight so that they do not have to withdraw.

Withdrawing from a class is commonly defined as dropping a class during the semester, past the penalty-free period (most schools have a week or two at the beginning of classes where students may drop a class with no effect to transcripts). When a student withdraws, a mark is added to that student's transcript, usually in the form of a W for the corresponding class.

As The Advisor mentioned, policies on withdrawing from classes differ from college to college. One thing is always true, though: A significant number of withdrawals can do harm to landing a good job or gaining acceptance to graduate school.

THE ADVISOR SAYS:

In graduate school, it can be more difficult to withdraw from classes, so getting used to operating that way can complicate life later.

Withdrawals stay on your transcript, and although better than an F, a large number of them can indicate a lack of commitment—something that anyone examining a school record will notice. For emergencies, such as a death in the immediate family or complete breakdown, it is completely appropriate to withdraw. That is just it; you as the student must have a reasonable explanation for any withdrawal. As an every-semester pastime, they will do nothing but hurt your record.

If you believe you are doing poorly in a class and may need to withdraw, see your professor. This may help you work through the problem and find an appropriate solution. You may end up withdrawing anyway, but you will never know unless you see your professor.

Visiting your professor may have benefits just beyond withdrawing or recovering in a class. Most schools have a designation (for extenuating circumstances) called an Incomplete or I. Being granted an incomplete means just that, you have not completed the course requirements, but will do so at a later date. Usually, incompletes are given at the institution's discretion (you are not guaranteed an incomplete). If you have a legitimate reason for needing to finish class requirements at a later date, be sure to speak with your professor about it. Lastly, if you do take an I, complete the requirements ASAP. Students have been known to push the deadline, only to realize they have forgotten much of the material.

THE ADVISOR SAYS:

Withdrawals may also hurt a student's financial aid—[financial aid] can even be dropped.

Remember Professors When Scheduling

My motto has always been that a determined student can do well in any class, regardless of the professor. Though this may be true, the difficulty level and teaching ability of the professor may differ, even greatly.

Most college students live by "the professor grapevine." The professor grapevine is the underground, informal rating of professors around any college campus.

"Never take Dunder for Econ., the guy is a nightmare!"

"Smith is, hands down, the worst professor on campus. Never take a class with him if possible!"

OR

"Jacobs makes the class so interesting, it's actually fun going to class."

"He's tough, but you'll learn more than you could ever imagine with Dr. Brown. His lectures are amazing!"

Though it has flaws, this informal network can be a good barometer for a professor. Do not be scared of a professor, though, just because the class is hard. Rather, be concerned if the class is outrageously boring, or if most people who have taken it learn little or nothing. Focus on professors who love what they teach and enjoy teaching. Not only will you learn more, but you will enjoy the learning experience much more (and maybe finish with a better grade for it!). For a virtual professor grapevine, check out http://www.RateMyProfessors.com.

Availability can be a factor as well. Some professors are extremely popular; unless you are a 10th year senior you may have a hard time finding a spot in the class. Look for the balance. Try to find a professor who teaches well and is somewhat available.

Take Your Time

College is not a sprint, it's a marathon. Of course you will want to take a normal amount of classes, but this does not mean attempting

> "If you have no way around it, just suck it up and take the bad professor. If you work harder than anyone else, you will come out on top. Giving 110 percent—no matter who the professor is—you will do well."
>
> —Senior, Microbiology Major

to defend your Ph.D. during your sophomore year. For example, many graduate schools would rather see a normal load of classes with great grades, than a huge load of classes with mediocre grades. Keep on top of things by

- finding a great advisor.
- staying up-to-date on scheduling.
- listening to the professor grapevine (to a degree).
- taking your time.

Remember the reason you are in college: To learn, not to get out!

THE ADVISOR SAYS:

Taking smaller steps and succeeding with those, even if it does take a semester or two longer, is the best way to handle college classes.

GETTING THROUGH AND MAKING THE MOST OUT OF CLASSES

Classes, even studying for exams, can be fun if you learn how to study and know a few secrets. You can knock out any college course and have professors eating out of your hand, if you do it right.

Well, something like that.

On a serious note, to do well in school, you have to want to do well. As the saying goes, "Where there's a will, there's a way." Excelling in college requires some will-power. So let's look ahead and start learning!

Six Strategies

Making the best of your classes requires attention and some TLC. If you follow these next tips and strategies, you will be alarmed at how productive your classes can be. Learning is fun, but sometimes classes are thought of as the downer part of college. There are no two ways around it, though—you have to get through the classes (and you can do it while having fun)! Much of the stress at school comes from classes; they can be long and dry, as well as difficult! But classes are where a lot of learning takes place, and doing well in them means big rewards later.

No matter what you think of your classes, they are going to be an everyday reality. So get used to the idea.

What are you more likely to do for a good time: go out to shoot pool with your friends or attend a class discussing political regimes of the Croatian region?

"Pick the classes around the type of student you are. Do you work better in the morning or evening? Then schedule your classes around that. If you are not a morning person, the 8:00 class? Don't do it! Getting your classes done early sounds good, but there are going to be times when you won't wake up. Schedule the classes a little bit later, around 9:00 or 10:00, so that you are still done early, but you will make it to class."

—Junior, American Studies Major

Do not answer—it is rhetorical, and hopefully obvious. Making your classes as fun as a night out with your friends may be a little far-fetched, but then, your classes do not have to be as bad as going to the dentist, either.

Classes do not have to be a place that you dread—though you are bound to encounter a couple that are about as exciting as a family reunion. To get the most out of classes and make them a little less boring, try some of these ideas that helped all kinds of college students, me included.

The Big #1: You Have to Go!

If you can get this part right, you are halfway over the hurdle already. Academics is like anything else; you have to lay a foundation to do well. On the academic side of college, that foundation is class, each and every one.

The student who rolls out of bed and shows up with only a pencil and a dumb grin every time the syllabus says there is a test? Well, that student can be out of luck sometimes—usually many times. Classes are an information session; they can give you all kinds of hot tips, including:

- test date changes (this is definitely known to happen).
- the professor's expectations on assignments and tests.
- what you should expect from the class.
- lessons on the material.

There are 1,001 reasons to miss class, and I am sure that we all can think of some great examples (beach, anyone?). Classes may have attendance policies. But you will most likely have a few that require you to take tests—and that's it! Though it is tempting to miss classes when you get to college because it may no longer be required, this habit can put a big dent in your GPA. And that little bit of help you might need from your profs some day (i.e., letters of recommendation, etc.)? Well, it is less likely that you will get that help if the professor does not even recognize you. Going to class each and every day not only helps with your college career, it helps afterward too. Developing the discipline it takes to attend every class can transfer to a similar determination needed to keep a job or to find one. So, in addition to just references and help from well-connected professors, attendance can benefit your career path as well.

It is a fact: Students who attend their classes religiously outperform their absentee counterparts on a regular basis. It is not that hard to pick your butt up and go, so do yourself a favor and make it—your professor may even let you bring a pillow (doubtful, though).

> "I came into college thinking that I would not be able to finish in four years. I promised myself that I would go to every class my first semester, and I did it. I knew that I had to start strong and made sure I did not miss anything or have any excuses for myself. It was a big step for me, setting the standard for how I wanted to succeed."
>
> —Graduate, Media Communications Major

> "Pay attention to your biorhythms; schedule your classes around them as best you can. It will make it easier to go, and easier to succeed in the course."
>
> —Senior, Education Major

Some easy ways to get more from your classes and make them more fun:

- Stay awake.
- Make friends.
- Pay attention and ask questions.
- Be creative when it comes to lectures.

Stay Awake!

This can definitely be a challenge in some classes. For most college students, it is the morning rather than afternoon lectures that kill. Although a boring class, no matter what time, can make counting sheep seem invigorating. To help you stay awake:

- take some coffee (if your professor allows it).
- splash cold water on your face before you head in.
- shower and get dressed before class instead of just rolling out of bed; you will feel more ready for the day. Feeling ready for class is a big help. Maybe shuffling to class in your pajamas will work for you, but many students feel as if they are still curled up in bed.

Make Friends

If you know people in your classes, you will look forward to going and meeting up with them. Friends can help make it more fun and exciting and give some help when it is time to study. If you are sick or out of town, you can also get the notes and lecture info without having to tell the professor that you couldn't make it.

Some accountability never hurts either. If you feel lazy or tired, you will know that someone is going to ask where you are. So your crew can help keep you in check.

STUDENT PROFILE—Todd H. on Accountability

Playing a sport, there was accountability to other players. We had 8 to 10 players in a group that held each other accountable for going to class—that is good in anything when trying to succeed. After high school, when your parents are no longer on your case, it's good to have someone who wants you to succeed, but isn't in your business. By holding each other accountable, not only did we go, but we formed better friendships—and class was a little more fun.

➤ *You may not play a college sport like Todd, but name one way to make yourself accountable for class attendance and assignments.*

Just be sure to hook up with the right people in class. The friends thing can backfire if you are best friends with the class clown and the professor starts to dislike you, too!

Pay Attention, Ask Questions, and Take Notes

A boring lecture can actually jump to life if you start to really listen. Paying attention not only helps you learn the material, but it might even help you keep both eyes open!

You are guaranteed to pass the time quicker and learn more if you get involved in the lecture. I remember working in a restaurant at the beach one summer. Not only did we make better tips when the place was busy, but work blew by! When you feel like class is dragging along, really pay attention, keep your mind busy, and you will have learned something and be done before you know it. And if you tend to have a dreamy mind, the easiest solution is to sit near the front. The closer you sit to the professor, the more likely you will be to get interested (and the more likely the professor will notice it, too).

Asking lots of questions can help clarify the material and make class seem shorter than a director's cut of *Gone with the Wind*. Also, you will get a better handle on the material. Keep in mind, the only dumb question is the one not asked. Do not be afraid of asking your question, no matter how simple it may seem. Chances are, others in the class would like to know the same thing! Once again, the teacher will notice your interest, too, and that never hurts.

Consistently paying attention adds to your retention of the material as well. Regurgitating a bunch of facts for the test, after which you forget everything, is not the mark of a truly successful student. Retention comes from understanding the material, and learning to retain information will be important not only for college, but for your career. Pay attention in that lecture—it will help the material sink in so that you will understand and remember, not just know it.

Note Taking

If you are lacking in note-taking skills, you certainly will need to bring them up to speed for college. Good note taking is partly good listening, and learning what is and what is not important. There may be a course at your institution in which note taking is addressed.

The skill of learning what is important comes with practice and getting to know your professor. But, at the start, if you are lacking either the practice of ever having taken a class with that professor, go see the professor to get the best advice for that class on expectations and note taking.

"For people who attend a large university, getting used to the huge classes can be tough. I found sitting in the front few rows gave me the feeling of being in a small classroom, and made class more bearable."

—Senior, Biology Major

Be Creative When It Comes to Lectures

If you are anything like many college students, it is hard to take great notes and still listen to every word or example the professor utters. Most professors do not mind if you bring a small tape recorder to class and record the lecture—as long as you are not selling it, of course. If you are not sure that taping is allowed, just be sure to ask first.

By taping the lecture, you will be able to add more detail to the notes you took in class. And you can listen to the lecture a tad more closely when laying around your dorm or cruising around town. One student had a 45-minute commute to school and used this time for listening to her professor's lectures. Her 45-minute commute ended up shaving off some traditional study time and was put to good use.

There is another good reason to tape lectures if you can. We all tend to space out here and there. Or maybe, if you had a late night, uh . . . studying, for instance . . . you could even be a little tired. (Imagine that, a college student being tired at an 8:00 A.M. class!) Class after lunch can also put you right out, making that seat in Critical Thinking feel like a La-Z-Boy.

Tired, zoned-out, whatever—what I am getting at is that very often, for one reason or another, we miss small but important details that are given in lectures. Recording the class is yet another tool to ensure that you cross your t's and dot your i's.

Just because you record the lecture does not mean that you should sit there and not even try to pay attention. Also, for those of you who are tempted to skip class and try to listen to your friends' recordings—not a good idea. There are always examples, figures, or problems that the professor shows on the overhead, board, or computer. These cannot be revisited by a tape alone. The recording is there to supplement your understanding of the lecture, the one you did your best to stay awake for. So use it as a tool, not as a ticket to skip out on class.

If you must go out of town, listening to taped lectures is the best way to catch up. In addition to speaking with your professor, listening to the missed lecture—verbatim—will help keep you on top of your work.

How James Bond Tapes a Class

If you are a little bit uncomfortable bringing a tape recorder to class (if it isn't normal at your school), tuck it away. Most recorders will work stuffed in the top of your book bag (leaving the top unzipped, of course) or slipped under your seat. Before you record though, make sure that your professor allows it.

Trade-offs

A great way to get a mix of learning styles is trading off duties with a friend in class. Before you make any arrangements, though, make sure that the other individual is as committed and dependable as you are. You may switch note-taking duties every other class (this is something many graduate schools students do, like medical school students). As you know, it is basically impossible to listen perfectly and take great notes all at once. So, in addition to taping the lecture, ask a friend to partner up with you. It will be a great mix to keep you fresh at every class.

Do It For You

Going to class and taking school seriously is up to you. If you are not serious, it will definitely show.

Classes Can Involve Working with Others

College may be the first time you have ever needed to work as a team with your peers. Many high schools require few, if any, team projects, but learning this skill is ultimately very important in college and the future beyond that. Working as part of a group can be easy if you have great partners, or a real struggle if you get stuck with some lazy students.

Classes That Require a Group Effort

There are many college courses that require working with one or more students every period. Lab classes are the most common classes that use this type of format.

Working with a partner in a lab class can be tough. If you are taking, say, Analytical Chemistry, and your grade depends on making a certain amount of the desired compound (and you only have one shot), it is important for you and your lab partner to be prepared.

To work with a lab partner, start with these suggestions:

- Lay out expectations at the start.
- Meet before the lab class (that's days before, not hours) to make sure that you both are prepared.
- Split the work, if necessary.

Just as you would do with a roommate, laying out your expectations at the start of class can potentially diffuse big problems down the road. Not only will it help the person learn and get used to your expectations, it will also determine whether that person is a good partner or not. If you can find this out early, so much the better. Usually, it is possible to switch partners at the start of classes if you need to. Waiting until later can make it impossible.

Meeting a number of days before class begins can also ease stress when it is time to get busy in the class. There is nothing worse than arriving and having to direct everything your partner does because he or she did not read the assignment. It is far better to avoid this by meeting early and letting your partner know what you expect. So meet prior to discuss any problems. If you cannot

"If you are just going to school to make your parents happy, you will get grades that reflect it. When you get to a point where you are goal-oriented, there's a difference. You get out what you put in. Once you are focused, you are more driven."

—Senior, Civil Engineering Major

figure out the issue between the both of you, you will still have time to attend the professor's office hours to ask for help.

Split the Work

If your professor allows it, split the work between the two of you. Focusing on different ends of the board can help you both to complete it quicker. In addition, during the meetings, you can teach your side of the experiment, not only helping your partner, but increasing your own understanding as well.

PROFESSORS

Never underestimate the power of a well-educated, well-connected professor. Professors are the brains of the university, and they are there to help you (partly anyway). So use their professional advice and make sure to

- get to know them.
- ask for letters of recommendation.
- take their recommendations.
- use their office hours.

Get to Know Your Professors

Becoming acquainted with your professors is a surefire way to

1. get more interested in the class (more interest translates into better grades).
2. get a highly educated (and many times, interesting) perspective on many issues.
3. keep you motivated to do well.
4. set yourself up for a great letter of recommendation.

Professors can help cultivate more interest in their courses by telling you about the cool stuff. On almost any subject, there is a great deal of interesting information behind the scenes that professors, because of time constraints, do not have time to touch on in class. Remember: The more interested you are in the class work, the easier it is to handle.

Besides handling the workload, it is also important to learn about issues and the different perspectives on them. We all know that professors are usually a rather interesting and unique group of individuals. This is partly due to the passion many of them feel about their particular field, and partly because of their high level of education. This education and expertise often provides insightful views that will help you widen your scope of thinking. So when

> "Professors are exciting because you can talk with these people who are sometimes pushing the edge of knowledge, and gain insight from them."
> —Graduate, Chemistry Major

you go to visit them, let them talk. Listen to what they have to say—they will love you for it, and you will learn a lot. Although they are not always right, they can make you think about their side of an issue, helping you to become more well-rounded and better educated.

Motivation is another reason for getting to know your professor. Being accountable for his or her class adds extra incentive for you to do well. Once they get to know you, many professors will ask how you are doing in the course or take note of when your grades have slipped. But do not look at this as interference. This is just one more strategic move in keeping yourself cranking out top-notch grades.

Letters of Recommendation

The excellent grades are not the end of the line, though. Whether you plan to go to graduate school or head out to get a job after college, connections never hurt. Getting to know your professor can set you up for a great letter of recommendation, which is crucial to being accepted to graduate school or landing a sweet internship.

Tips on Getting a Great Letter of Recommendation

1. Get to know some of your professors, and only approach those you know the best for a letter. Asking a professor you only saw during class to write you a stellar recommendation is not a wise move (and it probably will not pan-out well).

2. Ask the recommender to write you a *strong* letter. If there is a large hesitation or a "No," you will definitely want to find another person to write your letter. A mediocre letter is not something that you want in your file/application.

3. If you are asking for a recommendation from someone other than a professor, be cautious. If the individual does not usually write recommendations, give him or her a complete packet of your accomplishments, if so agreed. In this packet, it is certainly appropriate to include some help such as "10 Tips for Recommenders" from the grad school section of http://Accepted.com (see Table 6-1). This can help the recommender write you a better letter.

But a good recommendation is only the beginning. Getting to know your professors and having them get to know you keeps many doors open for whatever you end up doing postgraduation.

Take Their Recommendations

If you plan to get something like a letter of recommendation, advice on internships, or research opportunities, flatter the profes-

Table 6-1. 10 Tips for Recommenders[29]

1. Review a copy of the applicant's personal statement or application essays so that your letter of recommendation can dovetail with—not conflict with or duplicate—the rest of the application.

2. Ask the applicant to supply you with additional information like a résumé.

3. Describe your qualifications for comparing the applicant to other applicants.

4. Discuss how well you know the applicant.

5. Choose two to three qualities that you observed in the applicant.

6. In discussing those qualities, support your statements with specific instances in which he or she demonstrated those attributes. Be as concrete and detailed as possible.

7. Try to quantify the student's strengths or rank him or her vis-à-vis other applicants that you have observed.

8. Avoid generalities and platitudes.

9. Include some mild criticism, typically the flip-side of a strength.

10. Discuss the applicant's potential in his or her chosen field.

"Tips for Recommenders" by Linda Abraham from www.Accepted.com.

sors a little and take their recommendations! When a professor says in class "It may be a good idea to get this book," or "It might be good to review the class Web page," do it!

Aside from showing them that you are smart, taking your professors' recommendations will impress them when you approach them outside of class. Profs love to know that students are working, especially above and beyond what is required. Taking and discussing their recommendations is a surefire way to impress them. And you never know when that is going to come in handy.

Use Office Hours

You know those two-hour windows when students assume professors are sitting in their office and doing nothing but playing computer games or talking on the phone? Well, this nifty playtime has a formal name: Office Hours. And they are there for you, the student; so use them!

> "I'm a person who did not always excel in academics, so I would advise someone who was not a straight 'A' student and probably needs a little extra attention to use their professors as much as possible. They can really help you understand the material."
>
> —Junior, Business Major

Use the office hours. Anyone on a college campus will tell you that many students fail to take advantage of them. Since the whole purpose behind this book is to learn to set yourself apart, what better way to set yourself apart from the entire class than by going to see the professor during this time? If you have questions or comments, bring them on. Stuck at an 89% when you are dying for that A? A steady stream of visits to your prof could be the deciding factor. The professor will get to know you on a personal level, and you will not just be another face in the crowd. And you will surely pick up tidbits of information during the visit that make all the difference.

Not all professors will want to know you, or have time to know you. Some college professors are very busy people who write textbooks, do consulting, and constantly travel. If you ever happen to have professors like this, do not hold it against them—they are just busy!

Professor Problems?

Professors are not perfect. If you attend a large university, they may be teaching several classes, each one comprised of hundreds of students! As with all of us, mistakes happen. When they do, and whenever dealing with professors, it is important to take a professional approach.

The Right Way to Complain

One of my professors had a great approach for any complaints about grading. The student was to attach a piece of notebook paper to the original test, explaining which question was graded wrong, and why. This was to be done at home and turned in one week after the test, rather than immediately after the tests were returned. This helped keep students from blowing a gasket. (After all, a mistake in grading can be really upsetting to some students.) So, rather than the professor trying to explain the mistake while the student was already upset, the student had a chance to rationally and carefully state his or her case based on the facts in the test, not on how he or she felt at the time. The professor would return both sheets, and explain his decision, within a couple of weeks.

Many fellow students complained, but hearing the professor's reasoning helped me to understand. In the real world, or in any type of job, problems have to be handled in a similar way. Marching into the boss's office, shaking a piece of paper, and complaining is a sure way to get oneself fired.

So if you do have an issue, with grades or anything else, try addressing it in a professional way. Of course, if this does not work, you have other avenues, like approaching the head of the department. Most professors, though, will respond in a kind and timely manner if they are treated with respect.

MAJORING IN *HUH?*

Some students attend programs solely for the purpose of learning a particular skill. Others know (and have always known) exactly what they want to do with their life. For the large number of others, here we go.

When I first started as an undergrad, I intended to do extremely well. I even had my mind set on the career I thought was sure to make me a success. Yet soon after I arrived, that all changed. Before I knew it, I was frustrated, bewildered, and downright clueless as to how to pull everything together.

What happened? I lost my motivation.

You can guess what this turned into: not-so-hot grades and a lot of wasted time. But I am not one to quit when I am down. I slowly started to piece together ideas, facts, and strategies to help myself understand how I could do better. I did a lot of soul searching and finally discovered what I was really interested in, rather than just picking out a sure-fire successful career choice. I finally listened to my interests, got focused, and changed my major.

So what happened after such a big decision? My brain caught fire, my GPA shot through the roof, I had time to work out more, and my social life was still fun!

I had discovered that my interests are my true motivations (hel-lo!).

We all know that one goal of college is to get the proper training for our career choice. One big question remains: What is that career? Which some students believe, means, What is that major (which is not so true as you will find out later)?

Picking Your Major: A Start

How do you find your interests? You must know what kind of questions to ask to find your interests, right?

This can get a little tricky, kind of like trying to predict the future, with or without a crystal ball. After all, how are you supposed to know what type of demands, personality, and thinking it takes for certain careers?

CollegeView.com Questions[5]

Most people can get a realistic idea of what college major their interests best match by looking through the common ways of thinking that each major demands. Let's take a look at these basic questions, which will get you started in finding the right direction (see Table 6-2).

STUDENT PROFILE—Randy S. on Picking a Major

I started college wanting to be a Physical Education major so I could teach and make an impact, like my teachers had on me. But I subsequently switched majors into broadcasting by taking some classes and falling in love with it. I worked at the radio station on campus, did some things there, and with my passion for sports, was able to carry that into radio by calling some school games. I had found something I wanted to do. It was kind of weird how it happened. I just got on the radio and things flowed pretty easily—it came kind of naturally.

➤ *Which approach is better: Planning every step of your life from the start, and why? Or, do not plan anything and see what happens, and why? Or a combination of the two, and why?*

Table 6-2. Major Questions

Arts and Entertainment

❑ Are you talented, creative, and self-confident?

❑ Do you have a passion for drawing, painting, designing, singing, acting, or directing?

❑ Are you willing to work hard doing what you love, even if the pay is low?

Business and Finance

❑ Do you enjoy organizing or watching over details?

❑ Do you like to interact with people, selling them on your ideas or products?

❑ Can you type well, or analyze large sets of data?

❑ Are you a leader in school clubs, sports teams, or your community?

Computers and Technology

❑ Do you enjoy sitting in front of a computer for hours, perfecting your projects, programs, and designs?

❑ Do you see yourself as a logical, analytical thinker?

❑ Do you excel in math, science, or philosophy?

❑ Can you communicate ideas creatively and effectively?

Table 6-2. Major Questions *(concluded)*

Construction

- ❑ Do you get a kick out of making things with your hands that are tangible and useful?
- ❑ Do you have experience with carpentry, plumbing, or electrical work?
- ❑ Do you enjoy managing or designing large projects?
- ❑ Can you work hard, sometimes in unpleasant conditions?

Education

- ❑ Do you enjoy helping your peers understand things you are learning?
- ❑ Is reading one of your favorite hobbies?
- ❑ Do you like working with and helping children of different abilities and maturity levels?
- ❑ Is there any field of study that really excites you and that you want to continue learning about?

Engineering and Mechanical

- ❑ Do you like to build, repair, or improve things?
- ❑ Are you inquisitive about how things work?
- ❑ Can you think through a problem step-by-step mathematically?

Environment or Conservation

- ❑ Do recycling, energy conservation, and wildlife relocation excite you?
- ❑ Do you enjoy spending time outdoors, hiking, camping, bird watching, and the like?
- ❑ Can you manage large projects, working both individually and with groups?

Human Services

- ❑ Do you like caring for, listening to, or serving others?
- ❑ Do you enjoy doing community service projects?
- ❑ Are you good at interacting with people from many different backgrounds?

Media and Communications

- ❑ Can you play with words, either verbally or on paper?
- ❑ Are you good at getting ideas across to others?
- ❑ Do you enjoy experiencing or making music, drama, or films?
- ❑ Do you enjoy reading or writing for books, newspapers, or magazines?

Medicine and Health

- ❑ Have you always been someone who took care of other people?
- ❑ Are you able to work well under pressure and in uncomfortable situations?
- ❑ Do you want to help people become healthier every day?

The bottom line is, take a hard look at what you like to do, the things you enjoy spending your time on, and that you are good at. Chances are, that particular area is most well tailored to you. Do not forget that what you end up becoming is all up to you and how badly you want to get there. The amount of effort you put in will determine where you go, not just your major. Go ahead and complete the "Finding Your Major" Worksheet.

Do not worry if you have not yet decided on a major. Many students do not pick a major until their sophomore year. There is time the first year and into the second to kick the tires on different programs at your school.

WORKSHEET 6-1

Finding Your Major

After reading the Major Questions in Table 6-2, fill out the following:

Choose three categories that you most closely identified with:*

1.

2.

3.

Now, schedule an appointment with your college's career center. Here you can meet with a career counselor and take an aptitude test.

Appointment Date: _____

Appointment Time: _____

And, bring this sheet!

———————
* In line with your aptitude test and goals, discuss with the counselor any opportunities to further develop your interests in these three areas.

THE ADVISOR SAYS:

A good number of first year courses will go toward any major, so the first year is somewhat flexible.

When to Freak Out and When to Calm Down

It is totally unnecessary to freak out about picking a major. Picking a major is not like picking a husband or wife. Here are some reasons why:

- You can dump a major after a short time.
- If you choose to stick with it, the commitment only lasts until college is done, then you can do whatever you want.
- It is less trouble to change a major than get divorced.

See? Compared to marriage, a major is a relatively small commitment.

There are many examples of graduates gaining acceptance to grad schools and landing job offers that have nothing to do with their undergraduate major.

Just a few examples:

- French major in medical school
- Music major in law school
- Engineering major in business
- History major in finance
- Philosophy major in banking

A Larger-Than-Life Example

Jack Welch, the legendary CEO of General Electric Corporation, was a chemical engineering major at the University of Massachusetts, and received a Ph.D. in chemical engineering from the University of Illinois.[6] Yet for most of his career, he dealt with business negotiation, strategy, and motivation and training. Not exactly chemical engineering!

Two Rules

1. **Quit the What If? game.** Unless you are sure that another major is exactly what you want, do not change. The What If? game can be dangerous when you talk about constantly changing majors. As they say on multiple-choice tests, unless you are sure the answer is wrong, do not change your first solution. The first solution can, many times, be your true, gut feeling—and the right answer.

"I'm different because I'm 30. I didn't know if I wanted to go to school and dive into college, so I went to massage therapy school. I liked it, and it got me excited about the healthcare profession, so after a couple of years, I began working towards my AA degree. From there, it was a series of small events that led me to finding my current major."

—Senior, Microbiology Major

"Chase those things that you find mildly interesting, and slowly you will find your way. Put time into those things you are accidentally a little bit better at, or vaguely interested in—start investing in that. Start looking, reading, and trying because that is where you can find the rewards."

—Graduate, Chemistry Major

"Picking a major does not limit you. You can do anything you want after college, just try something you like."

—Graduate, Graphic Design Major

> "Your major never really reflects what you end up doing in life. Study what interests you the most. It's your chance to become somewhat of an expert in a certain field. You will learn important life lessons no matter what you study."
> —Graduate, French Major

2. **Indecision is worse than any old decision.** If you are having trouble deciding between your top choices for a major, just pick one. In a situation like this, do not rush the decision, but when the time is down to the wire and you have to choose, choose! Indecision is worse than any decision. If you pick something you are halfway interested in, this is a better way to go than hanging back and extending graduation because you just want to make sure. More school is more money, and though it should not be rushed, the process should not be held up by indecision. If you find an area of interest but a double major would require more work than you are willing to give, consider a minor or concentration. This way, you will receive credit and training in that area and not have to stay for years extra.

As stated before, look into something you like. It won't necessarily hinder your future, you can still major in chemistry and end up in business!

In addition to the worksheet you did on picking a major, there are additional ways to continue the choosing process.

DOING

> "Learning about something and living it are completely different things, but they complement each other well."
> —Graduate, French Major

If you have trouble deciding on your major, think with the previous section, and learn options to do in this section.

Why is learning these options so important? Paralysis by analysis is thinking too much and acting too little. It is just the opposite of impulsive decisions like crossing the street without looking. But neither condition is good. One or the other of them traps some college students and leads them to make either a snap decision about their major or no decision at all until it is too late to graduate on time. To keep this from happening to you, combine the thinking with the doing.

Students who have really questioned their major area of study and how it relates to career goals have done just that—a lot of thinking. Thinking is great, but can only take you so far. At a certain point, you should venture out and experiment by doing with any area of study you have in mind. If you've been thinking a lot and cannot decide, that might help solve your dilemma.

Ways to do:

- Working a college job
- Volunteering
- Shadowing
- Interning

Working in College

Getting paid is the simple reason most students work in college. Even so, working may be one of the most practical ways of learning by doing. We will go more into jobs in Chapter 13, but if you would like your work to also help you explore your major(s), here's a rough idea of what to look for.

It Is More Than Pay

Sure, you want to pay the bills, but you will also want a job that teaches you about something you may want to know. This job could be during the school year, in the summer, or both.

For example, you are an Engineering major who thinks managing a big construction firm might be a good way to use your engineering degree. You might even have a particular company in mind. In your case, you could gain valuable insight from working a summer for that company, perhaps even as a laborer. Sure, you might not be the site manager of a construction project, but you can see what the site manager directs throughout the day while you are working. Not only would you develop an appreciation for the work that is done at the site, but you will also begin to see the practical applications of your schoolwork—how what you are learning is put into action.

Working in a situation like this might really motivate you to buckle down in your studies and become more excited about your major. Or, with your new insider knowledge, you might rethink your major or decide to explore other ways to put your engineering degree to work after graduation.

No matter what your interests, working in different positions at different jobs will help you to see what some jobs are really like. And this will give you better insight and direction with your studies at school.

For college jobs:

- It has to pay the bills.
- It should teach you about an industry you are considering.
- It can be fun with the right attitude. And as we know, attitude is everything.

Two Notes on College Jobs

Every type of student, at one time or another, entertains the idea of getting a part-time job or really needs to. When it comes to getting a job while in school, consider these aspects of the ideal college job:

1. Work as little as possible while still paying the bills.
2. Work somewhere that interests you.

> "My part time job enabled me to get by with spending money and groceries. I worked on campus because I could not find better flexibility anywhere else. My $7/hr. was earned, but it was low stress and very flexible."
>
> —Senior, Physical Education Major

"Get an on-campus job. I only had to work during the week, 10 to 15 hours per week. It's not a lot of money, but it's easy and you may be able to get some studying done."
—Sophomore, Undecided Major

This is the best way if you are not in a hurry to find just the right job. If you are short of cash and the only job you can find is working at a restaurant or in a mall, take it. Bills do not wait. At the same time, making a few extra bucks can pale in comparison to the value of a college degree with premium grades. So when you can, make your job an enhancement to your college career rather than a chore. Whether it is working at a doctor's office or a hospital if you want to go into healthcare, or working at a law office if you want to go to law school, if possible, use this time to get an idea about the career you are interested in. Not only will this help you when you apply for a job in that field or for graduate school, but it will also make the time you spend at your job more meaningful and enjoyable.

Volunteering

Volunteering is the craze these days. To graduate high school, many students must perform a certain number of hours for an organization. Although in some ways volunteering has become somewhat of a chore (because it is required), it can be very rewarding, both personally and professionally. Balancing your way to success in college means more than just pleasing yourself. To draw true satisfaction in college, you have to give of yourself, too. Volunteering allows opportunities for leadership, experience, research, and giving back to the community.

"I volunteered in a medical setting, became an EMT, then saw it upfront and said; 'Wow this is what I want to do.' I was able to see everything written in the textbook—it was awesome. If you do something like that, it will motivate you to do it even more. You are doing the dirty work at that point, and if that does not turn you away from it, you will go even harder for it."
—Senior, Microbiology Major

Quick and Dirty

Here is the quick and dirty for volunteering:

- Look for opportunities in the field(s) you are considering. If you do not know any volunteer organizations, pull out the Yellow Pages again, ask around, or look at *A Student's Guide to Volunteering* by Theresa Digeronimo.
- Take a leadership role as soon as you can. (Volunteering is a chance to prove your leadership abilities.) If it is not possible to do this, conduct yourself as a leader would anyway. You will gain the respect of your fellow volunteers, and your maturity and serious-mindedness will be noticed by all.
- Take pride in your service, and yourself: You are giving back to the community while discovering things about yourself.

Try Shadowing

Shadowing is a valuable tool to help you decide on your major. Shadowing is similar to apprenticing (not quite like Donald Trump Apprenticing!). When you shadow, you are working around or with a professional in the field you have chosen.

Shadowing could be considered a subdivision of volunteering. Unlike working at a low-level job (which most jobs are in college) where you do not really get to see what the boss does, or volunteering where the director may be in an office or another city, shadowing gives a truer perspective.

STUDENT PROFILE—Nathan A. on Shadowing

Many people think real estate developing would be a great career to enter, but they do not understand the everyday operations—and whether they would really like it.

I felt this way, but decided to take the plunge to really find out. To begin understanding real estate development, I shadowed the owner of a small real estate corporation. During that time, I learned all the highs and lows that go along with the business; how politics play a huge factor in the process of zoning and re-zoning, and the great feeling when a petition is approved.

Now, I work for the firm, but started my job with a true perspective on the business. I now have the real view of real estate development, not only the glamorous view I knew in the beginning. Through this whole process, I have learned the importance of gaining hands-on experience in making up my mind, and how learning on the job can actually lead to a job.

Perhaps you want to be a nurse. Working in the hospital or volunteering there would give you a general perspective about the hospital environment. But it would not show you a true picture of what a nurse does. If you are able to shadow a nurse, though, you can get a glimpse, firsthand, at what they do. This is still volunteering, but at a different level. It is a view directly into the particular job and its challenges and rewards at the front line.

The biggest benefit from working around a professional is that you get a direct, firsthand demonstration of what they do every day. This can be valuable in choosing a career. After all, if you work around a stockbroker and you cannot stand what he does, you might want to change your job aspirations.

Here are two ideas to help you be successful at shadowing:

- Do not be afraid to approach individuals and ask to shadow them. The worst they can do is say "No."

- Learn as much as you possibly can. Once you land the opportunity, do not take it for granted.

To get the most benefits from shadowing, shadow in any type of job you are thinking about. It might help you narrow your choices and get you more excited about certain fields than others.

STUDENT PROFILE—Lauren B. on Finding Opportunities

I did not know anyone when I transferred colleges. But I did know that I wanted to go to medical school. I knew it was important for me to have experience shadowing a physician. I did not know any other way to get started, so I pulled out the Yellow Pages and began calling offices. After a huge number of 'no's,' one doctor was impressed by my approach and allowed me to hop aboard.

Students ask me all the time how I landed such a great opportunity. I tell them that I kept calling and never gave up hope that I would find something.

If you have an interest, be bold about finding opportunities; they are always there.

➤ *Whom would you like to shadow and what would be a bold way to approach that professional?*

Be Creative

Let's say that you are interested in business. For one reason or another, owning a chain of delis is your dream job, and you want to see, firsthand, the everyday workings of a deli.

Owning any business surely has its challenges, and they are unique to each type. After all, it may sound great to be a deli owner, but do you really want to be figuring inventory, making sandwiches for unpleasant customers, and constantly hiring and firing workers (some of the more negative, but real aspects of owning a deli)? Just making sandwiches in a deli might not teach you what you want to know. And maybe you do not have time to work your way to manager. So, how about volunteering your time for a week or so to the owner to get a behind-the-scenes view? If you have a relative who owns a business or a family friend who deals in this work, ask if you can work at the establishment for a week.

On the other hand, if you only offer to work for a week, you might not find a deli willing to train you for such a short time. If you cannot find a deli, try another type of small business. Many times, small businesses face similar problems. Working at a small grocery store might give you a similar perspective (especially if it has a deli!).

When looking at different careers in deciding what you may like to study in school

- be creative.

- use connections (any friends, family, etc., who can help you).

Shadowing uses your extracurricular time to your best advantage, and you will get some firsthand experience at what is coming down the road. If you decide that you do not like it, you have not wasted years working toward the wrong goal. Plus, that kind of experience can only help in your quest for a successful career after college. And the networking you will do while shadowing never hurts—important contacts for jobs or letters of recommendation are fringe (but extremely useful) benefits.

Interning

Interning is another tool to use in the process of making up your mind. After you have worked, volunteered, and shadowed a professional, you will most likely be pointing in a certain direction. That is the time to begin searching for an internship opportunity. Although not every type of after-college plan will require an internship, it may still be advantageous to pursue one. You will get a larger glimpse of the prospective field, while having more responsibility (most likely) than a student shadowing.

Do not be picky. As said before, many types of work share similar challenges with other jobs, so take what you can get and learn the most you possibly can!

USE RESOURCES THAT WILL HELP YOU SUCCEED!

Maybe you are in a big lecture class with really hard-to-understand material. You do not understand it, you cannot make it to the professor's office hours, or maybe you just feel like everything is caving in. Do not forget about campus resources. Keep in mind that the university is there to help you. The better you do in school, the better it reflects on them. So look into some of the great (often free) places to get help.

Tutoring Centers

Most schools have programs in their academic success centers with free tutoring. Most subjects are offered, and a block of time (usually one hour) is set aside for your questions. If you sign up, though, show up. If you do not, you may be barred from being tutored again. Do not burn that important bridge.

In addition, if you have done well in a certain class, tutoring could be a part-time job for you. It is a fact: Teaching a subject will help you to learn and understand that same subject at a different level. Tutoring can also be a great way to help you study for a standardized test. Both the GRE and MCAT (standardized tests for graduate school and medical school) have plenty of class-related information that needs to be studied in depth. Teaching the associated subjects will improve your understanding and mental agility with the concepts.

The Library

The college library is the largest resource on campus, especially with the help of online books and journals! If you have a question, chances are you can find the answer in the library. Besides being a great research tool, it is a great place to study if you need some peace and quiet. I don't know if it is a law of nature, but the more time you spend in the library, the higher your GPA goes. And today's college library is more useful than ever. Even though you may have the Internet in your apartment or dorm, the library has access to more than you could dream of—like millions of important research articles in online journals and subscriptions, which can supply any information you need for classes or personal projects. Some campuses have free printing; others usually have cheap printing. So if you find an article or review you would like to keep in hard copy, you can print it out.

In addition, the staff at the library can be a huge help. These individuals' jobs are to find anything you might want or need in the library's resources. Having so much information readily available is great, but searching through it can sometimes be tedious and frustrating. The staff can lend a helping hand, showing you search techniques and places to find what you need.

If your college has an introduction to the library class or meeting, go! Learning your way around can save you hundreds of hours in the next four years, just with research papers and assignments. Finding the information you need is the toughest part of most projects, so saving time on this can simplify your life on campus. Definitely know where the library is and how to use it—you will never be sorry!

Computers

Have some massive Internet research to do, and all you have in the dorm is a dial-up connection? A project that has to be done by tomorrow and your computer just crashed and burned? Get yourself to the computer lab right away.

Not everyone has a personal computer at college, or high-speed access to the Internet. Even if you do bring a computer, ink cartridges run out and computers can break. For these and other reasons, college computer labs are a great resource. Computer labs are commonplace on college campuses everywhere now. They have any program you will need to use, and at some schools, even free printing. Also, most schools have staff (usually students), either in the computer lab or somewhere else on campus, who can help you figure out the program you need to use.

Learning the ins and outs of the computer programs you will use in college will be a necessity for graduate school, work, or anything else. Most employees are required to use computers today. Investment bankers need Excel to build financial models; mechanics need computers to fix cars because of on-board computer chips. Medical professionals use computers with increasing frequency, as do all types of service industries. Did you visit the local deli for a sandwich this week? Likely, your order was rung up on a computerized cash register. See a movie last weekend? You guessed it, almost all movie theaters use computers to schedule movies, sell tickets, and keep track of the snack bar.

So unless you plan to be left in the dust in the years to come, it is important to get comfortable with computers and technology. But, you do not have to go it alone. There is help when you need it, and even before you need it. Head to your computer lab!

Counseling Services

Depression and other similar issues can be real problems at college. You might feel overwhelmed at one time or another, especially in the first few months. Or, you might not be sure of what to do if you have problems with your classes. Whether the problem is small or large, use what is there for you and resolve it. Many colleges have student counseling services to help with a variety of issues.

Psychological Counseling

If you feel like your world is caving in, you will not be able to focus on your classes or anything else. So your health and your sanity are your first and foremost priorities in college. We have talked about time management, and we will talk about exercise and eating properly later on, because these are ways to preserve that upbeat attitude you need. Letting your life stay in an unplanned, jumbled mess is the exact reason why so many students are stressed today. Like most other things in life, some problems are easy to fix, and some take more work. So when student counseling is not enough, you will want to look into this option.

Psychological counseling services may cost you a fee. But because you are a student, and compared with private services, they are quite cheap. And if you need it, you might be surprised at how hard your counseling center will work to help you afford counseling.

It is important to remember, too, that you come first. If things do become too much, use the psychological counseling services. They are provided for just this reason—to help you get a handle on what's bothering you and get back to feeling successful at college.

Table 6-3. Self Test

Take the following self-test to determine whether a visit to the counseling office might be helpful. Answer True or False to the following statements:

1. At times I feel stressed and anxious and don't know what to do about it. T F
2. Sometimes I feel down and I can't seem to shake the feeling. T F
3. I often feel as if my goals and the course of action to achieve them are not clear. T F
4. Sometimes I have problems with a peer that I can't handle. T F
5. I find that I use alcohol or drugs in place of problem-solving. T F
6. I often don't know how to handle problems with my boyfriend or girlfriend. T F
7. Sometimes I have problems controlling my anger. T F
8. I frequently have difficulty balancing school and family responsibilities. T F
9. I have trouble dealing effectively with persons in authority. T F

If you answered True to any of these statements, it may be an indication that it is time to speak to someone in the counseling office. With the help of a trained professional, you can explore ways to cope more effectively and prevent small problems from becoming larger ones.

Segadelli, Jane, Ph.D. "Take a Self Test." In *Psychological Counseling Homepage* from Nassau Community College.

Career and Other Counseling

THE ADVISOR SAYS:

The career center has many assessments that will help students confirm their interests.

Still not quite sure what you would like to do after college? Need advice on classes? Take heart, because there are many places to go to get help and advice about these important issues. Most universities have a career center, with multiple counselors to help with your career selection. These centers can provide

- aptitude tests.
- mock interviews.
- résumé-building help and workshops.
- internship information.
- alumni networking opportunities.

The centers can also provide other resources to help you decide the area that best fits your skills and talents.

For academic counseling, advisors usually fill this role. This is part of the reason for getting a great academics advisor. They will not only help with class selection, but also advise you on just about anything to do with your college major and scheduling.

There is always a lot to be done at any stage in life, but organization and management of your life will help reduce the stress and improve your productivity. Your college is just as interested in your success as you are. So look around a little bit, even do a little digging, and you might be surprised at all the little-known programs most colleges have to help students.

CHAPTER 7

Schoolwork, Studying, and Test Taking

"Do a little more each day than you think you possibly can."
—Lowell Thomas

CHIP AWAY

We have talked about the importance of performing well in school for reasons like your future career, graduate school, a safety net, and a confidence builder. Here, we are going to talk about how to start doing well in school.

When it comes to tackling schoolwork, the first piece of advice is to chip away at the block.

Over the course of a semester, think about how much work one class takes. Now, take that and multiply it times four or five to get an idea of how much time a full semester load of classes takes. When you think about it all in one chunk, that is a lot. In fact, it's kind of overwhelming!

To get past that Mount Everest of work, break it down into small chunks.

What sounds more doable: running 365 miles in one year, or running a mile a day for 12 months?

That is exactly how you need to look at classes: two full days staying up to the wee hours of the morning and worrying yourself sick, or studying an hour a day for a few weeks.

Breaking tasks into smaller chunks is the best way to preserve your sanity, especially when dealing with something as tough as a full load of college courses.

RESEARCH PROJECTS AND OTHER MAMMOTH ASSIGNMENTS

These never seem to go away. At every level of schooling, there is more and more research to be done. And each time, the papers have to be longer and more in-depth. But rather than throw your hands up in defeat, learn how to handle them with style, not with stress. The following sections will help.

Writing a Research Paper

This is a skill you must master through college; you will be required to write a number of these papers. Learning to write a stellar paper will help you improve your written communication skills, which are important in your after-college life, too. Composing memos in business, publishing research in science, teaching English—great writing skills can get you ahead in any path you choose to go.

Starting: The Blank Screen

With any undertaking, beginning is the most difficult part. As I discussed in Maximizing Time and Energy, it is important to just start! One terrific tool to begin with on a writing project is called stream of consciousness. Just write down all the random thoughts racing through your head (preferably on the subject of your paper). This is the shotgun approach, kind of like a one-person brainstorming session, where you will discover the mental pathway down which your writing is leading you. Using the stream-of-consciousness style can get the boulder moving.

Let's say that you have an assignment to write a research paper on a sport —you decide on golf. The first step in writing your outline is to determine the purpose, audience, and thesis.[30]

Purpose: To show the development of golf from its rural beginnings to the popular sport it is now, used for pleasure, business, and fellowship

Audience: Golf aficionados interested in how the game started and has matured to its modern standing

Thesis: To explain golf's development and transformation from a game only played in the Scottish countryside to a sport with international presence used for pleasure, business, and fellowship

Introduction

I. The Old Golf: An Early History
   A. Scotland: Golf's Home
   B. The Original Game: How It Was Played
   C. The Early Players

II. Historical Evolution
   A. The Change: From Rural Game to Stylish Sport
   B. Golf's Large Expansion
   C. Golf as a Traditional Sport

III. The Role of Golf in Today's Society
   A. Modern Golf: Is It Truly the Same Game?
   B. Golf's Entrance into Everyday Life
      1. The Business World
      2. Fellowship
      3. A Way of Life
   C. Golf's Place as a Spectator Sport

One amazing professor taught me that to be a great writer, one must continuously read, write, plan, and revise.

Read. Why read? Reading other great writers' work will help you learn to write better. You might think of it as learning from the best. Reading stimulates your brain; imparts knowledge to you (the reader); and improves your writing, grammar, and vocabulary. You do not even realize that it is happening, but it does. Obviously, it is a great way to knock out many things with one stone.

Write. In addition to reading, nothing will improve your writing skills quite like writing! As the saying goes, practice makes perfect. Perhaps your writing will never be perfect, but if you practice writing, I guarantee you it will greatly improve. Taking creative writing and other similar courses during college gives you the opportunity to write, and have others share opinions on your writing. Getting these opinions—especially from professionals—is a great benefit to taking writing classes. But the writing will also help you improve.

Plan. Planning is crucial to great writing. Stream of consciousness gets the pen moving, but for any large-scale project like a research paper, it is necessary, at some point, to plan. For many people (including me) planning can be the most difficult area of writing. Knowing how much of what subject will fit where is tough and intimidating. The proven and easiest way to plan is to

- start with stream of consciousness.
- write a brief outline and let it sit.
- continue returning to that outline and improving it. (This is why it is best to start your writing early, and not under the gun. Quality work will take shape with effort and time. There are no substitutes.)

Revise. The last point here is also the last component that determines great writing: revision. Even the best writers must revise their work—and continuously! *War and Peace* was not jotted down once, never to be edited again! This is another reason to begin your paper early. The best product will come of frequent reviewing and revision of your last draft. If you cannot find a friend to help you, try the college writing center. They will review and suggest improvements for your work.

Try these tips, and you will see that great writing is earned, it does not just appear out of nowhere. You will also see that you can improve your own writing, and be confident in the papers you hand in.

Plagiarism in Writing

Plagiarism is a serious offense. Copying another student's paper (in whole or part) or using other writers' work without giving them credit can land you in big trouble. Plagiarizing can have devastating effects on your job search or graduate school application, too. And, perhaps even worse, you will lose the trust and respect of your professors.

Many students believe that directly copying information that someone else wrote is the only form of plagiarism. That is dead wrong. Summarizing others' research and writing or taking only bits and pieces without citing the source is plagiarism too. Basically, you should cite any piece of information that is not common knowledge. I have heard it put as, "Cite anything you did not know before the course began." On some papers it may seem that every other line has a citation attached! As always when it comes to plagiarism, though, better safe than sorry! When citing your sources, there are different ways of doing it. Each professor chooses which reference style your paper should conform to, like the APA, MLA, or other similar style. So find out which one your professor prefers and find the correct handbook in the library. (Almost every college library carries these.) Some professors even maintain a Web page with the appropriate information and other helpful tips. If you are still not sure how to cite material, approach your instructor, who will be more than happy to clarify the information for you. Doing the proper research for a paper, however difficult, is satisfying. Integrity in your work is something important to uphold, not only for your grades but for yourself.

Remember that professors can find out! Universities are investing more money every year in software programs to detect plagiarism. By electronically scanning your paper into the program, professors can match the wording in it against large databases that include common sources like encyclopedias, published articles on the Internet, and past students' papers. If too many phrases match or other red flags appear, expect to be called on the carpet, pronto, to explain yourself! Better to just do the work yourself and cite the source of everything else you use. As an old saying goes, "When in doubt, cite it!"

Timing It Right

When a 15-page research paper is assigned at the start of the semester and is due at the end of the semester, this is a sign. The teacher is probably trying to get a message across to you: START NOW!

But, as usual, we do it our own way, starting the night before the end of the semester.

Well, that was the old you. The new you is going to take on large projects and papers as soon as possible.

Sure, everyone has excuses:

"I just can't force myself to do it until I absolutely have to."

"I cannot write a paper in segments, I have to do it all at once."

We college students are creative when it comes to excuses—seems like half of our time is spent making or explaining them!

Make It Due Earlier

A simple trick to get those uberdifficult projects done is to make a due date for yourself early on. Set a date to have certain segments of the project done—for example, outline by October 1, introduction by October 15, and so on.

Not only will this lighten the load for the end of the semester, when you have exams and everything else in the world due, but also the start of the semester is usually pretty low-key as far as workload goes. Nobody likes those sleepless nights during finals week because for the past four months we did absolutely nothing.

Breaking up the work not only makes it seem easier, but the quality will go up a level, if for no other reason than you actually slept the night before.

The Pre-Grade

Here is something you might not have heard of. Try having your professor pre-grade your papers. Not all professors will do this, but if yours is willing to, you can basically end up getting a perfect grade by taking each revised edition back for a once-over.

If your professor will not pre-grade, take it to a teaching assistant, another professor, or the writing center at your school (most campuses have them). No, they will not be the final authority, but they will at least give you some pointers on sentence structure, diction, and grammar.

Let's face it, compared to all the last-second papers handed in with hardly any revisions, just taking a second look and spell-checking will set you up for a higher grade.

There are both projects and classes that will require a team effort. Once you have learned how to write a great paper, you are not off the hook quite yet. Piecing together top-notch presentations is also important for you, the successful college student.

SCHOOLWORK: WORKING WITH OTHERS

Throughout college, you will have to work with others. Group assignments are becoming more common on every campus today, mostly because working with others is the real world! This is an important skill, so let's get to it!

Presentations

If you major in a business major, like marketing or communications, these types of assignments will be more common than in any other major. However, an education, science, or history major will most likely have to piece a few together, too. To complete a group presentation with a top grade, you will need to learn how to do a number of things:

- Lead
- Delegate
- Assess progress

You might be the type to always lead the group or the type to hang back a bit. Either way, it will be to your advantage to lead a group at one time or another. True, taking the lead role puts a large amount of the responsibility in your lap. You will be the final decision maker on everything that goes into the presentation. But even if being the leader sounds intimidating (or even if it doesn't), you must have a well-thought-out plan. If you assume (or are assigned) the leading role, make sure to arrive at the first meeting prepared.

Have a Plan

Yes, a plan. Blowing smoke on the process will lead the group absolutely nowhere. So come prepared with

- a brief outline or bullet points you would like to address.
- a rough idea of the project's length and organization.
- an open ear and open mind. Be ready to listen. Brainstorming may reveal a better organization or some creative ideas for the project.

Delegate

To be a successful leader, it is necessary to learn the fine art of delegation. I have always enjoyed delegating tasks, because it means one thing—less work for me! If you learn how to do it well, you will have the same happy outcome.

To successfully delegate, you must know how to manage the projects you have handed out (we address that next). Whether you go into business, teaching, law, medicine, or any other profession, you should be able to delegate some responsibility. Some of the greatest leaders have only been experts at handing out assignments to the right people; after all, one person can only do so much! So, picking

---

A Presentation Outline

Here is an example of what to bring to a meeting for a group-presentation.

Assignment: Critique of marketing techniques used by Abercrombie & Fitch

Must address:

- Introduction to the company
- Who are the target customers of the current ad campaign?
- What media (TV, magazine, online ads, etc.) has the company used?
- Has the campaign been successful? Why or why not?
- What would your group do differently to promote the brand?

Presentation length: 20 minutes

Number of group members: 4

Due date: 2 weeks

Specific assignments:

- Andrea will find basic facts about the company, the target customers, and media used.
- Edward will find example ads to show the class and use press releases, news, and other information to determine the success of the campaign.
- Jose will determine different ideas that the company could implement to garner higher sales.
- Tiffany will design the presentation (PowerPoint, images/videos) and organize speeches.

Andrea's and Edward's assignments are due 5 days from today. Jose's assignment is due 9 days from today. Tiffany's assignment is due 12 days from now. The day before the assignment, we will have a practice session (as many as it takes to work out the kinks). The following day we will give the presentation.

the right people to study with, assign projects to, and be friends with in general is a major component of succeeding in college.

While working in a group setting, to delegate properly, you must listen. If a certain person in the group is crazy about one aspect of the assignment, put her on the case. Many times, through listening, you will be able to understand who is best for what portion of the work.

Be Well-Organized

People will be willing to take you seriously only if you present yourself that way. As a leader of the group, it is your responsibility to bring structure to the project.

Work With the Group

Blazing in to a meeting with your group and dishing out work without any regard to the group's needs and abilities is . . . well, let's just say that it will not turn out well. Work with the group on decisions, knowing that if a split decision arises, it is you who can make the consensus. On the other hand, never take your role as a leader to imply your superiority. On the contrary, become a uniter between the members. If you do, the best results will follow.

Assess Progress

To successfully perform in college, and especially in a group project situation, you must be able to assess progress. When you initially commit to goals, you will obviously want to examine your progress, and dealing with schoolwork and especially other people makes this a necessity. The best way to organize these assessments is to break the project down into segments. Each week (or whichever interval you choose), the group should meet to compare their progress and encourage or troubleshoot with one another on problems or holdups. Better to find out that someone in the group is lazy at a group meeting than on presentation day! The opportunities to assess the progress toward the completion of the assignment should be considered to help each other. At each meeting, participants can review each other's work making suggestions and constructive criticisms to better the project as a whole.

It is important to note that sooner or later you may be partnered with a student who chooses not to do his or her share of the work. In this situation, it is important to work hard and do your part, but also to let the professor know. You may do it discreetly during office hours or however you prefer, but make the problem known sooner rather than later. You will have a more difficult time explaining the situation after receiving your grade, so speak with your professor early.

Do a Run-through

After you have finished the project and are ready to present it, it is important to do a run-through of the final version. This will help you identify problems before standing in front of the class.

For example, most professors allot a certain amount of time for the presentation to make sure that every group fits in. Unless the group goes through the whole presentation at least once, it is impossible to gauge the total length. There is no sense in losing valuable points because your group went over or under the allotted time. In addition, if you have a computer program with slides that accompanies the presentation, working the kinks out is important. You must keep up with the slides and determine the order and setup.

Never overlook the run-through. It is one of the simplest and most important aspects of the project.

Making Your Assignments Interesting

One of the most challenging parts of writing a paper or designing a presentation is making it interesting. Even if you are composing a paper on 1970s architecture, it is important to keep it interesting. Here are some ways to keep your audience engrossed.

Writing Assignments

Sure, there is less flexibility in writing assignments for creativity. But there is still some room for excitement. Your professor has to grade many papers along with yours. To get a better grade, try to create an exciting piece of work. First, it is important to understand that exciting writing usually takes longer to write than boring writing. The first step to making more exciting writing is to know your subject.

This is probably obvious, yet it is one thing most students lack when it comes to writing papers and assignments. To get a clear picture and write an interesting piece, do your research. Not only will you have more knowledge to draw from, but you will probably discover small, interesting facts about what you are investigating. And sometimes, it is these somewhat random pieces of information that bring together what you are writing in a captivating way.

Presentations

Presentations can be one of the most fun parts of college. Unlike papers on medieval cultures that only tell, there is a huge amount of room for creativity when you can show what you have learned. Just like papers, presentations must be accurate, interesting, and (sometimes) entertaining. Moreover, showing your creative abilities is the best way to give a top-notch presentation. Nothing is worse than looking around the room and seeing everyone passed out—and it is because of your boring presentation! Think about it: Students hate it when professors give lackluster lectures. So why should your lecture be drab? (No, don't say "for revenge." Remember, you are a college student now, and past such petty thinking.)

Consider this example of a terrifically creative presentation. In a meeting put on by a Fortune 500 pharmaceutical company to a group of top physicians, the presenter used quite a bit of creativity. He presented all the medical jargon in a rhyming fashion, using Dr. Seuss as his theme. Just like Seuss's writings, the presenter rhymed his way through the presentation with colorful slides, including Seuss cartoon characters. Not only was the message very effective and accurate (your information must always be correct), but the audience was enthralled because of the way in which it was presented. Picture that—a bunch of big doctors loving nursery rhymes! The ploy worked, though, and is a testament to the power of creativity—you will get your message across much more effectively!

Use the Tools

Your parents did not have PowerPoint and other great programs when they were in college. Nowadays, there is no excuse for poorly done presentations. Using these programs is not difficult or necessarily time-consuming. It is easy to find slides that cater to any look you are chasing, whether purely professional, professional mixed with comical, or just plain funny. Many types of slides come with the program, and if you do not own a computer, your school most likely has access to one.

Some tips to making your presentation better using these tools:

- Add pictures. A picture is worth a thousand words. Never forget this when designing your presentation.

- Add movies. I remember doing a group presentation on Levi's jeans in a marketing class. We integrated a Levi's commercial via an Internet connection. Doing this allowed us to not just talk about but also show what we were talking about. The ploy proved very effective, and everyone (including the teacher) thoroughly enjoyed it.

- Use some color. With these programs, there is no need to show a black-and-white presentation, even if your materials are not in color. Simply including some attractive colors can improve the project.

Make Sure

When making any type of presentation,

- do your research and make sure that your information is accurate.
- if in a group, use the skills described here for group projects.
- be creative. What will be your "Dr. Seuss presentation"?

So when it comes to papers, presentations, and all other work in school, learn to live by these three rules:

- start early.
- be diligent.
- be creative.

STUDYING

Remember studying—that concept you and your high school friends joked about while comparing your decent grades?

Believe me, in college, the ability to get by without studying fades rapidly with every succeeding year. In college, you are faced with a ton of new information to learn. You will have to know how to study if you want a decent grade.

But do not worry. Most universities offer courses on the development of good study habits. Do not be afraid to use the resources of the college you attend!

STUDENT PROFILE—Kyle R. on Study Habits

I had a big shock coming when I transferred colleges. At my previous college, the professors had time to go into depth and really teach, whereas at my new school, the professors had huge classes and gave watered down lectures—I had to teach myself. So, unless you are used to teaching yourself, be prepared. Work on your study habits, that way if your professor is not too helpful, you'll have something to fall back on.

➤ *What study skills do you possess to fall back on?*

➤ *Name one area of studying that you could improve, and how you plan to do it.*

If you are too busy or maybe do not have the option of a study skills class, here are some pointers.

Know What to Study

Before delving into the material, you have to know what to look for. You would be surprised how many students study a limited amount of material—diving into just the book or only their lecture notes, for example—without thinking about the specifics that the professor talked about.

Paying attention to your professor and reading over the course syllabus will give you clues to what kind of questions or material the tests and quizzes will focus on. Also, thanks to the Internet, quite a few professors put older practice tests on the Web. Some even hand them out. Looking these over can give some great clues and some practice for the real thing. Even if the exact same questions do not come off the practice tests (which they sometimes do), you will get valuable study time.

Of course, you should not limit yourself to only what has been announced and handed out, because there will always be other information on the tests.

The Nightmare Scenario

Here is a scenario that comes to mind when I think of studying for college tests.

Scene: In class the day before the test . . .

Student: "Professor, what should we look over for the test? What are you really going to concentrate on?"

Professor: "Well, if you know everything, you should not have any problems."

Okay, so maybe this prof took it too far. But he is right, you know. If you read the book, go to class and listen, and do the practice problems—in other words, know everything—you will not have any trouble.

Think about it—all semester long, the professor has been giving clues about the material you will be tested on by how much time was spent on certain topics. Pay attention to your prof, study regularly, and you will be prepared.

How to Study: Learning What Works for You

Just as every person has a unique personality, physique, likes, and dislikes, everyone has a certain way of studying that helps him or her learn the best. Some people are visual learners—they read it and are fine. Some have to write key things out. Some have to hear it. You probably already know what type of learner you are. If you put that knowledge to good use, you will learn better, faster, and with less frustration. If you do not know, do a little self-analysis.

It will not take many questions like this to figure it out. But no matter what type of learner you are, many students coming from high school lack good study skills. Therefore, they are clueless when confronted with a large load of schoolwork. If this describes you, here are some tips that can help. Like figuring out how you learn best, learning how to study is trial and error. Try a certain technique. If it works, stick to it. If it does not, give something else a shot.

More Options

Here are a couple of places to start when figuring out what works best for you.

1. **Rewrite your notes.** This is very popular. Rewriting notes helps ingrain them into your head. Also, the sooner after a lecture you rewrite your notes, the better it works. If you do this soon after, many times you can add in small examples and facts that the professor presented, ones that you still remember but did not necessarily jot down at the time.

2. **End of chapter questions.** Answering questions at the end of the chapter, whether it is history, business, or physics, will help you learn the material. It also gives you an idea of which areas you are a little rough on so that you can ask your professor. Remember: Professors love students who ask questions, because they know they are working. Never pass up a chance to gain distinction in the professor's eyes.

3. **Group study.** Some folks cringe at the idea of studying with other people, but this can be a very valuable tool. Study groups are great if you are getting a little burned out with the Lone Ranger style of studying. Plus, they can help you remember more than you would be able to do alone. I remember a certain class where the whole lecture was notes, notes, notes, and more notes. Overwhelming! Yet when I got together to study with a couple of other people in my class, between the three of us, we were able to make sure we had notes on everything that was talked about. Having company can make the work seem much less like work, too.

Read the Book!

So you are in one of those classes where all your classmates tell you, "Don't worry. Everything on the test is from the lecture. Don't even worry about the book."

Three Types of Learners[32]
Visual

Do class lectures bore you to tears, but you seem to be able to get everything you need from your books?

Visual learners work best with graphics, pictures, and reading. Flash cards or note cards may be a big help to this group.

Auditory

Do you hate to take notes, but can usually listen and easily remember the main points of class lectures?

Auditory learners are very careful listeners. They learn well by discussing their interests as well. If you know people who may just listen in lecture and not take notes, chances are they are auditory learners.

Kinesthetic

Do you love lab classes or rewriting notes to help the lecture sink in?

Kinesthetic learners get to know their information by doing. Some type of physical manifestation of the subject (like lab classes), or otherwise physically engaging activity, helps this type of student learn better.

"In contrast to just reading my notes, I actively learned the material. I would take my class notes, read through and write down anything I did not know. After repeating this process many times, I had learned everything—by writing it down and reviewing it."
—Graduate, Computer Science Major

> "I make note cards after every lecture when the material is fresh. It helps solidify everything in my mind."
>
> —Senior, Psychology Major

> "The first week of class, I look at the kids answering the questions or adding some kind of intelligent input. Afterwards, I introduce myself and ask if they would like to put a study group together."
>
> —Senior, Microbiology Major

> "Hit the ground running. Take that first week and take advantage of it. Read the first couple of chapters or meet with the professor. Most people just take off that first week and think it's nothing—and then next thing you know, there is two weeks of work piled up and a test."
>
> —Senior, Microbiology Major

> "Knowing to take a break every now and then to go out with my friends was useful. Be willing to take out some time that you probably would have spent procrastinating anyway."
>
> —Graduate, History Major

Do not take this advice literally! Yes, the professor might concentrate more on lecture, but even if that is true, the book is not a worthless resource. The book tends to tie together the ideas and thoughts presented in class. This makes a complete story that is easier for you to remember what may, at times, seem to be unrelated facts.

Here is the best way I can think of to explain it. Remember those books in high school like *Lord of the Flies* and others that were required reading? Well, do you also remember searching like a crazy person at all the local bookstores the night before the test for the *Cliff Notes* version? Oh, if only you could get them! They were the answer to every 10th grader's prayer!

Yet most of the time, you got them, and they did not even help that much. Right? Here's why: Even though *Cliff Notes* gave a great overall picture of the book, they still did not cut it at test time compared to really knowing the material.

Well, guess what? By just reading and memorizing the lecture notes, you are doing the whole *Cliff Notes* thing all over again (and you should have learned the first time)! Reading the book helps give you a better understanding of the big picture and brings dates, names, and obscure facts together into a sensible group of information.

So do not just memorize and regurgitate—understand what you are reading. If you need help doing that, ask! This will make the class easier, and you may even get something out of it.

Stay Ahead of the Game

Keeping up with classes is good, but staying ahead is great. This means staying ahead from the beginning of the semester, it can give you a nice boost of momentum to help through the rough times. This means keeping up with your reading and attending lectures—and reading before lecture is best, you will better understand difficult concepts and will be able to ask more suitable questions.

Take Breaks

Every hour it is beneficial to give yourself a brief mental rest. Forgoing this can result in trouble concentrating and less productive time with the books. If you are going to study, you might as well get the most out of it, right?

TEST TAKING

Test taking never fails to freak out students. Yet if students follow two simple strategies, their problems will usually seem more like molehills than mountains:

- Be prepared.
- Gain control.

Being prepared is the first line of defense. If you go into a test without having studied enough or properly, there is no saving the day. Bottom line: If you have not learned the information, you will not be able to recall it. Preparation for tests involves the techniques discussed earlier in this chapter, along with the discipline and determination I talk about in Chapter 5.

Learning how to control yourself while taking a test is valuable in the quest for college success. This has much broader implications. Learning to settle your nerves and get a hold of yourself for the new job you start after college, the start of a graduate program, or any other nerve-racking situation will get you far in life.

For test taking, it does not matter how much you have studied or how prepared you feel. When you combine test taking and anxiety, there is often trouble. Many times, the more people have studied and the better they know the material, the more anxious they get about taking the test. The fear of taking tests is something that countless students try to deal with—and unsuccessfully.

If you spent all that time studying the material and know it that well, why blow it because you blaze through the questions too fast or lose your train of thought because your paper is soaked with sweat?

Although knowing how to study is very important, do not underestimate the need for test-taking skills. The bottom line is simple: Stay as calm as possible and keep your head about you. (Sounds like you are training for a boxing match, huh?)

No matter how you do it, you want to reduce your level of anxiety. Being extremely nervous about a test has negative effects on your thought process and on your ability to logically approach the questions.

Some valuable advice came from my Organic Chemistry professor when I approached him about one of my tests. I had studied the material and knew it very well—pretty much inside and out— but I ended up doing poorly on that particular test. I was pretty peeved that I had done so badly. And the worst part was, I knew the material but had answered the questions in the wrong way!

Here is some advice he gave me, plus some I have picked up in other places. Even though it sounds kindergarten-ish, it certainly worked on the next test!

Test-Taking Checklist

- ***Chill out!*** When you come in to a test, do not stress about how well you are going to do. Trust in your ability and the time you put into studying, and leave the rest to the heavens.

> "Studying away from home can work to one's advantage. With all of the distractions, from roommates to TV to Internet, it was easy to put off studying for anything else. By going to a specific, quiet place I was able to focus on my work."
>
> —Junior, English Major

> "Find what works for you; I like music during studying, but some people like complete silence."
>
> —Sophomore, Undecided Major

- *Take a glance.* Taking a quick look over the test can ease your mind a bit. It can be nerve-racking when every page is like defusing one bomb at a time . . . red wire, blue wire. Take some pressure off yourself and take a look first.

- *Read the directions.* That's right, back to elementary school. If you do not read the directions first, you might miss something specific that you have to pay attention to as you take the test. If you do not know about that item, you are up a creek without a paddle. And yes, some professors still do that lame trick: "If you are reading this, fill in your name for an extra point."

- *Pace yourself.* Do not blaze through the test like a hot knife through butter. Slow down, take your time, and read carefully. But "pace" means even pacing, not slow as all get out, but steady. Go through the questions slowly enough to pay attention to details, but not to where you have left half the test blank when the time is up.

- *Star and go back.* If a test question gives you some extra trouble, do not sit there the whole time driving yourself nuts with "Is it A or B, A or B?" Put a star next to it, and go back to it when you are done. When you are finished with the other questions, this will give you some extra time to digest that question, and with less pressure too.

- *Double-check.* When you are finished, go back through and double-check your work. Especially those questions you had extra trouble on. This can help you catch any of those stupid mistakes that can, and oh yes, will be made somewhere during those 120 credit hours of college.

To Do's Before a Test

- Treat the day as any other day. Part of test anxiety is working yourself into a crazy state. Treating the day as some type of game-winning or -losing buzzer shot will directly work against you. Take the test seriously, but use that extra energy it would take to get upset to study harder before test day.

- Get plenty of rest. It is important to walk into your test having had a good night's sleep. This will allow you to concentrate better and recall information more easily. Going without sleep can make you moody, more prone to making mistakes, and less able to quickly recall information. Sleep at least eight hours the night before your exam.

- Avoid stimulants like caffeine. Unless you have the jitters without your coffee or soda in the morning, avoid it. It will make you antsy and less able to concentrate. Have orange juice instead.

- Eat breakfast. It is a fact that eating a well-rounded breakfast helps you to a better start. Your brain uses a lot of glucose (sugar) for energy, so if you would like it to work properly, you have to feed it properly.

Performing well in school is not a matter of luck. It is the result of a concerted effort, putting into practice the techniques discussed in this chapter. If they do not come naturally at first, continue to work on them, and before you know it, they will be habit!

Money, Money, Money

"Money is better than poverty, if only for financial reasons."
—Woody Allen

THE ABC'S OF CASH AT COLLEGE

If you want to have a successful and somewhat low-stress college career, learning how to handle money is important.

You probably have a different perspective than the next college student on money. Some students come from homes where there was never enough money. Others come from wealthy families, where money is no object. Further still, many students are paying for college themselves because their families cannot afford it. One thing is for sure, most college students have to worry about money.

Money in college comes from one of four places:

- Jobs
- Loans

- Scholarships and grants
- Parents and family

Jobs

THE ADVISOR SAYS:

It is when jobs take over that the problems begin. I encourage freshmen not to work at the very start of school; get used to the academic demands first.

Working for some or all money in college is very common. Most undergraduate students work, at least part-time, while they are in college. If you are supporting yourself, working while in school may be necessary. But to give a maximum amount of time and concentration to your schoolwork, work the least amount possible while living frugally. In other words, working to pay for things like tuition, books, and a small amount of fun money is all right. Working to pay for a Porsche should probably be left until after college.

Loans

THE ADVISOR SAYS:

Many students have large (monetary) obligations. Students can use the opportunity to speak with financial aid counselors and find another source of income to help them.

Cheap money: Not everyone is able to find free money for college. Though free money is not guaranteed to be around, plenty of places have money to lend to needy college students. The number of undergraduate students using federal loans to pay for education is steadily increasing. In 2000, 43 percent of undergrads were using some type of federal loan for college.[2] If you need money for college, whether it's a small chunk or every last cent, federal loans can be a lifesaver. Many times, the loans have generous interest rates and terms. Taking on these helpful loans can reduce that stress and uncertainty, giving you time to focus on the reason you are in college—to learn! You (and maybe your parents) will want to be sure to review all the fine print; with any loan, you will want to know what you are getting into. But overall, these can be a great alternative to working 40 hours per week in school. It is best to make an appointment with your financial aid counselor, but here is some basic information on student loans to get you acquainted.

The Three Major Student Loans[33]

Stafford Loans

Stafford loans are the four-door sedan of college loans. The interest rates are reasonable, as well as the terms. Looking into Stafford loans, there is an important distinction to be made between subsidized and unsubsidized.

Subsidized are the preferred type of Stafford loan because you do not pay any interest during school (the government pays the interest). You still must repay the loan, but you get a six-month grace period after you finish school (or stop attending) to begin repaying.

Unsubsidized Stafford loans are terrific for financing your education; they just are not as accommodating as the subsidized loans. The difference is that you pay the interest that accrues during school—you do not have to make any payments during school, though. The same six-month grace period after graduation applies.

To gain approval for Stafford loans (subsidized or unsubsidized) requires filling out a FAFSA (at www.FASFA.ed.gov). Also, the amount of money you may borrow depends on many factors, such as the number of years you have left in school and whether you are a dependent or independent student. For more information, check out *The Student Guide* at www.studentaid.ed.gov. After you have sent in your FAFSA, your eligibility for the different types of loans will be determined. Besides checking out the Web site for any questions, visiting your school's Financial Aid Office is the best first step. They will have information not only on Stafford loans but on many other types of financing as well.

Perkins Loans

Perkins loans are low-interest loans made to undergraduate and graduate students. As with Stafford loans, Perkins loans have a grace period before you must begin repayment (only it is nine months after leaving school to Stafford's six!). Once again, depending on your level in school determines the amount you may borrow. And, because Perkins loans are originated by your college, making an appointment at the financial aid office is the first step to gaining the financial help. To see more information on Perkins loans, visit http://www.studentaid.ed.gov and see *The Student Guide*.

PLUS Loans

Unlike Stafford and Perkins loans, which are made to the student, PLUS loans are made to the parents. The catch is that you must be a dependent undergraduate student to be eligible, and parents must pass a credit check and eligibility requirements. Also, there is no grace period with PLUS loans; payments must be made while you are attending school. So, PLUS loans are another tool to fill in the gaps of any more money that you need for your education. For more information on PLUS loans, review *The Student Guide* at www.studentaid.ed.gov or make an appointment with your school's financial aid office.

There are other avenues to obtain loans beside the federal government, including regular banks and loan institutions. The terms are not usually quite as generous; nevertheless, this is one more option if Stafford loans and other government programs do not fit your circumstances.

Scholarships and Grants

Definitely the best way to pay for college—you don't! Although full-ride scholarships or grants are relatively rare, you might be surprised at the number of students who are eligible for a few hundred (or even thousand) dollars per year. Plus, because scholarships fall into need-based and merit-based categories, there are opportunities for everyone. All kinds of organizations locally and nationally give money.

- The military
- Rotary Club
- Masonic organizations
- Kiwanis Club
- Lions Club
- Church funds
- Wealthy individuals
- Parents' employers

There are many Internet search engines to find scholarships, too. Some charge a fee (sometimes a hefty fee). But today, the only services you need to use are free. http://FastWeb.com is a reputable place where you can search through 600,000 scholarships worth over $1 billion. Although it may take a little bit of hunting, filling out forms, and writing essays, the payoff is certainly worth it.

In addition to using such a service, many schools can tell you about scholarships and grants, too. So be sure to ask the financial aid office at your university. If there is college money to be had, they will likely know about it.

Lastly, keep your nose up and sniffing around. Tell everyone you know that you are on a scholarship search. You will be amazed to find how many different scholarships and grants are out there. There may be a wealthy businessperson who played college tennis and majored in linguistic arts. If you have similar goals, that person may be willing to pay some (or all) of your college tuition!

Be creative when it comes to finding these opportunities, and never be afraid to take the time and fill out an application. It might just earn you some cash.

Parents and Family

Although a large percentage of students work while in college, many still receive some support from family. If your family has paid your tuition in part or whole, it's a great privilege. Work hard and do not take it for granted!

SETTING UP A BANK ACCOUNT

If you do not have one already, or need to change banks, one of the first things to do when you get to college is set up a bank account. Different banks have different terms, and specials on everything from checking to car loans. Many banks also have specials for students. With the competition among banks today, it can be pretty easy to find a bank with free debit cards, free or flat-rate checking accounts, and low-cost bill-paying services.

Overdraft/Keeping Track of Your Cash

When you are setting up the account, decide which features you would like to have, but be sure to ask questions about them. For example, overdraft protection seems good, but it is a double-edged sword.

Some surveys show that less than half of all college students balance their checkbook every month.[3] Not doing so makes it easier to bounce a check, and that means having to swallow at least a $25 fee for each overdrawn check. Overdraft protection can keep these fees from triggering, because there is an automatic reserve (usually $500 to $1,000) to cover the shortage. Sounds great, right?

Well, like the perils of credit accounts in college, overdraft protection can almost be thought of as a credit extension. If there is no penalty, and a large pool of funds is available, a student might throw caution to the wind and wind up using this protection as restaurant money. So, rather than overdraft protection, it is probably a better strategy to balance your checkbook often. If you have the discipline to keep your checkbook in check but like the added security of overdraft, by all means use it. You will have to make up your own mind regarding overdraft protection, but keeping things simple is usually the best way to go in college.

ATMs

Banks also differ by geography, and this might affect the amount of money you will pay in ATM charges. If you do a lot of traveling and like the convenience of a nationwide network of ATMs, a large bank chain might be the best choice for you, even if their checking account fees are higher. On the other hand, if you are a local yokel, a smaller local bank may do the trick.

Whichever route you decide, be very aware of ATM charges. Using machines that are outside your bank's network can cost a few dollars per transaction. These two- and three-dollar payments can add up if you use an ATM many times per month. But there is good news about that: Some banks allow the customer to use any ATM machine a set number of times per month for free. This is definitely something to ask about when setting up your account.

Consider Credit Unions

Some universities and organizations have credit unions for the students, faculty, staff, and alumni. These banks can be advantageous for students because they are not for profit. Many times, if a student is looking for a car loan, or any other type of loan, the credit union can give the best interest rate. Over the life of any loan, just a couple of points can make a substantial difference in the total money you will pay back.

CASH RULES!

These are some simple rules to successfully handling your money at school.

Buy Using Cash or Debit Card, not Credit Card

Credit is not quite the curse many make it out to be, but it takes discipline to manage it. It is not a bad idea for students to have one major credit card. In some emergencies, credit cards can save the day. If you are taking a road trip and forgot to get cash, what do you do stuck in the middle of nowhere and out of gas? It is perfectly appropriate to use credit cards in these types of situations. But students who get into financial trouble are not usually using cards in this way. These students are using cards to buy new clothes, presents, food at the grocery store, restaurant meals, and so on.

It might be okay to use credit cards for

- out-of-gas situations.
- car repairs needed immediately.

- needed medical visit. (However, check with the college clinic first; you might be able to get free or low-cost care there.)

But do not use credit cards for

- usual dinners out.
- bar tabs.
- beer, food, and the like.
- gifts or personal items.
- unneeded clothes.
- any item you want but do not need.

Credit cards should be used as the exception, not the rule. Though it is important to obtain one card to begin building a credit history, get used to using cash to purchase items. This will help filter out frivolous purchases. Debit cards are fine too, but just like a checkbook, you need to know the balance. Paying for overdrawing your account can add up to quite a bundle.

Learn to Live Frugally

There is a difference between being frugal and being cheap. Living frugally means cutting expenses where and when necessary. A frugal person can go out for a nice dinner sometimes, and buy a nice new coat when needed. Living frugally means (1) watching expenses without sacrificing well-being, and (2) making sensible decisions on how far to go to save money.

Being cheap is a characteristic of weaseling free money by constantly using friends, cutting corners, and (sometimes) living in a distrustful manner. Being cheap is not something to be proud of, but being frugal is.

Because frugal living is essential to most college students' successful college career, here are some pointers.

Cheap or Frugal?

Cheap

- Whenever pitching in for food, cab rides, or whatever, you are always short.
- You take advantage of others' generosity and never return the favor.
- You never have your wallet or purse with you.
- You live by the pointers given previously while always discussing how cheap you found an item and what you received for free.

Signs You Are Living Frugally

- Buying the chicken breast at half price.
- Remembering your discount card at the grocery store.
- Taking the bus or riding your bike sometimes when gas is too expensive.
- Buying your textbooks online to save money.
- Pitching in with friends to buy food in bulk.
- Knowing the specials around town—taco night, 2-for-1 night, and the like.

The running joke of college students having no money is not really a joke. Sure, there are the exceptions. But learning to stretch your dollars is a huge challenge in college. One of the primary reasons students spend too much is drinking. Going to bars, as many students find out, is very expensive. Paying $6 for a mixed drink when that same money could cover two meals is not money well spent. And, as many of us know, there are many college students who buy more than one drink. Keeping your drinking under control will not only keep your life less stressful and more healthy and productive, but will be easier on your bank account too. If you are using loans for college, that drink may be costing $9 by the time you add in interest and fees. Just a little something to keep in mind if you ever find yourself in a bar.

> "When going out at night, never bring a credit card —it's bad news. Plan how much you want to spend and bring cash. This will keep you from spending too much. It also stops those 2:30 A.M. 'drinks for everyone, it's on me' type of situations."
>
> —Junior, Political Science Major

Have a Plan

Perhaps the most important rule for being responsible with money is having a plan, commonly known as budgeting. Budgeting sounds much more complex than it is.

Making a Budget

1. Spell out the amount of money you will receive from parents, loans, jobs, and similar sources.
2. Allocate the amount of money you will spend, allotting the cash by category.

Next, keep track of your spending and how it relates to your plan. You might do this weekly, monthly, by semester, or by year. Usually it is best to combine these approaches and have a weekly, monthly, and yearly budget prepared. (All you do is multiply; it is not too hard to figure out.)

Figuring your income is not difficult, but many people are unsure about how to estimate what they will spend. The amount of money you will spend depends on

- your expected lifestyle.
- the college you attend.

Lifestyle includes a lot of variables:

> "I lived with relatives to save on rent and used the rest of the cash to pay off my car and stay out of debt."
>
> —Senior, Biomedical Sciences Major

- Clothes you wear
- Eating habits
- Car payments (if any)
- Going out (socially, clubs, restaurants, bars, etc.)
- Residence (To a degree, you can avoid living in the nicest place around if money is a concern, but you cannot help the high real estate prices in New York, for instance.)

The college you attend can include these variables:

- Public or private university
- Housing in the area: New York University housing will be more expensive than East Tennessee State University
- General expense of the area (a high-density urban setting with higher prices versus a more rural college town)

This may seem like too many variables to consider when figuring a budget, but help is available. Most of the time, the hard work has been done for you.

Many schools in their financial aid office have budget estimates for students, or even interactive budgeting computer programs. Many times, they have that information for both on and off-campus. Even though your lifestyle may differ (by more or less), this a great place to start. If the details are not spelled out on that budget, you can find them out by asking the office. This way, you can compare your spending and living expectations with that of the set budget.

> "It is okay to splurge every once in a while—that's what money is for! Know your means, though. You typically will not have to watch every penny, just be sensible with that occasional splurge."
>
> —Graduate, History Major

Use that provided budget as a blueprint to making your own plan. This will allow you an accurate account of how you can plan out your spending and lifestyle at school. And once you have a realistic budget and stick to it, you will not have to worry every month about having enough to last out the month. It is all laid out.

An important note: Budgets are not perfect. Almost no one will absolutely stick to a budget. There will always be emergencies that arise, so do not have a coronary if you miss the target by a miniscule amount.

Adjusting the amounts up or down is now up to you. If you are always on the phone, you may allow a bit more for that; or if you would like to live in a nicer apartment, up that category to your liking. Find your school's allowed budget from the Financial Aid Office or online and plug it into the worksheet in the Appendix. Here you can make a custom budget to fit your needs.

WORKSHEET 8-1

Budget Worksheet

Use information from your school's financial aid office, coupled with your own living preferences to fill in the worksheet.

Sample 20xx–20xx School Yearly Budget

Category	Yearly Estimate ($)	Monthly Estimate ($)—*Divide by 8 months, the length of the school year*
Tuition and ancillary fees	4200	n/a—usually paid in large chunks
Books	650	n/a—usually paid in large chunks
Entertainment	1020	127.50
Clothing	300	37.50
Rent	3200	400
Telephone	320	40
Utilities	480	60
Food	1600	200
Miscellaneous	600	75
TOTAL	12370	940

20__–20__ School Yearly Budget

Category	Yearly Estimate ($)	Monthly Estimate ($)—*Divide by 8 months, the length of the school year*
Tuition and ancillary fees		n/a—usually paid in large chunks
Books		n/a—usually paid in large chunks
Entertainment		
Clothing		
Rent		
Telephone		
Utilities		
Food		
Miscellaneous		
TOTAL		

Easy Ways to Save

As you know, it is much easier to spend money than save or make it. Following are some common drains on college bank accounts.

Books

Buying from other students can be the easiest and cheapest way to stock up on your books for the semester. Some college organizations even sponsor textbook exchange or buyback programs—a great place to get deals on books. Just be sure the book you are purchasing is the same edition being used now, or you may have to buy another!

Buying online is another option. Find your books early and order through http://Half.com or http://amazon.com and you can save 50 percent (which can be thousands of dollars throughout college). Also, selling your books on Half.com or comparable Web site can get you more money than selling back to the bookstore.

Computer

First, decide if you will need a computer or not. If your school is especially well-connected with 24-hour computer labs, you may be able to save buying a computer altogether.

If you do decide that a computer will be necessary, check your school's bookstore. Many colleges provide discounts on computers through the bookstore, and Dell™ gives discounts to students directly. If you decide to purchase, looking in August and September can be the most advantageous, when companies are campaigning hard for students' business. You can also save on software through the bookstore; and with Microsoft®, you can even download some software for free if you are pursuing a certain degree (like Computer Science, for example).

Cell Phone

If you have a cell phone, budget your minutes throughout the month, and stay a little on the underside. Phone companies will estimate your usage, and it is usually on the low end. If you are not careful, just a few minutes over can blow an otherwise perfect monthly budget. Here are some tips:

- Check your minutes weekly.
- Leave most talking until night minutes are in use.
- Purchase a plan that many of your friends have. Many companies will give you extra cell-to-cell minutes if you both use their company.
- Look into all available plans (family plans, no-roaming plans, etc.) to decide which will fit you best.

Parking on Campus

Be sure to park only in designated places. Universities are notorious for writing tickets. If you do receive a ticket, be sure to appeal it. Appealing a ticket usually requires taking a few minutes to fill out a form. You can do this at your campus parking or transportation office.

- Purchase the parking sticker.
- Know where to park.
- If you receive a ticket, appeal it.

Eat In

It is definitely more common for students to eat out at school, because time and/or convenience may be a factor. In fact, eating out is where students spend most of their money. But, that much eating out is not needed. If you have a meal plan, make the most of that. If buying groceries is left to you, watch for sales and specials and eat in.

> "If you have a date, try cooking at home instead of going out. A cookbook is $8 and is a one-time investment. Not only will it save you money, your date will be thoroughly impressed— even if the food doesn't turn out great."
>
> —Senior, Computer Science Major

General Guidelines for Saving at College

- Ask, "Do I really need this?"
- Make a budget.
- Stick to that budget.

   All of which will keep your life low-stress!

Sticking with the Budget

A couple of pages ago, you (were supposed to) set up your student budget. If you did not, go back and do it! Generally, sticking to your budget is the single most important part of successfully handling money through college, and life. If adjustments are necessary, by all means, adjust. Writing in your budget on the worksheet will not single-handedly solve your monetary problems, but it gives you a plan to live by rather than wing it everyday! Sticking to your plan will take some sacrifice and some determination, but the sooner you have a plan—a budget—the sooner you will begin to feel in control of this important part of college life.

MONEY $TRESS

We have talked about stress and how it can negatively affect your schoolwork and life as a whole. Learning to control money in a mature fashion can save you a lot of grief and problems through college, and contribute to your college success.

> "Money is the one thing students stress about more than grades."
>
> —Sophomore, Exercise Physiology Major

It Is Easy to Get into Debt

STUDENT PROFILE—Chris S. on Money

I witnessed others with whom I worked go out and get themselves into huge financial trouble. They then had no choice but to set school aside and pay off their debt. If anything, it was that alone causing them to delay or put off school as a lower priority.

Just seeing that, I knew keeping my nose above debt would be a key factor to staying in school. The less debt, I knew, the less I would have to worry. And the less worries, the more time and energy I could focus on school in general.

➤ *If financial worries take time and energy from your school work, discuss three ways to reduce your financial burden.*

Wrecking your financial credibility does not happen overnight. Students usually obtain a credit card, and over the period of months or years, they dig a hole that is difficult to climb out of.

Gaining access to money in college today is easier than it has ever been. Credit card companies love college students. Why? Because most college students, unlike most grownups, have little or no debt, and very few living expenses. People in those categories are more likely to pay their credit card bills. And even if students cannot pay, the companies know that guilt will compel students to put pressure on their parents to help them pay the bill. To credit card companies, college students give them a definite win-win situation.

Ask any college student: Almost every time they check the mail, there's an application, approval for, or already a credit card. When your parents were in college, they certainly were not bombarded as students are today with offers like this. Today, at any time, even without a job, a college student can obtain a credit card with a limit of thousands of dollars!

This is tempting, very tempting. Those new shoes you have been dying for, or that new shirt you just have to have but cannot afford, can be yours at the drop of a hat. The money is so easy to get, it is almost impossible to resist. And too many students fall prey to the temptation of a credit card, with little or no way of paying for it. If they cannot make those ever-growing payments on time, it is reported on their credit report.

Starting life after college can be a challenge, even with perfect credit. Beginning life after college with bad credit makes the difficult close to impossible. In addition, many jobs, especially in the banking and finance industry, check credit as a type of reference. Bad credit can actually keep you from getting a job! Because your credit can have a significant impact on life after college, keep your credit in good shape so that you do not have to start behind the eight ball.

Keeping Credit Cards to a Minimum

- Never fill out credit card applications on campus. On every college campus, there are constant promotions that give T-shirts, candy bars, or some other freebie to students. All they have to do is fill out an application. Harmless, right? Wrong! Avoid filling out even one. It is like giving your e-mail address to one Web site: constant junk mail forever after!

- Check your mail—and read it! When an application or card comes in the mail, check to make sure the company hasn't already signed you up. This could lead to open accounts on your credit report, which are nothing but a chore to remove. Even worse, a criminal could use these open accounts to ruin your credit, and that can take years to straighten out.

- Check your credit report. Every year, check your credit report to ensure there are no open accounts, credit cards you are unaware of, or large problems with your credit. It is relatively cheap (about $15) and worthwhile.

- Be firm. Banks and credit card companies would like to sign you up for 10 cards if possible. They will also try everything in the book to persuade you that it is a great idea. This is the first time most students are in charge of these kinds of responsibilities, and it can be difficult. If you do not want the service, make sure to be firm and tell them "No." Learning to say "No" is one key to having a successful college career. This is good practice for your after-college life, too.

Identity Theft [4]

Identity theft is a large problem and only growing. The complications of being a victim can be enormous. To prevent identity theft before it happens, follow the following simple tips.

When providing personal and account information online, make sure the business is legitimate.

- Look up the phone number in the Yellow Pages or another well-known source.

- Check with the Better Business Bureau.

In addition, make sure the site is secure by clues such as "the lock" on the bottom of your computer screen. Keep a record of your online transactions and review your monthly statement. If anything looks strange, contact your bank or credit card issuer immediately.

Maintaining Good Credit at School

- Too many credit inquiries lowers your credit rating. The bank sees people who constantly check their credit as itching to spend money. Only check your rating if you are seriously considering a purchase.

- Maxing-out credit cards lowers your credit score. The closer you get to the limit on your card, the further your rating will plummet—one more reason to keep from charging any purchases you do not absolutely have to.

- Do not charge more than you can afford to pay when the bill comes. If you lack the discipline for this, consider obtaining a card that must be paid off every month, like American Express.

- Credit cards are for personal use—do not share! Hunting down money owed you when a friend's charge appears on the bill is added stress on you and your friendships that you do not need.

If Problems Arise

No one can help emergencies in life, like

- health.
- transportation.
- family.

Health

Health is especially important. If anything is wrong with you physically, or mentally, such as depression or anxiety, do not hesitate to visit the campus health center. You may have to cover a $20 co-pay (or it may be free), but any price is worth your health.

If you have stuck closely to your budget, this should not be a problem. But even if it is a problem, forget about the cost and take care of yourself. Besides, relatives or others may be willing to toss in some extra money if they know you are sick.

Transportation

Transportation can throw a wrench into your plans as well. There is nothing worse than living a few miles from campus and the '84 Camry puttering to a stop. If this happens, here are some suggestions:

- If you can hurry and pay for repairs, do so.
- In the meantime, use a bus service or ask a favor from friends for a ride. (Simply buying them a cheap dinner here and there and/or chipping in on gas can be considered returning the favor.)

- If you cannot pay for repairs right away, and it is too much to ask a friend to pick you up, borrow a bicycle or pick one up at the pawnshop (cheap). Or, once again, ride the bus.

- And if you attend school in Minnesota and your car breaks down in the middle of winter, a bicycle might not be feasible. So once again, find a friend or use public transportation.

Family

Your time during college might coincide with a family emergency. It is not uncommon for a mishap to cause a health crisis or other problem at home. If anything like this does happen in your college career, you might have to get home in a hurry. If relatives are in a bind and unable to help, go ahead and assume the expense if possible. (Once again, sticking to your budget may take care of some of the problems associated with affording a plane or bus ticket home.) If it is an issue, this is one of those times when it is appropriate to use a credit card.

Stuff Happens!

So you are out of money and need clothes, shoes, toiletries . . . (fill in the blank). Many students run across this situation regularly. To tell you the truth upfront: there are no magic answers. You will have to be creative and resourceful in these sticky situations to meet your needs; I'll show you what I mean!

First decide—is it possible to get it or not? Here are some resourceful ways to find out:

- Can you borrow from a friend?

- Can you buy it cheaply (on sale, at thrift stores, or at discount stores)?

- Can you rent it?

- If it is broken, can it be repaired?

Borrow: These are all viable options. For small stuff like some toothpaste until you get paid tomorrow, there should not be too much of an issue as far as borrowing some. Borrowing does work for bigger stuff too, though just be sure to return the favor when asked—you likely will be.

Buy cheaply: For college students, Wal-Mart or other discount stores may become a staple. Items are usually cheap, and the store is always open (perfect combo for those late-night shopping trips). Shopping at secondhand stores is also a popular option. Not only is it acceptable, but a number of college students actually prefer the look of clothes from these stores.

If You Go Away to School —Cheap Options to Get Home

- **Bus.** The tickets are cheaper than airfare; the downside is the discomfort and length of the trips. You might have stops in every town from Boston to Reno along the way, and that makes the trip longer than a simple drive.

- **Trains.** Amtrak and other local lines are comfortable and cheap ways to travel.

- **Airlines.** Because of the competition and the industry trying to stay afloat, you can find some great deals for flying. There are discount carriers without all of the amenities, like Southwest and JetBlue, that have better-than-average prices. Checking rates on the Internet can be a great way to go, and student discounts can be found.

- **Ride Boards.** Some colleges have Ride Boards. Usually in the student union, these are listings of people taking trips home, looking for people to share the ride with. Just pitch in for gas, make a new friend, and enjoy the cheap ride home.

Web Sites for Travel Info

- www.Expedia.com
- www.Travelocity.com
- www.Southwest.com
- www.JetBlue.com
- www.Amtrak.com
- www.Greyhound.com

Rent: Maybe you cannot afford that snowboard, surfboard, or pair of skates, but still want to be part of the fun—renting may fit perfectly! Just be sure to understand the terms upfront and know what you are signing up for.

Fix it: Finally, repairs may be possible. For example, if you ripped your coat and desperately need a new one, try looking into repairs. Look up a tailor shop in the Yellow Pages and be sure to get a price quote. Compared to a new item, repairs can be quite cheap!

If any of these options (or others that you know) is appropriate, then go for it. If not, read on.

Work Around It!

Things hardly ever work out just how we like. There may come a time in college where you will have to bite the bullet and work around your needs. For example, if you need new running shoes but cannot afford them at the moment, find an exercise that does not require high impact absorbing shoes—biking, swimming, or other activity that you are able to do.

The bottom line is: Be creative and resourceful when it comes to emergencies. Usually if you apply both—Is it possible to get it, and if not, how can I work around it?—many problems can easily be solved!

HELP, I'M $5,000 IN DEBT!

It's a nightmare, and you would not believe how many students experience it. The following scenario is oddly familiar and consistent (girl or guy, the scheme can happen to anyone).

How It Happens

1. A student receives her first credit card.
2. That Friday, the student and friends have an outing at the mall, and she buys a few small items: a shirt, two CDs, and one DVD—$80 total. Not bad.
3. That night, its out to TGI Friday's for dinner, then out to a movie—$25.
4. Saturday. The students order delivery food in the afternoon, and our student finds that cool jacket on sale online for half price—$100.
5. She repeats this a couple times per month for a few months.
6. She makes only the minimum payments each month (which only pays the interest and does not pay toward

the money she owes), and lets interest accrue for a year or two.

7. Here she is now, thousands of dollars in debt.

A thousand dollars is quite a bit of money, especially to the wage-starved college student. But as you can see in this example, the ease with which one can accrue that amount of debt, and more, is deceivingly simple.

Like in the example, it is the little purchases, done time and time again, that get students into financial trouble. Of course, the best course of action is to tame your Visa trigger finger and stick to your budget. But if you did not choose the best course, there are some options left.

Getting Out

If you get into such a mess, it is best to get out—right away.

Approach Relatives with a Plan

If you come waltzing up to your parents asking for five grand, watch out. They probably will not just hand you the money and say, "Try not to do it again." Before you approach them, get together a plan.

- **Find out what went wrong.** Take a look at your billing statements and identify your problem. Are you a habitual shopper, restaurant customer, bar mainstay? Figure out your area of temptation.

- **Write a plan.** Figure a plan to keep you from spending money at this/these place(s) again. If you have gone overboard on spending, you may need to go overboard not spending to get back to square one. First, simply use the Budget Worksheet from earlier in the chapter (refer to Worksheet 8-1). Budgeting will help you stay focused on improving your financial situation by giving you a piece-by-piece plan to accomplish the goal. If you are still having trouble with your finances or feel overwhelmed, go to a not-for-profit credit counseling service to help (see Web sites provided).

- **Put the plan into action.** Put your plan into action for a while. If possible, give yourself a month or so to prove that your budget works.

- **Go ahead and approach.** Though all these pointers are great, they do not guarantee anything. Your parents or relatives simply may not have the money, or may not loan it to you, no matter what. It is their money, after all.

Not-for-Profit Credit Counseling Services

www.familycredit.org
www.nfcc.org
www.nccs.org
www.collegecreditcounseling.com

One thing is for sure, though: If you figure out what went wrong and have a plan in place to fix it, you will put yourself in a much better position to work out of the debt regardless of their cooperation.

If your relatives do accept, be sure to walk the tightrope. If you do not, burning this bridge may haunt you down the road.

Talk to a Bank Representative

Though it may be a bit intimidating, these people are here to help you. Make an appointment with someone at whichever bank you have an account with. The advice is free, and your debt reduction is in the bank's best interest too (they do not want things to get so bad that they never get their money!). There may be special plans, such as ones to consolidate your debt at a lower interest rate. These folks may be able to directly help, or at least they can refer you to an organization that can.

Get Rid of Existing Credit Cards

Whether you tear, cut, or burn (not a good idea, fumes from burning plastic are not particularly healthy) the cards, get rid of them. If it is absolutely necessary to keep one, you are the boss. But because you do not have such a great track record, it is probably better to remove all temptation. When closing accounts, be sure to call and cancel rather than just destroy your card (the balance will still exist!). Leaving open accounts on your credit report is not helpful for rebuilding your credit. Sacrifice and scrimp until you have some money put aside for emergencies and you can do without all the credit cards.

If You Do Get Into Debt, Stay Positive!

Many people have worked themselves into quite a debt in college, but many have worked themselves out. Paying down those credit cards is similar to schoolwork, exercising, or applying for a job. Consistency counts. Keep a positive attitude to stick with your plan. There will be times when everyone else is going out and you simply cannot, but swallow the unpleasantness and keep going. You will become a better person for it.

Social Life: People, Places, Dating, and Stress

CHAPTER 9

"Life is partly what we make it, and partly made by the friends we choose."

—Tehyi Hsieh

CHOOSE YOUR FRIENDS

Choosing friends will have a major impact on your college life. The fact of the matter is, where you hang out is going to be where you meet your friends. So choose that spot wisely.

The most common places in college to meet people are

- living space (dorms, apartments, etc.).
- social clubs (frats, sororities, clubs, organizations).
- hangouts (parties, pool halls, coffee shops, etc.).
- classes and study areas.

Of course there are the dorms, where everyone else is new, just like you. Sometimes, that makes meeting people easier. But not

> "If you want to be an intelligent person, it's a good idea to surround yourself with intelligent people. That is why I associate with people I study with—I know that their habits and tendencies will slowly become mine as well."
>
> —Junior, Art History Major

everyone lives at the dorms, and many may move out of them by their second year. So be sure to consider the other places on that list. Aside from your living space, the people you meet will often have similar interests to yours. For example, if you join a fraternity or sorority, these organizations tend to be more homogenous than, say, your classes, so you will be more likely to meet people with common interests. If you are an athlete and play sports for your college, you will draw common ground based on this, too. But beware: If you are constantly at parties and meet most of your friends there, you might spend a lot more time partying than you really should.

My Story

I met one of my good friends outside a professor's office. We both had questions from a past exam, and began talking about it out in the hall. After we met, we found that we shared an interest in fitness, and so we began working out together. Later on, we held study groups, and then hung out outside of school, classes, and studying. I gained a workout partner and great friend just by going to see my professor.

My experience is not to say that the only good friends you will find are in study groups—or in the hallway outside your professor's office! I have met some other great friends at parties, and some just by chance. Because you do not want to constantly study, or continuously party, have a good mix of friends. Mix them up so that no matter what, there is always someone to share time with.

Where It All Happens

What a Friendship!
While he was at Harvard, Bill Gates was friends with the person he brought on board to start Microsoft. The lesson: Be nice to your peers—they might make you a billionaire!

Bill Gates's relationship with his friend is probably rare, and this brings up another good point. Just because you are friends with someone does not mean that you will both share every interest. As I'm sure you know, there is nothing much worse than a boring discussion, no matter how much you like the person. Just because you absolutely love to talk about the scientific process behind processing oil into gasoline, that does not mean everyone else does. So, when you have interests that you love to learn more about and discuss with other people, join or start a club. Clubs allow you to make connections with people interested in similar issues, in a forum where discussions can go on for hours and people can form bonds and friendships. On top of just finding people who are fun to be around, clubs might enable you to get help on something you have always wanted to do. If you have wanted to design a Web site about college filmmaking, go to the film club. They might not be Web designers, but you might meet people willing to help you perfect your idea.

Take your friends seriously; take a look at what they like and their main interests, because chances are, those will end up being powerful interests for you, too.

GETTING INVOLVED

"Get involved" was one of the most common themes I heard as I interviewed students for this book. And they are right. College is unlike any time you will experience in your life because of the sheer number of activities and organizations available to you as a student. Getting out and exploring other places besides the dorms and classes can be fun. Doing this can also bring you some rewarding relationships, because the key to meeting people at college—dorms or no dorms—is to get involved. If you get out and get into new things, new people will come right along with it. There is no shortage of things to do or clubs to join on a college campus. And there are always people willing to hang out or get into something interesting. (Almost all activities provide a venue to try out leadership and help build your experience and problem-solving skills as well.)

> "My school has a Student Organization Night where most campus organizations have a booth. You can see the different groups and find out where you want to join."
>
> —Freshman, Undecided Major

Diversity Is Beneficial

Because going to college is about broadening your horizons, socializing with people from different backgrounds will add to the experience.

The people are as important as the education. They are an essential part of your education, so learn from a broad base of people.

> "Having a diverse student body to interact with is just as important as the academic aspect. Interacting with people of different points of view helps you to think in a different way."
>
> —Graduate, Economics Major

Chill Places in and Around Campus

In the dorm or out, making your new world feel like home means knowing where everything is, like your classes. But do not forget the fun. Many campuses, whether they are urban or rural, have plenty of student-friendly places in and around campus. Finding some of these hangouts can be the difference between feeling settled in or not. You may stumble on to them or find them by word of mouth.

During the Day

Some schools call it the Quad, some the Commons, and the list goes on and on. These nice, outside places are there for everyone to enjoy. Whether you go to school in California or Minneapolis, at every school there are times during the year to enjoy some time outside. Gathering on the Quad to play Frisbee, meet with friends, or even take a snooze between classes is perfect.

> "There are many advantages to the people you are around. They have a whole range of interests and experiences that you can tap into. You can find out how they have done things and how their choices have panned out—it is really very valuable."
>
> —Graduate, Chemistry Major

If it is not the right time of year to meet outside, find the indoor hot spot. The student union is a good place to start. These facilities usually have food, couches, and maybe a computer lab. Once again, this is a perfect place to check your e-mail or grab some food with friends during the day.

If you enjoy studying in a bustling environment, these places can be perfect. There is usually more than enough room to spread your books and notes out to study.

At Night

Coffee shops, game rooms, and pool halls are just some of the amenities many college campuses provide these days. If your campus does not have any, though, chances are you will find one somewhere close by. Sharpening your bank shot in pool or having a friendly conversation over a latte can be the perfect relaxation in the evening.

A Place to Relax!

They might be the same as some of the others, but these are places to get away for a little bit, whether it is with a friend or alone. (In spite of all the talk so far about meeting people, time alone is certainly important in college too.) One of the best relaxing hangouts is a bookstore. Bookstores, like Barnes & Noble and Borders, have big, comfy chairs and coffee bars. But even in independent bookstores, these are becoming commonplace. Take advantage of the reading material and laid-back atmosphere to relax, get some work done, or read the free magazines.

Special Events

Your school may have a great sports team (and great games), a barbecue night, or movie on the lawn. Getting out to these events can be a great place to bond with other students and meet great friends and create great memories.

Close to School

Not every fun gathering at college is actually on campus. There are community-based organizations that can be great fun for students. There is everything from car clubs to youth groups, or anything else that can be found. Of course, being in a city will broaden this category of events, but wherever you are, I am sure you can find a few opportunities.

"Going to football games on Saturdays or going to basketball games during the week was a fun diversion from schoolwork—whether it was a win or a loss."

—Graduate, Economics Major

"I have been going to a Wednesday night youth group with approximately 300 people, and it has been a very good influence. Afterward, everyone goes out to eat and it's a great way to meet people. I can go anywhere on campus and see at least one person I know, that I met at that youth group. It has really been a healthy thing to get involved in."

—Senior, Biomedical Science Major

CLUBS

The Video and Film Club, the Surfing Club, College Republicans, College Democrats—the list of clubs could go on forever!

Clubs are one of many unique and fun opportunities college provides. Not only do they provide people to mingle with and get to know, but they can be informative and fun. If you are in a political club, a local politician may come to speak. If you are in a real estate club, a local real estate investor or businessperson may come to spark ideas and lend advice. Clubs and organizations are a gold mine for the successful college student, so use them! If you have an interest, there is a club—or room to start one.

> "Have an experience to have an experience. I never wanted to be a DJ, but tried it out on campus and there I was—in charge of 10,000 watts."
> —Graduate, Graphic Design Major

The Options

- Politics: Republican, Democrat, Green Party, Libertarian, you name it! Many colleges have a number of political clubs to satisfy even the biggest election junkies. If you are not sure if politics is your gig, attend a meeting to see what goes on. You might love it.

- Outdoors: Hiking, fishing, rock climbing, or anything else—if you are interested in these activities, these clubs can get you access to venues where you can exercise your love of the outdoors. You will also find friends to accompany you.

- Business: You may have a gift for business, and know it early. Or you might just want to know more about what the business world is like, for after college. Business clubs can help to grow your interest and skills. In addition to a place for meeting people, business clubs often bring in successful business owners to speak and tell about their successes and failures.

- Religion: No matter what religion you practice, there are opportunities for developing a support network through either joining or starting a club. Many students enjoy sharing time with students of similar beliefs, while meeting others who may be new but interested in their religious beliefs.

- Arts: Film, drawing, painting, graphic design, music—for every creative outlet, there is a club. If you enjoy painting, drawing, graphic design, or music, an art club may be a great place. If you enjoy discussing art but do not necessarily enjoy painting, drawing, or designing, an art history or art philosophy club may be the best choice.

- Communications: Getting started in radio, television, or print reporting can be tough, because that is a tough industry. If you want to explore opportunities and gain knowledge to better your chances, explore one of these clubs. If you are starting a club like this, be sure to sign on a top faculty member in the appropriate department. He or she can help you get started and gain access to information, ideas, and speakers that will add a lot to the club.

- Society: Some students find philosophy and similar disciplines intriguing. Setting up a philosophy club can be as professional as PowerPoint presentations, speakers, and agendas, or as casual as meeting socially to debate issues. However you decide to approach things, these clubs can instigate critical thinking, and be a lot of fun too.

- Professional: Law, Medicine, Dentistry. Many schools have these clubs already in swing and established. If you are interested in one of these areas, these clubs are a must-join. They can be a doorway to opportunities for each profession. Interning at a law office, shadowing a dentist, or even watching an autopsy for medicine can be available through the club. And as with the other clubs, you will meet people who not only share similar interests but also may have an important impact on your after-college life, too.

- Automobiles: Cars, motorcycles, off-road fast cars and bikes are common interests of many college students. Clubs can bring together riding partners for motorcycle rides or friends to go mudding with.

If you join an existing club, and there are dues, most likely there is a reason. Your less-than-$20 will pay for pizza at meetings, speakers, and T-shirts, for instance. And the club experience need not take a lot of time. Usually clubs have meetings once a week for an hour or two, where they discuss interests and ideas or do their favorite activities. Perhaps two or three times a year, there will be special events that take more time but also increase the fun and involvement.

If you just cannot seem to find other people that have similar interests, finding a club that focuses on a hobby of yours is a great way to meet folks that you can make a connection with. On every campus, there is at least one club that will serve your interests. And if there isn't? You can start it!

Novel Club Ideas

- The Monopoly Club: People who absolutely love to play Monopoly can come here and play continuous games as well as discuss professional interests, such as real estate investing, and the like. Maybe strange, but a very inventive idea.

- Entrepreneurs Club: Students attending the meetings have the opportunity to meet others who are interested in starting a business. Here is a place to meet other creative individuals with a passion for building on their own ideas for the future.

Intramural Sports

Another terrific way to get to know people is by playing intramural sports. The great thing is that these are just for fun, and you do not have to be any good to play. Most of the time, they do not require much practice, so they really do not take up a lot of your time. They can simply serve as great exercise and a fun time to hang out and talk with friends.

There are tons of ways to get on a team. You can sign up and be put on a random team. Or, create your own with some of your friends. Nothing like a few good grass stains or sore legs after playing some soccer or intramural basketball!

The Options

There are many sports from which to choose, such as:

- Flag football
- Soccer
- Basketball
- Lacrosse
- Ultimate Frisbee
- Ice hockey
- Tennis
- Volleyball
- Softball
- Golf
- Water polo

If you played sports in high school and are itching to get back on the field but do not want to try out for the commitment-heavy college athletic circuit, try intramurals. Club sports are a great way to feel the thrill of the game throughout college, make great friends, and get a tough workout all in one.

STUDENT GOVERNMENT

You may be a more serious-minded person or want to have fun with more serious issues. Perhaps you are just interested in having a say in the operations of the university. Student government organizations (also known as SGs) are the perfect fit for a student who wants to practice leadership, decision-making, meeting new people, and gaining great experience for any post-college field.

Something you want to change at your college? Joining the SG can give you a say in changing it. There is another bonus, too: The SG is always a great extracurricular to list on a graduate school or job application.

However, the SG club is not just for fun. Students who get involved in this club often say how satisfying it is to make a difference in some initiative or action taken by the university.

STUDENT PROFILE—Dan R. on Student Government

I was active in the Student Government during college, and learned quite a bit. I served on the President's Committee on Ethics in Human Research. The committee reviewed research done by the Psychology Department involving students. It was our duty to determine whether the department's studies violated any ethical standards toward the students involved in each study. It was a rare opportunity, being on such a powerful committee, basically giving the yea or nay to a university department's research. It was also a great feeling, knowing I was contributing to the well-being of my classmates and the university at large.

➤ *Is there an issue at your college you wish you could change or contribute to? If so, how would you do it?*

Creating a platform can be a fun way to learn about accomplishing an objective. If there is a hot-button situation at your school (parking usually comes to mind), here is your chance to strike out and attempt to do something about it. Learning the ways to lead people toward accomplishing a goal is a fun and useful skill to begin learning in college.

Working for the student government can also be frustrating. Just like any government position, there is plenty of bureaucracy and red tape to deal with. But it is worth it. As a senator of the student body or in any other position, you will gain valuable insight into the workings of large organizations.

Putting together a campaign is another great learning tool that running for student government provides. You will have to articulate your positions on certain issues and lay out your plan to improve the school's situation. Running a successful campaign and achieving your objectives can be a tremendous confidence builder, and you will help other students along the way. The people skills you will develop doing this will be second to none. You will be sure to improve your

- personal interaction skills.
- public speaking skills.
- interviewing skills for everything from jobs to graduate school admissions.

GREEK LIFE: WHAT REALLY GOES ON?

Not every school has a greek community, but if your school does, this may be an important section. In every movie you have ever seen about college, how did they portray fraternity members? Big jocks wearing letters across their chests and dating ditzy chicks in pink sweaters, right?

> **What Is Greek Life?**
> Greek life refers to the fraternity and sorority communities on campus.

Although this is what people might imagine when they think greek life, like most movie portrayals, it is not terribly accurate. But because of those descriptions, greek organizations have more misconceptions to deal with than any other organization on campus.

Some Quick Greek Facts[9]

- Nine million people in the United States are members or alumni of greek organizations.
- There are 750,000 undergraduate members.
- Greeks are the largest network of volunteers in the United States.
- Forty-eight percent of all U.S. Presidents have been greeks.
- Thirty percent of Fortune 500 executives are greek.

Animal House?

If you look around, you will find a few fraternities and sororities that give *Animal House* a run for the money. But for the majority, this just is not true. Greek life is comprised of and incorporates just about every aspect of social life possible—not just partying.

> "If you are going to get involved with greek life, be really involved. There are many opportunities for learning leadership and skills, so use them to your full advantage."
> —Senior, Business Administration Major

THE ADVISOR SAYS:

There is nothing that brings you in holistically, as a person, and rounds out your education better than a fraternity or sorority.

By offering such opportunities as formal study hours, community service projects, and networking, greek life can offer the student great experiences in college and benefits after.

The Breakdown

There are many different aspects to greek organizations.

Academics

On many campuses, greek students have higher GPAs than their nongreek counterparts. No, you do not have to be involved in one of these organizations to do well. But belonging to a chapter adds extra incentive to work hard. The greek network of support keeps fraternity/sorority students more concerned about their grades. Most organizations set aside weekly study time for members and maintain old test banks to help members study and prepare for exams.

Leadership

There are also many opportunities for leadership roles in the greek community. From positions in the organization, to help in campaigning for a student government office, there is a definite push to build leadership. This development helps greatly after college when getting a job or applying for graduate school; the ability to function as a leader is an enormous plus no matter what field a person goes into. Greek organizations provide positions such as

- President. Duties range from presiding over meetings to setting the tone for what is acceptable in the organization. The chapter president may help in other areas also.

- Treasurer. The treasurer is responsible for collecting dues and budgeting for the current and upcoming semester. With the responsibility and position of leadership, being the treasurer can be terrific training for a future career.

- Rush Chair. This is probably one of the more outgoing and social individuals in the organization. The rush chair meets and talks with potential members, and is the first face of the organization that many people meet. This position is a workout in people skills.

- Secretary. Keeping track of what is discussed at meetings, who needs to be contacted, and scheduling is left to this position. These are important functions, without which the organization could barely function. The responsibility of serving as secretary is great practice for life after college.

- Other options, including Vice President, Social Chair, Philanthropy Chair.

STUDENT PROFILE—Henry L. and Responsibility

Assuming a leadership position in my fraternity was a great experience that helped prepare me for life after college. As president of the frat, I was responsible for running the entire organization, which sometimes included assuming other duties. One semester, our treasurer was unable to complete his duties, so it became my responsibility to complete the budget. It was not easy juggling the event planning, clothing, and other expenses to create a balanced budget. However, in the end I learned to multitask well, and a new skill—budgeting—which will all come in handy in the business world.

➤ *Do you think assuming a leadership position in an organization is a good idea? Why or why not?*

➤ *If you were able to choose, which type of position would you like to take?*

Connections

Excellent networking is available through fraternities and sororities. With over 1.3 million bachelor degrees projected to be awarded in 2005,[10] you need all the help you can get when it is time to find a job. Not only is a greek organization a respectable extracurricular and community-oriented activity, it may also be the perfect introduction to an interviewer. If the interviewer is an alumni of the same organization, that is one more way to make a connection and set yourself apart in the competitive world of job hunting. Being part of a greek organization points to the following:

* Ability to work well with people. Working in teams and groups is the rage everywhere from the new problem-based learning/ small-group teaching methods to a job in the corporate world. Being a member of a fraternity or sorority shows that you most likely have this ability.

* Commitment. To rush (the process of joining a greek organization) takes commitment. Commitment is important in every area of life. This is definitely a feather in your cap when applying for jobs or graduate school.

* Loyalty. Many fraternities and sororities hold loyalty as an important value. Knowing that you place a high priority on loyalty may add another positive to your application to graduate/ professional school or employers.

All these attributes will help you establish that important connection for jobs or graduate school after college.

The Social Greek

An undeniable part of greek life is the social aspect. Many non-greek students see paying dues as buying friends. Yet paying for a gym membership does not mean you have to get in great shape, or for that matter will get into great shape. So paying membership dues for a fraternity or sorority does not mean that everyone will be your best friend. Just like anywhere else, you have to make your friends in frat and sorority houses. Although many students in these organizations do become close, it is from fun times and shared experiences, not buying each other off.

"My sorority gave me a starting point socially. I met people everywhere, but having that base was important for me."

—Junior, Mass Communications Major

Though many folks think greek life is one big party, it can actually offer a more regulated lifestyle. Greek sponsored parties offer

- ID checks.
- rules about drinking and driving.
- a safe place for people to have a good time.

Compare this with an off-campus apartment party:

- No one cares who is 21 or not.
- There is less supervision over people who drink and drive.
- No one looks out for the safety of others.

These regulations certainly are not foolproof, but the greek parties are much more controlled than the average college student might suspect.

It is important to remember how important social activities are during college. Having a safe place to meet and enjoy the company of people with similar interests is an exciting opportunity. Greek organizations certainly are not the only place this can happen, but they are one large place.

The social aspect of greek life is definitely part of the experience, but it is only one slice of the pie. There is so much more to these organizations than just keg parties. Read on.

Community Projects and Service

"Frats do a lot of good. My frat went into the city for a day to some government projects and painted buildings and planted trees."
—Graduate, History Major

Fraternities and sororities donate millions of hours of community service annually, and they raise substantial amounts of money for charitable causes. Being involved in one of these organizations means that you do not have to go out on your own to find community service projects and ways to help underprivileged people. The organizations have projects put together for the chapters to do. Also, your involvement is applauded and supported by your peers, which makes these causes that much more enjoyable to participate in. Not only are you working alongside friends, but the service projects themselves are often pleasant too.

Fraternities and sororities have been known to organize events like the following to raise money for charities:

- Powder puff football games (girls play football, guys cheerlead)
- Charity baseball and softball games
- Spaghetti dinners
- Walks and runs to raise money for causes
- Building projects alongside such organizations as Habitat for Humanity

This is an abbreviated list, but it gives you an idea of the fun possibilities that may arise.

By becoming part of one of these organizations, you can help in serving the community and making a difference.

Why Doesn't Everybody Join?

If you are thinking about greek life, you might be wondering why everyone doesn't join. First, greek life differs from school to school. At some institutions, it is not as serious a commitment as others. And although fraternities and sororities can benefit you in several ways, they are not a necessary part of college life. For example, I am not in a greek organization because it does not fit in with my schedule. Rushing (the process of shopping and joining a fraternity or sorority) is a large time commitment. Many students who have been through the process claim that time management skills are the most essential component to arriving on the other side with decent grades. In addition, the school you attend may affect your decision of whether or not to join. Your surroundings may dictate the practicality of joining such an organization. After all, if there are no greek organizations, it is a simple decision! At some schools such as Washington and Lee University, most students belong to a greek organization.

Of course, some students wonder about fraternities and sororities after reading (and hearing) of horror stories stemming from hazing—initiation rights that can be humiliating and/or unhealthy. Students have died and been seriously injured from drinking too much alcohol at greek organization-sponsored events—this is a fact. Because of these and other incidents, both schools and the organizations themselves have begun cracking down on hazing in general, making the initiation process less malignant than previous years. Joining a greek organization is a personal choice, and you must consider all information. More important than deciding based on a small number of national cases, meet other students involved with the organizations at your school. What have their experiences been? What is the reputation of different organizations on your campus? The answers to these questions will provide you with the best information to make the most informed decision.

So if you are thinking about joining a fraternity or sorority, weigh your outcome for both—and do it on paper, sometimes seeing your thoughts can help you decide.

BRINGING RELATIONSHIPS

It is not unheard of to bring high school boyfriends or girlfriends to college. Many if not most of the people I knew at college brought

> "Our sorority was big on philanthropy. We wrapped children's books for Christmas presents, read stories to kids in hospitals, and dressed up at Halloween to see the kids."
>
> —Senior, Psychology Major

> "Dating factors into the balance thing. It's a large part of the social interaction at college."
>
> —Junior, Sociology Major

> "Long-distance relationships definitely change your college experience. But if the person is that important to you, it is worth it."
>
> —Senior, Psychology Major

significant others with them. But there are challenges in doing so. Relationships at school can be a bumpy ride at times, and a challenge to even the strongest couples.

It is vital to lessen your stress—the bad stress, anyway—so that you can live a successful college life. There is enough stress on campus just with the profs' high expectations, staying healthy, and staying in good shape. Eliminating stress from needless places is a must for the successful college student. Relationships, even when they are not perfect, are good stress, can lessen bad stress, and give you a happier college experience.

Maybe your relationship fits into one of the three categories:

- The good
- The bad
- The ugly

The Good

Your days are filled with small, "I was thinking of you" gifts and mementos. Phone calls are loving and giggly while you share meaningful and interesting conversation on both ends. "Ahhh," you think blissfully, "my life is perfect!"

Okay, this may be a little too dreamy, so here is a more realistic definition of a good relationship. Good relationships are made by individuals with common interests and fitting personalities. By "fitting," I mean couples who complement each other well—their interests are similar and their personalities accommodate each other. Two stubborn people interested in very different things will not make for the best romance! Though things are not always perfect, the good relationship runs relatively smoothly.

Having, and keeping, a good relationship in high school and keeping it through college is a rare feat. If you have something good, you will know it, and if things do not feel right, never force them. Above all, do not allow your away relationship to keep you from getting out and meeting new people. We have talked about the options and culture that college provides, so stay involved and always be open to new people and ideas. College is a time to enjoy new things. Whether you come with a partner or not, keeping yourself out of the social loop because of a significant other is not a healthy idea.

The Bad

Beyond being wearisome, bad relationships can wreak havoc on the best college student's life. These relationships can be characterized by love-hate feelings, constant fighting, and general problems often arising because of the relationship. If you find yourself in one of these situations, there are only two workable options:

- Fix the relationship
- End the relationship

Fix

Perhaps you have found that your antics are inconsiderate and not exactly kind to the other person. This is quite a *Eureka!* moment, and something you should be commended on. Not many people discover this on their own.

Now that you know there is a problem, fix it!

The fix can go one of two ways. If you are the problem, try to figure out why. Maybe you are partying too much and that is really bothering your partner. Or maybe you are obsessing a little too much about getting perfect grades and the extra study time is causing you to ignore the person who really cares about you. In either case, you can probably figure out ways to balance your time better. Or, maybe the problem is not with you. After close examination, perhaps you realize that you are not really the problem. In either case, some type of sit-down with your partner and a calm, collected presentation of what you see as the problem may do the trick. Sure, this can easily result in outbursts by both parties and a regression instead of progression of your relationship. But it may spark the change that is needed to fix the relationship. Whatever the case, it is worth a try. Communication, even if it brings conflict sometimes, is never a bad thing.

End

End is the option (the only option) when fix has been attempted but has not worked. Although a tough option to enact, sometimes that is the only option left. Neither one of you will be happy at the beginning, but in time each of you will be better off.

The Ugly

Ugly often comes somewhere before or in between fix and end. It is characterized by a day-to-day bewilderment over how and why the relationship has gotten this far. Each party hardly cares about the other, yet is comfortable with the way things are. That ongoing confusion usually comes with a huge load of stress, too. These relationships will die hard and fast at college, especially if the two involved are many miles away (which, many times is the case). Characteristics of the Ugly may be

- lack of any common interest.

- day-to-day disdain of one another (no love/hate, just the latter, and a sense that things are never going to get better between you).
- even violent outbursts.

These types of relationships need to let people go in their own directions. There is only one option with the Ugly: End it. There are good reasons for this. A bad relationship may turn ugly, if it is let go far enough. And, the stress can be enough to derail you from your goal of having a happy college experience. Lastly, you may miss the chance for a great relationship wasting time in an unhealthy and irreparable one. If you and your partner have an ugly relationship, save each other the grief and end it now. One warning: In many ugly relationships, one or the other partner will not want things to end. If things do get violent between you two, or there is the threat of violence or harm, you have the duty to report it. College campuses have police departments and professionals to handle these situations.

On the Brighter Side

I am happy to say that bad and ugly relationships are pretty rare in college and long distance can work if you (and the other person) are willing to do the work.

Most relationships are the good kind, and dating falls into that category, too. The relationship game is hot during the college years, so there are plenty of people to play it with. Dating can be a lot of fun, so have fun with it.

WHAT EXACTLY *IS* DATING TO YOU?

Dating and relationships are certainly a big part of college. There are plenty of places to meet people and plenty of people to meet. Plus, if you have been around one small group of people for years in high school, it is an exciting time because it is the first time you will be around new people in a while.

Dating can be a great thing, but just like with any relationship, beware. Make sure the person you are with shares the same values and likes to do the same things. If not, the relationship can be a major drag after a while. And no matter how much you share, watch the amount of time you spend with each other. Going overboard here can ruin any time management system.

Although some people consider dating a long-term relationship, it is usually just a lead-in to that. Dating is like tasting a sample at Sam's Club—it is a time to spend time with different people to find someone you think might have long-term potential. Or, it can just be a fun and social time with a new person. Some people take dating very seriously. Others find it an entertaining pastime. Whichever camp you fit in (or maybe somewhere in the middle), there are plenty of people just like you at college.

Fun Things to Do on a College Date

Chances are you will want to do something fun but not too ceremonious. Cancel the fancy dress or formal wear rental and consider these ideas:

- Bowling. Every college town has bowling lanes nearby. This may be the original cheesy date idea, but it still works.

- Exercising. Not up for something formal, or late at night? If you or the other person is into health and fitness, taking a jog, in-line skating, or bike riding together can be a nice stress reliever, and a fun and productive date. Plus, doing something casual during the day may lower the tension level if one or both of you are a little bit nervous.

- Group dates. Maybe you are not so comfortable one-on-one, or you do not know this individual very well. Go on a group date or just out with a group of friends. If you are constantly searching for the right thing to say, going with a group may be perfect. With other people there, the pressure is not always on you to have stimulating conversation ready at all times. So if you struggle with James Bond–esque smoothness, try going in a group.

- Meeting at the local coffee shop for informal conversation may be just the thing. You can bring your books to study before or after, or maybe even with the person if you both share classes.

Things to Avoid

- Movies in the theater. This is the ultimate date-killer usually, unless you already know the person quite well. Sitting in a dark room and not speaking with a person you hardly know is not the best way to find friendship.

- Anything too fancy. If this person is your girlfriend or boyfriend of 10 years, by all means, go to a five-star restaurant or the symphony if that is your style. If this person is the model you just met in English class, forget it. Grabbing a bite informally or making something yourself will certainly suffice. Likewise, a college-sponsored concert on the green will be a lot less pressured than a formal affair of any kind. Even if you really like this person, making a big move too suddenly will surely scare him or her off.

> "Going on dates does not always have to be expensive, or cost anything at all. Just relaxing on the Quad or going to a coffee shop to talk can work great."
>
> —Graduate, Computer Science Major

Student Date Ideas

- Museums, aquariums, the zoo— usually free or relatively cheap
- Barbecues, board games, or renting a video—fun, cheap, and plenty of chance to interact
- Picnics or a day at the beach— cheap, relaxing, and time to get to know each other

"Being totally self-sacrificing in relationships can be a problem in college. You have to look out for yourself first; if you try to help someone and put yourself in jeopardy at the same time, all that's happened is two people are now in trouble."

—Graduate, Biology Major

- Anything too dark. First dates should be fun, entertaining, and have plenty to laugh about. The Holocaust Museum as a first date may not be the best idea. Comforting her (or him!) as you leave a heavy movie like *Schindler's List* probably isn't the best way to win over a date.

Beware of the Pitfalls

Just because dating is fun does not mean it is without its pitfalls as well. Relationships can inflict major damage if let loose to run their (sometimes) bad course.

Break-up Rules

Ending a relationship is never a fun ordeal. There is usually a feeling of loss between the two parties, and the longer the couple has been together, the harder it is. These feelings are completely normal, there is really no way around them, but there are ways to deal with them.

If a relationship comes to a halt, try these break-up rules.

1. **Express, do not regress.** Many times, students become too caught up in a relationship, potentially inflicting major damage on their GPA and everything else. When a relationship goes sour, it is the natural tendency to constantly replay reasons and issues in your mind of why this or that happened. Sure, it is a good idea to figure out what went wrong so that you do not make that mistake again. However, do not dwell on it. Dwelling breeds more unhealthy feelings and insecurities and complicates the already-less-than-ideal situation. Express your feelings, but do not regress back from whence you came.

2. **Let bygones be bye-gones.** Many relationships end, especially when you are young. And when they end, it is normal to feel generally upset and even a little depressed. (If you feel extremely upset, do not hesitate scheduling an appointment with the counseling services at your school.) It is a simple but tough solution to let the past go. This parallels many pieces of advice in this book, especially one: One way to lower the bad stress in college is to realize when a situation is out of your control. Though it can be a tough thing to accept, it is the healthiest thing to do. Learn to let past things move on and out of your life.

3. **Occupy your time.** When relationship pitfalls come—and they will for many people—occupy your time with other things. Whichever activity you choose, make it a consuming activity. For example, watching television is a poor

choice. Watching TV lets our minds wander and begin to think about things that are bothering us. If your relationship just ended, your mind will definitely wander there. Try an activity where your mind is alive and thinking and processing other intriguing stories, facts, or skills. Here are some ideas:

- Reading. Probably one of the best all-around activities, reading lets the mind be creative and sharpens the intellect at the same time. Best of all, there are books on any and every subject imaginable. Whether you head to the library, bookstore, or read on the Net, this is probably one of the best occupiers.

- Social activities. So you have had a rough day? Head over to a friend's house and relax for the evening. Talk about anything and everything—except your old flame. A little bit of laughter and companionship might be just the thing for a sulking relationship casualty.

- Exercise. Maybe you run or walk, or lift weights, or play a sport. Any of these activities keeps your mind focused. Play some football—try running a belly option while thinking about your ex! Not easy. Trying to score in a field hockey game is an impossible time to consider where that ex-boyfriend is at the moment.

Rationalizing

Rationalizing is trying to use your mind to put a nicer spin on something. To a point, rationalizing can be healthy, but it can quickly spin out of control into much more than it needs to be. It is okay to take time to reason out the problems that were present in the relationship. This is a good thing, because you can apply what you learned to future relationships. But rationalizing does not mean a one-month hiatus of meditation, or spending a whole weekend staring at the ceiling, agonizing and regretting every detail of the relationship.

If you are in a similar situation,

- review the problems.
- store solutions for similar future issues.
- move on.

STRESS, DEPRESSION, AND PERFECTION

There is no doubt that college is a tumultuous time in people's lives. Sure, there are plenty of positive things to look forward to, and these will keep you busy and your head full. On the downside, the negative issues that college presents—like doubt, insecurity, and fallibility—are limitless. And often, the positive and negative are coming at you all at once.

- You get a great grade on a paper—the same day your boyfriend is seen making out with another girl, for example. (This happens, but perhaps that is an extreme example.)

- Your roommate borrowed your last clean shirt and you have a date in an hour—and the only open washing machine in your dorm is sporting an "Out of Order" sign. Then you remember that your paper is due tomorrow!

More Ways to Help

When these highs and lows fall together, you do not want to be squashed in the middle like a bug. In an earlier chapter, we briefly outlined some safeguards that you can put in place to soften the blow when these issues surface (and they will!). Here are some more ideas to help you deal with the inevitable "slings and arrows" of college life.

- Staying healthy will build the baseline for a productive day, week, month, and semester. This includes exercise and eating a healthy array of foods to keep you energized throughout the day.

- Plugging away at academics will build confidence and, to a degree, direction into your life. Staying ahead in school is the best way to keep stress low and performance high.

- Staying social will keep stress low and enjoyment high. People crave interaction, and feeding this hunger is not only fun but a necessary part of a healthy college life.

It is necessary to keep up a vigilant effort toward these ideals. A slipup is nothing to lie awake about, but a diligent and determined effort over time is the goal. College is a marathon, not a sprint. Above all, remember that you will have bad days and good, and by the end of the four years, the good will outweigh the bad.

Get Rid of Stress!

THE ADVISOR SAYS: *I wish I could say that students are any different from humans in general, but not so. Sometimes we get absorbed with minutia, which is an unhealthy way of living. Do your best to avoid being absorbed in the small, inconsequential happenings at college—and in life.*

Stress is the most common issue that students face on campus. So eliminating bad stress is the name of the game in college.

Good and Bad Stress

Deadlines—Due Dates—Tests. When most people hear any of these terms, a bell sounds that signals anxiety and discomfort. These are just two by-products of stress, and they are not surprising. Stress is a force exerted on us by pressure—pressure created by our circumstances and (most of the time) ourselves. Sometimes though, this anxiousness and discomfort motivates us to move in an attempt to eliminate the stress.

It might not sound like it, but this is the benefit of stress. Because stress is a pressure, it pushes us to move. If stress pushes us in the right direction, this is for the better. So eliminating all our stress would create a less-than-productive environment. With absolutely no deadlines, expectations, or work required of us, we would fulfill the expectations placed on us—doing nothing! This certainly would not lead to the level of success we expect in college.

But then, there is bad stress, too. It is important to understand the difference. Stress that pushes us to excel and meet (or hopefully exceed) expectations is good stress. Bad stress is anything that pushes us to worry excessively—sometimes too much over large things, but many times over small events that are blown out of proportion. So the difference between good and bad stress can be the amount, as much as the reason.

Some Things to Quit Stressing Over

You can still care about these things, just do not have an aneurysm over any of them:

- Past happenings. These include, but are not limited to, yesterday's test grade; how horrible last semester was; the impression you made at last weekend's party; the job interview you attended yesterday. Focusing too much on things like this only takes away from finding solutions for present problems and issues.

- Happenings over which you possess no control. Your best friend's outfit for the sorority party; what others think of you; the letter you just got from your sister back home, giving all the details of your little brother's latest speeding ticket (or worse). This is the past and nothing can change it.

- Insignificant ordeals. Whether the dinner for your date is perfect or not; you do not have the coolest shoes (or jacket, or car) of anyone on campus—in four years (or maybe tomorrow!) no one will care about any of these things, so you should not either.

> "The stress in college will test your mettle. Most students at one time or another will think, 'This just isn't for me,' but sticking to your goals is the only way to beat it."
> —Senior, Chemical Engineering Major

> "You won't remember that biology test you were stressing over, but you will remember the friends you made."
> —Graduate, Philosophy Major

Signs of Stress[7]

Physical
- Trouble sleeping
- Rapid or irregular heartbeat
- Tension or migraine headaches
- Stiffness or tightness in back, shoulders, or neck
- Rapid breathing or shortness of breath
- Sweaty hands
- Upset stomach, cramps, heartburn, nausea, or diarrhea
- Fatigue

Behavioral
- Irritability
- Anxiety
- Drastic mood swings
- Difficulty concentrating
- Memory problems
- Conflicts with coworkers or friends
- Doubts about your ability to accomplish tasks
- Social isolation

"Work hard, play hard. Doing really well on finals, then throwing a huge party was my favorite pastime in college. Work hard to accomplish those goals, but celebrate when you do it."

—Graduate, Political Science Major

"Outside activities help me deal with stress. When it gets very bad, I will go surfing, or turn to my faith. You have to find something that gives you peace."

—Senior, Microbiology Major

Dealing with Stress

THE ADVISOR SAYS: *Living a healthy lifestyle is paramount. Students have this and that to do, all the while forgetting to take care of themselves. Many students take yoga, swimming, and the like to relieve the stress of college.*

Proper rest (approximately eight hours per night), frequent exercise, and relaxing time with friends can help you manage your stress at school and keep it under control. In addition to these, it is beneficial to let loose and reward yourself when you have survived a stressful period—like final exams! If any of these issues begins to seriously interfere with your life, be sure to see a doctor or counselor. There is no shame in getting help when you need it.

The Trouble with Perfection

No matter how hard we try, being perfect is impossible. With ever more focus on success in our lives, it can be easy to let things get out of hand, and it is happening in the college world. Duke University in Durham, North Carolina, is dealing with this very issue now.

The term "effortless perfection" may not mean much to you, but it does to a large number of students at Duke. The term has emerged as a hot topic to describe what some students feel is the attitude of the female student body to perfectly balance academics, exercise, social life, and many other activities without apparent effort.[28] The feeling is that many students (mostly female) at Duke feel an overwhelming pressure to pursue many different interests, perform exceptionally well in all of them, and come off as hardly trying. Some females at Duke see the beautiful, well-kept, thin, well-dressed, smart leading girl to be doing all these things with no effort—and believe they must do the same.

The issue with effortless perfection is not the push to do well and balance important activities, but the concern for other people's approval. Working your hardest and putting forth your best effort is always a commendable way to live. At the same time, you cannot let others' opinions affect your life to the point of driving you mad.

To keep yourself (guys and girls) from feeling pressures of this kind, commit to your own personal success. Earlier in the book, we defined personal success, and that is what we are discussing through this entire book. Do YOUR best, and forget about other people's opinions of your accomplishments. If they congratulate you, appreciate it, but do not run your life by the opinions of others. If you look to others for happiness, you will never find it. True happiness comes from within. Keep up your effort, but instead of effortless perfection, focus on effort-filled perfection!

Depression

In addition to stress, many students suffer bouts with depression. When you first arrive on campus, you might wonder how anyone could be depressed; or you may feel that the start of college is extremely difficult and tough to handle. Some students find the years as an upperclassman particularly uncertain and difficult. Whether you find your new surroundings great fun or full of hardship, somewhere along the line you will feel overwhelmed in college—every student hits ruts occasionally and may feel depressed.

Depression Is Not a Flaw

Perhaps you (or the people around you) still think of depression as a character flaw, that people who suffer depression are weak or lacking in self-discipline. It is true that in extremely mild cases some focus and discipline can overcome the problem. But for many, depression needs more help than that to get better. Depression is a biological condition having to do with the complex chemistry of the brain—not something you can stop just by working harder or thinking positively.

Whether it is you who feel depressed or someone you care about, be careful not to place the blame solely on the person's character. Instead, be supportive and understanding. Friends and family should be there to support one another, not to cast judgment. Suggesting to a roommate, friend, or family member that they try counseling is not out of the question, if you do so in the proper way. Take the self-test at the end of Chapter 6 to see whether you may need counseling. If you see any signs of depression, the mature choice is to seek help.

THE ADVISOR SAYS: *It takes a lot sometimes to accept all of the responsibility. That goes along with being an adult, and many students are not prepared at the start. Many schools have 10 free counseling sessions for students who need it.*

How to Deal with Depression, and How Not To

The stress level on campus is higher today than it has ever been, and many students feel the effects by experiencing depression.

It only follows: When we hurt, we want to stop hurting. That applies to a sprained ankle, and to emotional pain, too. But unlike a sprained ankle, there is still shame attached to emotional pain. A student who is too embarrassed to ask for help might try to fix the situation the misperceived easy way—with alcohol and/or drug use.

The Signs of Depression

The fact is that many students do not even realize they are experiencing depression. To keep abreast of your health and mental outlook, watch for the signs:[8]

- A loss of interest in activities or hobbies you once enjoyed
- Trouble sleeping—insomnia or oversleeping
- Problems concentrating, remembering, and/or making decisions
- Changes in appetite resulting in weight loss or weight gain
- Fatigue and a general feeling of being slowed down
- Recurring feelings of guilt, hopelessness, and pessimism
- Thoughts of death or suicide

Other less common symptoms include:

- Complaints (such as headache and stomachache) with no physical cause
- Weight gain instead of weight loss
- Sleeping too much

"What Are the Symptoms of Depression?" In *Health Guide A–Z* from www.WebMD.com.

To a depressed person, this might seem to be the simplest and quickest solution, but it is not. Not only does this prevent fixing the problem, it can create larger and more serious problems—like even worse depression, failure at school, alcohol poisoning or a drug overdose, legal woes, violent or self-destructive behavior, and even suicide. All for a disorder than can be easily treated!

So, rather than self-medicate depression and risk making things worse, see a professional. Your college either will have a counseling center on campus or can refer you to one close by. If you or the person you are trying to help does not feel comfortable seeing someone in person, get advice from some national hotlines. Almost every college bulletin board has one or more hotline numbers you can call. Your student handbook will likely have at least one number, too. There is a listing of some of them here in the accompanying sidebar. Your identity is kept secret when you call, and you will find out how to get the help you or the person you care about needs.

So, if you or someone you know is battling with depression, do not stress about it—take action!

Family Can Help

If you are feeling depressed, and need help, remember your family. They are there for support. Even if you hail from a less-than-supportive household, you may be surprised how much they truly care. Always keep in contact with your family because you never know when their support will be needed.

PHYSICAL CHALLENGES

Beyond just the mental challenges of college are the physical challenges (which have mental consequences). Getting sick or hurt on campus can be a tough time, especially if it is your first time away from home. At school, there is no one to take care of you, bring you an ice pack for your injured leg, or fix you soup and orange juice. (Well, maybe there is if you have made some wonderful friends.) However, if you know how to prevent illnesses and injuries or deal with them if they happen to you, you can prevent the negative stress they bring.

Staying Healthy

- Proper rest
- Exercise
- Well-rounded diet

Depression and Suicide Hotlines

- National Foundation for Depressive Illness— 800-248-4344
- United Way Helpline— 800-233-HELP
- National Hopeline Network— 800-784-2433
- Help Line USA— 866-334-4357

"Keep healthy, because if you get sick, and you are not a beautiful girl, nobody cares and the paper is still due."

—Graduate, Graphic Design Major

Treating Problems

- Common cold—get plenty of rest. If it lasts longer than two weeks, see your campus clinic—could be allergies.

- The flu—get your flu shot every season; use over-the-counter treatments such as TheraFlu®; get plenty of rest.

- Muscular aches/pains—use a general pain reliever. If pain persists, see your campus clinic.

During orientation, you probably received some good advice about what to do if you get hurt or sick on campus. And because you have probably experienced the most common bumps, bruises, and cuts before now, that advice will probably come back to you pretty easily when the time comes. (And no, you won't be considered weak if you call or e-mail home for a little reassurance, too!) But there are some things that can happen at college that never happened to you before, maybe even things you never dreamed could happen to you or someone you care about. And if they happen, you might panic and forget what you learned. Because these all relate to relationships, I would like to spend a little time here discussing them.

Sex

You know that it is a real part of college life, displayed or shown in one form or another all over campuses today. There are many viewpoints on sex and how to approach it, but you are in college, and I thought you should make the decision while I present you with some facts. The first and most important issue to understand regarding sex is that you are accountable! Sex can come with a lot of baggage, from emotional attachments to pregnancy or sexually transmitted diseases (STDs), so it is important to know what you are getting into—because deciding on sex is up to you!

STDs are a real issue of concern. These diseases not only have a physical impact but, many times, an even rougher psychological impact.

STDs

There are a number of STDs, including:
- Chlamydia
- Genital herpes
- Genital warts
- HIV/AIDS
- Syphilis
- Gonorrhea

These diseases can range from uncomfortable to inconvenient to fatal. Sadly, they exist on college campuses today in fairly scary numbers.

One of the worst things about STDs is that people can be infected and not even realize it. And yes, even good people can get an STD. So even honest and straightforward people might not know they are carrying a disease. People, by not realizing they are carriers, can easily spread it to others. This is why it is your responsibility to be safe when it comes to sexual encounters.

In addition to students who honestly do not realize they have an STD, some students will conceal their problem and continue their sexual lifestyle without mentioning it to their partners. Whether it is from embarrassment or disgrace, these individuals end up spreading the infection.

To prevent the spread of STDs, follow these guidelines:

- Steer clear of any form of sexual activity. That is the safest and only sure defense against these troubles. But if you do choose to engage in sexual activities, a condom is a must.

- As far as relationships go, it is important to stay monogamous. Think how you would feel if your partner cheated on you, contracted a disease, and gave it to you. Angry and betrayed are just a couple of emotions that come to mind. You would not want anyone to do that to you, so do not do that to others. If you are going to engage in a physical relationship, stay faithful to that person!

- If you suspect any symptoms of a problem, see a physician immediately.

Substance Abuse and Sex

Avoiding substance abuse is another important strategy. Although it might not seem related to preventing STDs, it is.

Stories like this next one have happened in college. Do not let this be you.

Vanessa: Hey, Ashley, where did you stay last night? We were waiting for you to come home, and when we called your cell, you sounded really drunk!

Ashley: I . . . I do not want to talk about it. . . . Ugh, I feel horrible.

Vanessa: Come on, what happened?

Ashley: Okay, well . . . you know that guy at the party I thought was really cute?

Vanessa: The guy you were talking to when Jenna and I left?

Ashley: Yeah. We basically hung out through the whole party.

Vanessa:	What was his name?
Ashley:	(long pause) Honestly, I cannot really remember. It was John, or Jake, or maybe Joe. I'm not sure which one.
Vanessa:	You hung out with him the whole party and don't remember his name?
Ashley:	I had a lot to drink and . . . well, it's kind of fuzzy.
Vanessa:	You didn't stay with him, did you?
Ashley:	(longer pause) Yeah. And I'm pretty sure we had sex, too. Vanessa, I feel so bad today, I just want to cry.

Most college students will not go through something like this, but a good number will, or know someone who will. If there is enough out-of-control drinking, it can easily happen. In addition to just having sex, binge drinking increases the chance that an individual will also have unprotected sex. Beyond Ashley just feeling bad physically from drinking all night and emotionally because of what happened, she now must be tested for STDs at the clinic. Not only can this be humiliating, but it is also a whopping bagful of stress, not needed.

Once again, we come to the issue of lowering the bad stress at college. One-night stands are just one experience that load on more bad stress. In turn, bad stress can lower the quality of your college life.

Success in college begins with lowering the bad stress, so learn from Ashley's experience that overdoing alcohol can result in less-than-ideal consequences.

Pregnancy

Probably the biggest nightmare of any college student (girl or guy) is a situation involving pregnancy. Do not misunderstand me— babies are a great thing, but a surprise in this department can be unpleasant. Unprotected sex can easily lead to pregnancy, no matter what techniques you have put into practice. The only sure route is staying away from sex altogether.

Knowing college students, though, this might be a bit of a stretch. If you do choose to have sex, be sure to use a condom— always. It is a good idea for both girls and guys to carry condoms. This way, no one is caught unprepared. And being on birth control does not mean condoms are no longer useful. They are another layer of protection as well as helping in the prevention of STDs.

If by chance the unforeseen does happen, go to the campus health clinic right away. They may recommend counseling or other services to help you through the pregnancy. This also goes for the guy, because a pregnancy is the responsibility of all involved.

The bottom line is that sex does have consequences, and pregnancy is a real possibility. If you are uncomfortable with this risk, you should definitely think twice before having sex.

Recap of Sex at College

To recap, if you plan to have sex at college,

- use a condom.
- stay monogamous.
- keep alcohol intake under control.

Most of all, avoid the bad stress that sex can create through avenues like guilt, depression, and confusion. Sex is a powerful act, and it raises powerful emotions. These can have a significant impact on your college life. A heavy relationship that includes sex, even casual sex, can reduce your confidence and self-esteem. And to be successful, you will need plenty of both.

Partying for the Successful Student

"Enjoy present pleasures in such a way as to not injure future ones."

—Seneca

THE FUN FACTOR: MANAGING YOUR FESTIVITIES

College may be a challenge, but it is also supposed to be fun. Partying is not bad in and of itself, but it does need to be managed. Your whole life at college comes down to balance, and the partying scene is no different. After all, there is a fine line between having fun and having enough fun that you are mistaken for a long-lost member of Motley Crue. If you have found your balance of work and fun (which is the goal), congratulations! If you are still working on it, or have not arrived at college yet, you can start by making a plan. The plan for keeping college life running smoothly while having fun consists of

- setting priorities.
- staying confident.
- making your own rules.
- finding alternatives to partying.

Setting Priorities

If you do not know where you are going, it is tough to make a plan for getting there. Setting your priorities is like laying out a road trip. If you are starting in California and want to end in Florida, but would like to see Montana, you would take a different route than if you would like to see Texas along the way. Similarly, your personal goals in college will determine your route and what you decide takes precedence over another area. Social activities, including partying, will fall into this mix somewhere, and only you can determine where.

Take a minute to write down your priorities, starting with the most important and ending with the least important. You might include items such as family, friends, relaxation time, grade point average, exercise and health, fraternity/sorority, social life, career choice, graduate school—whatever factors into your life during college (see Worksheet 10-1).

Staying Confident

Now that you have your priorities (if you did not write them down, go back and do it!), it is important to stay confident about them. One issue common in some colleges is people who want to party all the time trying to get you to do the same. This is exactly why you wrote down your set of priorities, to keep you on track for being the person you are working to be. Other people's priorities are their own, and just as you would not push your life on others, you would expect the same, right? Too bad that it is usually not this simple. People will ask you, no matter what your list looks like, to go against what you hold important. You just have to learn how to say "No."

Confidence to Say "No"

Saying "No" to partying plagues a good number of students, so that is what we will deal with. If you can succeed in saying "No" when you need to, not only will you gain self-respect, but others will

WORKSHEET 10-1

Priorities Worksheet

List your priorities from most important to least important. This list will give you the means to make a schedule and plan what activities get the most time, energy, and commitment.

1.

2.

3.

4.

5.

6.

7.

8.

9.

10.

> "It takes willpower, motivation, and self-discipline to keep the partying under control in college."
> —Junior, European Science and Policy Major

respect you, too. And if people respect you, they will not be offended if you refuse to go on a five-day bender. In fact, in the end they will respect you more! Be proud that you were smart enough to get into college, are determined to succeed, and are working toward a respectable end. This makes it much easier to say "No."

Saying "No" to Smitty

At some point in college, you will most definitely meet the person I call Smitty. Smitty is loud, he is funny, and he is the biggest party animal this side of the Mississippi.

Smitty is the person who pops into your dorm to get you out on Monday night, and Tuesday night, and . . . well, you get the picture.

Smitty is the guy who barely gets by in any class and does not seem to care. Even worse, he does not understand why you do not feel the same way.

Needless to say, every campus has a Smitty, and everyone likes him, which makes it that much harder to say "No." Consider the following typical Smitty scenario.

Setting: It's Wednesday night. Smitty approaches Jack (who is studying for his Business Management test) and lays into him.

Smitty:	"So, you going out with us tonight? We're all going to Building 14 for that huge kegger. Tommy says you can't hang, but I was hoping you'd prove him wrong by comin' out. So whaddya say?!"
Jack (smiling):	"That's what I like about you, Smitty. You believe in me. Now believe that I'm gonna ace this Management test. And while you're out, have a drink for me!"
Smitty:	"You're not coming out!? Come on, man, just for a little while . . ."
Jack:	"I'm goin' out on Friday with some people. We'll all hang out then. (Another smile.) You guys have fun tonight, and I'll be here in case you and Tommy need a ride."

(Smitty says that they have a ride but thanks Jack anyway and says they will definitely see each other on Friday.)

If you act like it is no big deal and you have things to do, no one will be too hard on you. Even if they are, forget it! Jack was strong in his stance and lighthearted at the same time. This is exactly what you want: to get your point across, but not to come across as a stuck-up jerk.

Be confident, stand up, and say "No" if you do not want to go. It may save you and your GPA!

Making Your Own Rules!

We all know that most college students do not have issues with partying too often, but a large number do. Studies show that nearly 23 percent of college students have performed poorly on a test/ other project, and one third have missed class due to one type or another of substance abuse![11] Just by the numbers, it is fair to say that setting some ground rules for yourself would not be a bad idea. If you never need them, you will not have wasted too much time.

Find what works for you, but here is one student's example of a rule she made for herself to keep ahead in classes while always having a fun time. She called it "The Week versus The Weekend."

The Week

Leave the week for school.

This does not mean that you cannot hang out for a while and go over to friends' places during the week, but the late nights should be left for the weekend. Relaxing a little can actually be a great way to wind down, but leave the time-hogs like playing video games and watching TV for after you have gotten your needs like going to class, studying, and exercising taken care of.

Leaving the week for school is a relatively small sacrifice. If you go to classes throughout the day, go to the gym in the late afternoon and study in between, then you will be done by about five or six o'clock. Voilà! Now you have your night free to hang out, watch some TV, or do whatever.

It is easier to talk about it than to do it. It is easy to get caught up in the Thursday night "sink or swim" (college lingo meaning "Get drunk or drunker"). But remember: The week is your school and study time.

We talked about momentum earlier. Trust me, starting to go out on weeknights is definitely getting the ball rolling in the wrong direction! At first you will say, "Oh, it's already Thursday, what could it hurt?" Maybe it doesn't, that one time. But maybe, because that Thursday worked out, then next Wednesday starts to be okay. Before you know it, any day of the week is game—or even all of them.

The Weekend

Now this is the time to enjoy yourself and relax. To get the most out of college, you have to be aware of how much time you spend relaxing. But this does not mean that you should not have some enjoyment! Going to a party for a few hours on a Friday or

Saturday is not going to ruin your chances of getting good grades or put a severe dent in your plan to get (or stay) in great shape. In fact, it will actually do you some good!

On the other hand, going to a party does not mean doing five-minute keg stands either.

Give yourself some flexibility—most college activities are scheduled for the weekends, but occasionally, they are not. Sometimes, there is a social event during the week you might attend. Just use the weekend as your main source of downtime, and from there you can adjust according to your individual needs and preferences.

The bottom line is that weekdays are school time and weekends are playtime.

This is one student's example of setting rules for her college life. If this does not appeal to you, don't do it! I want to help you spark ideas, not command your life! Find what helps you stay productive, and make your own rule based on that. Your rules will become part of your plan for success in college!

Finding Alternatives to Partying

It is fun to go out, but it can get so common that students begin asking, "What else is there to do in this town?" It does not matter which town or city you attend college in, there are always other things to do. Find alternatives to partying.

- Take up a sport and vow to become an expert at it. Golf sure takes a while to master. If you want to learn golf, enlist a friend to practice with you! If that is not your thing, join the lacrosse club or soccer club.

- What about learning to play an instrument? You can buy a guitar at a pawnshop for what it would cost one night at a bar!

- Learn to draw, paint, or write. With the Internet as a resource these days, you do not even have to go to the library to find free instruction and information on anything that you want to learn.

There are endless ideas that you can do solo or with others. The same goes for writing, drawing, or anything else. If you choose to find a partner to help you learn, you can compare your work and help each other become better—and you will not have any regrets or hangovers the next morning!

If you open your eyes to see them, there are endless opportunities. Everything I have listed here is possible in almost any place! And that is just the tip of the iceberg. I'm sure there are things that you have thought about doing but never tried. Give it a shot, put some time into it. Find some alternatives!

> "A couple of nights a week, some friends and I get together for air hockey tournaments. It's a little stupid but a lot of fun."
> —Sophomore, Physical Education Major

> "Some nights, I did some reading on my own or caught up with friends at other colleges on the phone or Instant Messaging. Whatever I needed to do for relaxation."
> —Junior, Biology Major

SUBSTANCE ABUSE

Substance abuse is common on almost every college campus. Steering clear of it may save your college career. Here is some information on different types of substances being abused:

- Alcohol
- Marijuana
- Cocaine
- Ecstasy
- Prescription drugs
- Heroin

Alcohol

It is just a fact that binge drinking, using drugs, or any other destructive behavior is not helpful in college (or any other time). Unfortunately, too many students believe that these activities are rites of passage or traditional and therefore have to be experienced. Many students, after the fact, can tell you that excessively engaging in these behaviors has done them no favors.

I know myself that drinking in college did me no favors. I made mistakes, and it took time for me to learn and recover from them. There is a saying, "Smart people learn from their own mistakes, and really smart people learn from others' mistakes." Be a really smart person and investigate other successful people who have come before you. You may just realize that the ol' college tradition may not be all it's cracked up to be. As one student put it: If you are expecting college to be like Hollywood—too crazy and too much fun—you may end up disappointed. College is a lot of fun, but not quite in the spirit of *National Lampoon's Van Wilder*.

> "Party in moderation. It is definitely good just to release some of the angst at college, but if you overdo it, you will create more."
>
> —Senior, Accounting Major

Binge Drinking

Binge drinking is defined as "the consumption of five or more drinks in a row for men and four or more for women at least once in the past two weeks."[12]

The Reality

Drinking is around in college, and you will be confronted with it. You might even choose to drink at some point; many successful college students do. As I said before, "No" is a learned tactic, and it works in many cases—but not all the time. There are going to be times when you will go out and maybe even drink. But if you do, watching how much is really important. Here is why: Binge drinking can have all kinds of negative effects—from big problems with the law, relationships, and sexual situations, to smaller ones like interfering with classes or a workout schedule. So it is important to be the boss of your drinking habits; and above all, do not drink and drive!

If you feel drinking might be a problem for you, stay away! It is not worth sacrificing your health and long-term goals to be "accepted." You will not be alone or uncool if you decide not to drink. No matter what you have heard or what you have been told by the Smitty types, many college kids do not drink regularly. If you choose your social activities and not let them choose you, you will be okay.

Drugs

Drugs comprise most other substances harmful to college life. Although people break drugs into different categories, I believe they all can be harmful, each in their own way. In addition to being physically and mentally harmful, getting caught with drugs can even jeopardize your loans for school. Federal student loan programs may not help pay your way if you have a drug conviction. Do yourself a favor and learn what these drugs do, and stay away from them!

Marijuana

Maybe marijuana will be legalized in the future, but for now, it is illegal—that in itself is the first problem. More of an issue than the laws about weed is the problems it causes users. Pot has been known to drain motivation from people who use it, which is a sure way to fall behind in your plans. When you set goals, it takes a high degree of purpose and motivation to follow through, something that we all possess but something that takes a lot of our energy and enthusiasm to awaken. Draining your motivation is like drilling a hole in the gas tank of your car—your motivation will run out pretty quickly! To keep functioning at your highest level, put something else in its place. Remember finding alternatives? Find an activity that you love to do, and put some time into it.

Cocaine

Though an overwhelming majority of students would never try this drug, it is around on college campuses. Cocaine is unhealthy and downright dangerous. People have died from heart problems brought on by this drug, among other ailments. The solution is simple: Stay away from the crowd involved with cocaine.

Ecstasy

This drug's popularity has grown over the past few years, and so has the list of potential complications associated with it. Beyond being potentially fatal, the drug and circumstances surrounding its regular use may induce (among others)[13]

- depression and anxiety.
- increased blood pressure.
- dehydration.
- brain damage.

For your health's sake, stay far away from this drug, as it is very harmful—no matter what you have heard.

Prescription Drugs

Oxycotin and other pain medications and Xanax, Valium, and other tranquilizers are the most commonly abused. These drugs are health hazards when taken without a prescription, but the most disturbing fact is that many people using these pills drink alcohol with them. This combination can be deadly and has killed or put many people in a coma. Only take these medications with the direction and a prescription from your doctor.

Heroin

Heroin is another very serious drug. Heroin first became popular in the 1950s, 1960s, and 1970s, and there has been a recent resurgence in its use. It is highly addictive and dangerous. I think that staying away from this drug or anyone using it should be obvious.

Life is difficult without vices such as drinking or drugs. Make life easier on yourself and avoid getting into them.

> **Getting Help**
> If you or anyone you know has a substance abuse issue, try this hotline:
> - Center for Substance Abuse Treatment 800-662-HELP

PRUDENT PARTYING

Sure, guys have problems with partying, too. But girls have some unique problems, including quite a bit of attention from guys. Invitations to parties are very common. It is not necessarily a bad idea to go to some of these parties, just make sure the organization is legitimate or that the party is in a public location. Every year, there are stories of girls being drugged at an event and unfavorable outcomes ensuing. So if you decide to attend a gathering, be very careful.

> "Have a good friend you can trust, who knows if you are over the limit, to watch out for you."
> —Junior, English Major

Always Be Careful

- Bring a friend (at least one, preferably more) and watch out for each other.
- Get drinks yourself. Do not accept one from a stranger.
- Check your drink before gulping it down. Even better, do not leave it out of eyesight until you finish it—if you need to, find a trustworthy friend to hold it.
- Stay in the main area of the party around everyone else.

By following these guidelines, the chances of anything happening are extremely small—exactly how you want them.

Date Rape

When many students think of rape, they imagine a masked character grabbing an unsuspecting victim in a dark alley. Though this can happen, most sexual assaults are committed by someone the victim knows—this is date rape. Date rape occurs everywhere, and college is no exception. I am not saying this to scare you but so that you will be prepared to handle situations to stay safe. To steer clear of a bad situation, follow these guidelines:

- Before you get to know a person well, spend time together in public places or with other people.
- Avoid alcohol and drug abuse. Many bad situations begin with some type of substance abuse.
- Learn to say a forthright "No." Let the other person know you are not kidding around when you say it.
- Tell a friend where and with whom you are going out with.
- Take your cell phone with you, if you have one. Designate a time to call your friend, so that you both know that each other is okay.

If you do get into a situation where you feel you have been raped, contact the campus police or a responsible adult for help. In addition, there are crisis hotlines in most areas. Look under Crisis Hotlines or Social Services in your phone book.

Beyond partying and staying safe at college, something else is vitally important.

BE WHO YOU WANT TO BE!

There is one great thing about coming to college: You have a clean slate. No matter who or what you were in high school, if you want, you can reinvent yourself. If you were a big party girl and want to get out of that scene a little, college is the perfect place. Maybe you never got out in high school and want to create more of a social life. You can do that in college, too. In college, you do not have your old reputation to live up to, or drag you down.

At the same time, it is easy when you first get there to fall into the guaranteed way to be accepted—going boozin' with your new friends. If you want to meet people to party with all the time, it will not be hard in college.

But if you do not want that, there are many other things to do at college, things that do not compromise the goals you have set for yourself. And yes, you can still have a great time.

It is harder to pick friends in college. It is more than just finding places to meet them. Just like anywhere else, there are people that will help you, and there are people that will hurt you, whether they mean to or not. It is not always easy to know this at first. Hanging out with people who have your same values, people who want to accomplish goals similar to your own, is a great way to start your college life. Pick the places you spend your time instead of being dragged to places you do not want to go. And pick friends who will help you to your goals, not drag you down. Use college to catapult toward success, and make friends with people who want to do the same.

CHAPTER 11

College Fitness

"Use it or lose it."

—Jimmy Connors

FITNESS HAS POWER

No two people are alike, and different remedies work for different people. So something that worked for me may not work the same for you. But I think you should know my story.

My Story

Working out did not just improve my college experience, it made it! I was very uneasy starting college, because for the first time, everything was up to me. There were no classes that I had to take (okay, English 101, but you know what I mean), none that I had to attend, and none that I absolutely fell in love with. This left me with one big fuzzy, messy idea of where I wanted to be and what I wanted to do.

My first couple of semesters did not work out so well. I was performing poorly in my classes and enjoying myself a tad bit too much. There was nothing grounding me, holding me to any standard or responsibility.

Call it pure luck, but exercise helped solve the problem. It gave me a positive and defined channel for my energy and enthusiasm, and it taught me discipline. I did not begin to perform better in school immediately, but it came soon after. I learned about the many great traits that I already possessed, gained a few more, and increased my health, energy, and confidence. Soon after being tethered by my workouts, I began to see things more clearly and define my interests better. It led me down a definite path. I am not trying to tell you that the exact same experience will happen to you, but it might.

As someone I know said, "I don't know about everyone else, but I can sure tell you what worked for me." Well, exercise did work for me, and I am not an exception. Every study, expert, and health-conscious student will tell you that exercise is positive.

Because campuses all have gyms and recreation centers (usually nice ones, too!), there is no excuse not to give it a try. You will find out some basics about working out and learn some of the tools to help you achieve your goals. Let's get to it!

Fitness is an important but often overlooked part of college success. Because many students coming from high school are not overweight and do not have health problems, it just seems like one more chore. What they do not realize is that exercise is an opportunity to change your life, not just your body.

The Benefits

- Promotes self-confidence
- Improves mood and focus
- Is an outlet for tension
- Increases energy
- Helps develop a great work ethic
- Lowers stress

I don't know about you, but that list looks great to me—well worth devoting a half hour or so every day to those results!

Staying in shape in college should not take a backseat to your other goals, but it often does. For one thing, many students are confused about what fitness means. Look at almost any magazine. There are about a million different diet tips and "30 Seconds to the

World's Greatest Physique" articles. And most contradict each other. In this chapter, I cut through the junk, give you some real advice, and share a real workout that works.

To get started, let's go through a little question-and-answer session on some common misconceptions about exercise.

Fitness Q & A

Q: I have never worked out before. Is college too late to start?

A: Anytime is a good time to start taking care of your body. You will feel better, look better, and have more energy to cope with what you have to deal with in college. You may even find it easier to start in college. For one thing, you might have quicker access to fitness equipment than you did at home. And no, you will not be the only one who is starting out. Because our society is a sedentary (inactive) one, most young people do not get enough exercise. So you will likely find others who, like you, are making a first-time commitment to fitness. Just start slow, track your progress (see workout charts in this chapter and in the Appendix), and get ready to be amazed and proud at the results!

Q: Do women and men have to train completely differently to get in shape?

A: No. Male or female, the principles are the same. Losing body fat and gaining muscle should be the center of any fitness plan. Small adjustments, like choosing the proper number of repetitions, might be necessary, but the underlying basics of training are the same.

Q: Women should not lift weights because they will get bulky and muscular. Right?

A: Wrong. Strength training should be a large part of any woman's fitness plan. Women will not get big and bulky, because they do not have the same amount of some hormones as men—the hormones that make a guy's voice deep, his jaw large, and face hairy. These hormones are also the biggest factor in building muscle. Because girls produce such a small amount of these, they do not have to worry about getting bulky.

Q: Isn't it impossible to gain strength and lose weight at the same time?

A: Absolutely not. These two almost go hand-in-hand. Building muscle increases the metabolism, which in turn, burns more fat. Because muscle takes more energy for upkeep than fat, building more muscle assists in burning more fat, even if you are just sitting on the couch!

*Q: **Cardio is off limits for someone trying to build a more muscular physique, correct?***

A: Cardiovascular exercise—exercise that strengthens the heart, like running, biking, and swimming—is good for everyone. To get lean and have your hard work in the gym show, cardio is a must! This type of training helps burn fat and improves endurance. Compared with the benefits of cardio, the hindering of muscular growth is minimal. Building muscle will happen if you train hard and eat right, period!

*Q: **Doesn't just doing sit-ups get you a six-pack?***

A: First of all, you do not get a six-pack. Just as everyone has a biceps or calf muscles, everyone has abdominal muscles. Cardio and resistance training both help in removing the fat. When you reduce the fat enough, you will see the six-pack. But there is no such thing as spot-reduction. When you burn fat, it comes off everywhere. Sit-ups will tone, define, and strengthen the abs, but if fat is covering them, they are not going to show!

*Q: **When should I start?***

A: The sooner you start, the better. Of course, exercise is rigorous, and it is important to check with your physician before beginning any kind of program.

> "Staying in shape is one of the best things anyone can do while in college. Schoolwork is demanding and you are sitting at a desk, computer, or chalkboard, getting a mental workout. If you neglect your body, your mental capabilities will lack endurance too. For me, running and lifting weights is a way to relieve stress and work my body."
>
> —Senior, Biomedical Science Major

THE SKINNY ON WORKING OUT AT COLLEGE

The quickest way to get in shape is to make your workout long enough to use all three parts of the typical workout system: weights, cardio, and stretching. Whether you are male or female, in shape or out of shape, designing a program that hits on all three parts is the key to your overall development.

The Basics

Weight Training

Actually called resistance training, weight training includes (surprise!) weights, Nautilus-type machines, and body-weight exercises—pull-ups, push-ups, sit-ups, and the like. The big-picture purpose is to stress your muscles enough to improve their coordination, strength, and appearance.

Cardio (Cardiovascular Training)

Most people think of running or biking when they hear "cardio." These are definitely options, but do not fool yourself into thinking that the treadmill or recumbent bike is the only way to get a workout! Tons of fun stuff can fall under the term "cardio," and many colleges have options like the following:

- Kickboxing
- Basketball
- Racquetball
- Rock climbing
- Group aerobics
- Rowing

Stretching

Stretching helps prevent injuries, and gives you a nice warm-up. Plus, it is an easy way to get over the number one exercise hurdle— getting started. Some people love stretching, and others hate it. Some people make stretching and flexibility an entire workout. Others just do a few minutes at the beginning and end. Even if putting your ankles behind your head may not be *exactly* what you had in mind, a few minutes of stretching before and after your workout will be a big plus.

Stretching at the start of your workout is best preceded by about five minutes of warm-up. You can jump on the stationary bike or treadmill to get the blood flowing and your body warmed up before stretching.

The Campus Workout

Sorry that I have to be the one to tell you this, but there is no 3-Day Hollywood Diet for getting into great shape. It takes work, focus, and consistency to improve your body. The workout in this section is a plan to get your body jump-started and start you off in the right direction. It is definitely necessary to gain the insight of your physician before beginning an exercise program, so hurry up and get to the Campus Health Center (see Worksheet 11-1).

As you will note, the weights are divided into two sections— upper body and lower body—and the cardio is done every workout. Stretching should be done at the beginning and end of each workout. That will give you a total of four weight-training sessions

WORKSHEET 11-1

Monday	Tuesday	Wednesday	Thursday	Friday	Saturday	Sunday
Upper body and Cardio	off	Lower body and Cardio	off	Upper body and Cardio	off	Lower body and Cardio

per week (two upper and two lower), and four cardio sessions. This is all you need at first, especially if you are new to exercising. In the following pages, you will find the exercise list, as well as charts to fill in for weights and cardio.

Exercises Using Weights

The first step is making sure that you hit the right exercises for the muscles you are trying to work out. Working all parts of the body is important. That is why your upper and lower body gets the same amount of time.

Guys beware: The Popsicle syndrome is easy to catch. Getting it will make you huge on the top and like a tiny stick on the bottom—not the best look to go for! And ladies? Working your legs is great, but do not forget about the other half of you! Balance is the goal.

For the upper body, do these exercises:

- Bench press. With feet flat on the floor, lay on the bench so that your upper back and neck are supported. Place hands shoulder-width apart on bar and lower to the midline of the chest. Press weight back until arms are almost locked, and repeat. Be sure to use a spotter, and lift the weight in a controlled fashion—no bouncing off of the chest.

- Lat (latissimus dorsi) pulldown. Sit on machine with feet flat on the floor and grab bar above with hands shoulder-width apart. Pull weight down to the top of your chest and lift back upwards. Repeat.

- Military press. Sitting upright on a bench with back support, raise weights from shoulder level to above the head and back down. Repeat. Be sure to keep your back straight, use a spotter, and wear a weight-lifting belt.

- Bicep curls. Stand holding weights, flex arms up from your sides and back down. Repeat.

- Triceps cable pressdowns. Stand against back support and grab rope or bar with a close grip. Extend arms from starting position of parallel with the floor to ending position where arms are extended close to the point of elbows locking. Repeat.

For the lower body, do these exercises:

- Lunges. With hands at sides, step forward. When rear knee comes close to the floor, push back up. Repeat with alternating legs. Be sure to push through your heel, not toe, this reduces stress on the knee joint.

- Leg extensions. Sit on machine and put shins under the padded bar. Extend legs. Repeat. Make sure to keep your butt firmly on the seat.

- Leg curls. Lie on machine and put legs under padded bar. Flex legs. Repeat. Make sure to keep your body flat on the bench; do not let your hips raise.

- Calf raises. Sit on machine, place toes on bar and get knees under padded bar. Push up on toes, flexing the calves.

For the abs, do these exercises:

- Crunches. Lie on floor and pull knees up. Place hands in front of your head (never behind, you may strain your neck) and curl toward knees. Repeat.

Always warm up before working out (five minutes on the treadmill), use a spotter when exercising with weights, and be sure to check with your physician before beginning an exercise regimen.

Filling In the Charts

- First, write in the exercises for each part of the body (either upper or lower). (See Worksheet 11-2 and Worksheet 11-3.)

- Second, put in the number of sets and repetitions. Two sets of each exercise should be what you start with, and the number of repetitions can be found by looking at the Rep Chart. Remember, you will want 6 to 8 reps in each set for strength, 8 to 12 for overall fitness, and 12 to 15 for toning/defining your muscles.

- Third, decide on the weight to use. This one is trial and error, but there is a basic rule to follow: The weight should push your muscles close to failure on the last rep of each set. In other words, by the end of each set you should not really be able to do any more repetitions. If you have any doubt, start with a low weight, and then move up if you do not feel enough resistance. You will soon find the right weight for the results you want.

- A word to the wise: Using too much weight can hurt! You can suffer a multitude of injuries by overdoing it, so be careful and always have someone spotting you on exercises. One more reason to work out with a partner!

Make sure that you

- keep the correct form on each exercise—follow the descriptions given here.

- wait 60 to 90 seconds between each set.

- push yourself ahead as soon as you start feeling that you are not challenged anymore.

A set is a certain number of performed repetitions (reps) for an exercise. For example, one set of bench press might be 10 repetitions with 100 pounds of weight.

Rep Chart

Plug the number of repetitions in for the desired effect (6 to 8 for strength, 8 to 12 for overall fitness, and 12 to 15 for toning/defining).

WORKSHEET 11-2

Weight Chart

Upper Body   Date: _____

Exercise	Weight	Reps
Bench press		
Lat pulldown		
Military press		
Biceps curl		
Triceps cable pressdowns		
Abs—Crunches		

WORKSHEET 11-3

Weight Chart

Lower Body   Date: _____

Exercise	Weight	Reps
Lunges		
Leg extensions		
Leg curls		
Calf raises		
Abs—Crunches		

Cardio

With cardio, there are three things you have to fill in on the chart: Type, Time, and Intensity (see Worksheet 11-4).

- Type is easy. Choose an activity you like, whether group or individual. Perhaps you will want to try one of the options mentioned earlier or some other activity popular at your college.

- Time. When you are trying to burn fat, time is more important than intensity. Doing 30 to 45 minutes of low-intensity cardio is the best fat-burning exercise. If you cannot start at that level, begin with 15 minutes and work up a few minutes per week until you reach the right range. You are not trying to beat someone else's record. Instead, you want to condition yourself while gradually increasing your time to 30 to 45 minutes.

- Intensity. Low intensity means that you are huffing, puffing, and sweating, but not absolutely dying. On a scale of 1 to 10, you should be working at a 6. Remember: As time decreases, intensity increases. So if the 45 minutes sounds like too much, or you are running short on time one day, shorten your training time, but increase the intensity. In other words, the less time you have to devote to cardio training, the more intense it should be. True, a longer time is optimal, but you can burn a substantial amount of fat with short, intense cardio too. This type of training also tends to get you in better cardiovascular shape, because it improves your stamina a bit more than the slow, steady type of training. And when you are trying to cope with a busy college schedule, stamina is everything!

WORKSHEET 11-4

Cardio Chart

Date: _____

Type	
Time	
Intensity	

Stretching

After all the real working out, it can be easy to forget stretching, especially if you are short on time. But take a few minutes before and after you exercise to do some basic stretches and loosen up.

Make sure that you stretch slow and steady! Bouncing can do damage, so stretch by slowly leaning down and holding for about 15 seconds.

THE RESULTS

A fitness routine is not a short-term, quick solution. Fitness should become a part of your life, for the rest of your life. To successfully make it a habit, starting at YOUR pace is the key. Regardless of your starting point, building a slow, steady fitness regimen is the best approach. Do not try to blaze through by setting unreasonable goals at the beginning; you will end up disappointed. To get the results you want, set realistic goals and then follow through on them.

Just Do It

Working out at the gym does not just happen. It is work, and sometimes hard work at that. To get yourself moving on those tough days, just do it! Quit thinking and do! Getting in shape and feeling better will take a commitment, but it will pay off in the end. Just as placing money in an investment can be a bit painful in the short run, in the long run, it will really pay off. Exercise is no different. It will take a little pain up front and a commitment, but it will make you a better person in the end.

STUDENT PROFILE—Taylor B. and Commitment

I was a track athlete at my college, and while on the interview trail for medical school, I had to miss a few practices. One morning, while staying with a host student, I woke at 4 A.M. to do my sprint workout and running routine. I knew the team was practicing, and I was fully expected to do the same while gone. The people I stayed with may have considered me crazy, but I had a commitment to the team, one that I would not break.

➤ *Would you have woken up with Taylor to make up a practice? Why or why not?*

➤ *Explain what commitment means to you. Cite at least one personal example.*

Working for success in college will take some sacrifice, hard work, and commitment. You do not necessarily have to wake up at

4 A.M. and work out, but you do need to do whatever it takes (that is honest and fair) to achieve your goals.

If your goal is to lose weight while shaping up, read on.

Goals

- Decide the exact amount of weight you want to lose, a definite number of pounds. If you have a lot of weight to lose, break this goal into manageable chunks, like 5 or 10 pounds at a time.
- Decide what body fat percentage you want to shoot for by looking at the body fat table (see Table 11-1).
- Make sure the goals you choose can be measured. In other words, "lose 10 pounds" can be measured by a scale; "getting in better shape" is too vague to be measured.
- Make sure the goal is possible. "Lose 1 to 2 pounds per week" is possible. "Lose 10 pounds" is reasonable, too. You can even put an end time if you want, such as "Lose 10 pounds in two months." But "Lose 10 pounds by Friday" is not a reasonable goal, nor is it a safe one!
- Use the three pointers from Chapter 9: Your goals should be unmistakable, measurable, and possible.

How to Measure

Measuring progress is best done these three ways. If you can, do all of them:

- Take a picture the day you begin working out, and every four weeks, take another.

> "People set their workout goals too lofty. They say, 'I'm going to run 7 days per week, every week.' Of course, they'll be unable to achieve their goals or get injured. They leave it as an all-or-nothing proposition— 'Now, I can't run 7 days per week, so I won't run at all.' It's much more productive to set something realistic and meet or exceed it."
>
> —Graduate, Economics Major

Table 11-1. General Body Fat Percentage Categories[22]		
Classification	**Women (% fat)**	**Men (% fat)**
Essential Fat	10–13%	2–5%
Athletes	14–20%	6–13%
Fitness	21–24%	14–17%
Healthy	25–31%	18–24%
Obese	32% and higher	25% and higher
Reprinted with permission from the American Council on Exercise (2003) *ACE Personal Trainer Manual, Third Edition* (www.acefitness.org).		

- Get your body fat measured. This can be done at a school gym, or if that is not an option, local gyms will usually do it for a few bucks. Get this done every month.

- Weigh yourself. This is not as accurate as body fat for measuring improvement, but still should be noted.

These measurements are to measure progress, not to obsess over. As with any other plan, you have to know where you stand if you expect to make improvements. Use this information to help you, not hurt you.

WORKSHEET 11-5

Fitness Goals

Fill in all the information to find your starting point, then make your goals to begin heading toward the finish line!

Starting date: _____

Attach personal picture (below):

Body fat measurment: _____ %

Weight: _____ pounds

Starting date: _____

Goals:

Body fat measurement (examine body fat table to estimate):_____ %

Weight : _____ pounds

Goal date : _____

Making It Happen

If you find yourself using these excuses too often, they are not excuses, they are cop-outs!

- I'm too tired.
- I'm worn out.
- I can't find the time.
- It doesn't fit with my schedule today.
- It's too inconvenient.
- I'll get to it tomorrow.
- I can't.

Occasionally, these are legitimate claims. Just be careful how much you use them. Quit with these and find reasons why you can do it!

Exhausting days come around now and then, and there is a solution. The most successful exercisers are not sprinters, but marathoners. So, when those exhausting days do come around, do a workout, but make it lower intensity, or a little bit shorter. This is part of training yourself. Make going to the gym mandatory. No matter how horrible it may seem at the moment, you are reinforcing the idea that workouts happen every day, rain or shine, no matter what. This is the essence of commitment.

On those tired days, do the following:

- Keep an abbreviated workout in mind to pull out on those days. (Important note: If you are doing the abbreviated workouts every day, you may want to reevaluate. If you are this tired and exhausted constantly, go to the campus health clinic.)
- Try a more relaxing workout, like yoga or a flexibility session.
- Enlist a workout partner to get the fire in your belly going.
- Stick with it. Bad days do not last forever, and a workout may only be 30 minutes to an hour. I know you can handle it.

> "Working out with a partner is crucial to success. They will push you on those tough days, and you can do the same for them."
> —Graduate, Computer Science Major

Finding Time

Contrary to some people, I strongly believe that there is more than enough time at college to work toward your goals and have some free time. Finding the time is essential to lowering the stress in your life. After all, if one of your goals is to get into shape, but you constantly skip workouts for lack of time, you may become stressed. That is why making that rough schedule of your day is one of the most important aspects of time management. By laying out the schedule, you are essentially creating time.

With school, friends, a job, and so on competing for your time, the time you need to stay in shape will not magically appear. So

> "By exercising and working out, I use my time more efficiently, but also having more energy so I create time so whatever else I am doing, studying or whatever is more efficient because I am mentally more alert."
> —Graduate, Economics Major

you must find and make time. Plus, you will need to figure out the best time for you to work out, because what works for others will not always work for you.

When to Work Out

It is best to work out in the morning, because your day will start on the right foot, and you will definitely never miss if it is the first thing you do! But for those of you who are not morning people, realize that the most important part is doing it!

Making time for your workouts does not mean you have to get up at 5:30 A.M. before your morning classes to do an hour on the treadmill. In the end, it is not the time of day that will make the difference. What will make a difference is fitting that workout in whenever you can every day. Nothing substitutes for consistency and hard work when climbing toward a tough goal, and reaching it makes everything worth it in the end!

So make time for your workout whenever it is most convenient for you, and do not worry about whether it is the perfect time.

Be Patient

Like I have said before, it takes a lot of work to improve your body, so be patient with the results. If you are not approached by Abercrombie model scouts the first week, take it in stride, you are still improving! If your goal is to lose weight, expect to lose between one and two pounds per week: If you lose more, it is either water or mostly muscle, and that is not healthy.

Forget Intimidation

For those of you who are a little worried about starting to work out in the gym: First and foremost, face your fear and go! Yes, the gym can be an intimidating place if you have not had much experience there, but put it out of your mind! People tend to have some common hang-ups:

- You don't know what you're doing.
- You would like to work out, but everyone in the gym is perfect looking and you feel intimidated.

For the first one, most gyms have floor trainers (yes, even colleges have usually sprung for this) and employees that will give you a quick rundown of the machines. Also, most weight machines have information on them explaining how to use them and what muscles they focus on.

The second hang-up is so common, and so unnecessary. For one thing, if you are trying to improve yourself, the last thing you

Consider Alternatives*

There are alternatives to the school gym. If you do not enjoy the atmosphere or cannot make it occasionally, consider an apartment setup. A doorframe pullup bar, a set of dumbbells, and a stability ball (those big bounceballs) will do it. This way you can hit all your major body parts in a quick workout at your own place.

Chest—dumbbell bench press using the stability ball as a bench. With feet flat on the floor, lay on the ball with your upper back and neck being supported. With dumbbells in hand, press the dumbbells from your chest upward, then back down.

Back—pullups are perfect. Place hands shoulder-width apart and pull up your body weight.

Shoulders—military press using the dumbbells. Sitting upright on the ball, raise dumbbells from shoulder level to above the head and back down. Be sure to keep your back straight and wear a weight-lifting belt.

Arms—curls using dumbbells for biceps and triangle push-ups for triceps.

- **Curls:** Stand (no ball) holding dumbbells, flex arms up from your sides and back down.
- **Triangle push-ups:** Assume normal pushup position, and make a triangle meeting your thumbs and index fingers. Do push-ups!

Legs—squats. Place the stability ball between your back and the wall, and then squat!

Abs—sit-ups. Support your back and neck on the ball, feet flat on the floor and do crunches (see earlier description).

*As with any other exercise program, see a physician before starting a routine such as this. See! For very cheap, you can have a home gym.

need to worry about is other people. Realize that they do not care about you; they only care about what they look like. Never let someone else—especially whatever someone else thinks—stand in the way of your goals. Besides, those perfect looking people rarely think they are flawless. Many of them have a more distorted body image than many out-of-shape folks.

Both hang-ups can be overcome, and here is one way to do it: Remember when I talked about making new friends in college? Well, this is one of the best benefits to doing that. Ask one of your friends to visit the gym with you! Chances are that your friend has thought about starting a fitness program, too, but has the same hang-ups you are having. If you take the lead by asking first, you will be helping a friend overcome shyness, and you will both gain courage because you do not have to go it alone.

Stuff You Should Know

- People in the gym—like trainers, employees, and others working out—will more than likely be glad to help you get started in the gym.

- Perfect people do not exist. Even if they did, how would that help or hinder your success anyway?

- Worry about improving yourself. Measuring your own success is the only way to go!

Is It Possible to Lose Weight in College?

Back in Chapter 1, this was one of the Insert Questions—of course it is possible! So many people gain weight during college, and many people have asked me how difficult it is to lose weight in college. My answer? Not hard at all. Compared to undergraduate college, many graduate school programs are more difficult—a lot more difficult. Even so, I know of one medical student who lost 65 pounds in medical school. If he can accomplish that feat in grad school, I believe we all can keep that up in undergraduate school!

SUPPLEMENTS

Not only is working out confusing these days, but so are all the enhancers that go with it. When you are already working hard in the gym, it can be tempting to try to speed up your progress with supplements that supposedly increase everything that you will want—fat loss, muscle gain, speed of getting in shape, you name it. But—and it's a big question to ask . . .

Do Supplements Work?

There are some supplements that may enhance your efforts in the gym. But to make the long explanation short, I am not telling you not to use supplements, but it is important to realize that supplements are not regulated by the FDA and therefore are not required to undergo the stringent testing required by the government. Not only have they not been formally tested by the government, many have not been around long enough to really know whether they are safe and/or effective.

Consider the Source—Buyer Beware!

The sources for much information about supplements are fitness magazines and Web sites. But please understand this: Honesty is a big problem for many of these so-called supplement reviewers. Many of the large fitness magazines (not all) also operate companies that manufacture fitness products. The tendency in these magazines and Web sites is to give great reviews for these products, no matter what the true information says. Often, these reviews are backed up with studies that look impressive but are really bogus or questionable. In spite of that, these studies are preached as the gospel by the company owners. Furthermore, much of the information presented as an actual review section of the magazine is an ad, conveniently not mentioning the fact that it is an advertisement, or doing so, but in print you might need a magnifying glass to read. This is not to say every company is guilty of lying and cheating, just a number of them. So read these types of articles and reviews with a grain of salt.

Supplements to Watch Out For

Ephedra

Although it was recently banned by the FDA, there is still plenty of this fat-burner around. A number of people have died, and their deaths are suspected to be related to the use of this supplement. Baltimore Orioles pitcher Steve Belcher, who was 23 years old, died after using the supplement, and many have implicated ephedrine as the culprit. Though there has not been an absolute decision regarding the compound's danger, it is probably best to steer clear until better information is available.

Creatine

Creatine has not been proven to harm your health, mainly citing the lack of long-term studies on the supplement. There are claims that using creatine improves strength and performance, but with the long-term effects unknown, it is safest to leave the creatine supplements on the shelf.

Protein

The Meal Replacements (MRPs)

Some people think of these as supplements, others as meals. Really they are kind of a mix. Items that mainly fall under this category are protein shakes and protein bars.

Too much protein can be detrimental and is definitely a waste of your money (it just is eliminated from your body after a certain point of saturation). On the other hand, athletes have been shown to need more protein than their nonathletic counterparts. If you are constantly exercising, it is fair to consider yourself an athlete (I do). With your increased protein needs, it might be an advantage to use a shake to supplement your regular diet. Be sure to watch out, though. Some of these shakes can contain a bunch of other additives you do not want or need (including supplements you might want to avoid).

You will most likely need a blender or something similar to fix these MRPs. And usually, the price is proportional to the taste— the most expensive taste the best and the cheapest taste the worst. So if you can handle the chalky taste of some, your dollar will go much further.

Protein bars are great, because you can usually find ones with balanced nutrition (a good blend of protein with other important nutrients), and they are convenient. Unlike the shakes, for which you have to use a blender, you can stuff the bars in your pocket or book bag. Although they are a bit more expensive than your typical candy bar, you can find them for a reasonable price if you look around on the Internet and in discount stores. Some choices are given here:

- Balance
- Myoplex
- Powerbar
- Luna
- Lean Body

Even though they have advantages, and I will admit they are convenient, MRPs can be very expensive for any college student. If you decide to use these, try to order them from the Internet or from discount vitamin stores. If you just walk into GNC and buy them, you will probably pay quite a bit more.

Places to Buy MRPs

Web sites (buying online is the cheapest):
- www.Netrition.com
- www.HealthNutWarehouse.com

Stores (not the best selection, but good prices):
- Sam's Club
- BJ's Wholesale Club
- Costco

Using supplements of any kind is a personal decision. However, it is fully possible to get in great shape naturally. Before you jump into using a supplement, do a little bit of research and find out what you are getting into. Using a daily multivitamin is all right and can help make sure that you are getting all your nutrients. Just make sure you know the distinction between these and other supplements.

Be Consistent, Do Not Be Obsessive

Exercise has many benefits—basically everything you have read thus far. It is important to note, however, that, like anything else, it can be taken too far. Exercise disorders have grown, probably stemming from our culture's obsession with outward appearance. There is nothing wrong with wanting to look nice, but things can be taken too far. If you constantly obsess over your weight or appearance and act out by exercising for hours per day or other unhealthy behavior, talk with someone. You may schedule an appointment with the counseling services at your college or with your physician.

Steroids

- The health problems associated with steroids are well documented. Because they unbalance the body's hormone mix, steroids can cause men to grow breasts, induce testicular shrinking, and cause fits of anger to materialize. I cannot imagine any college student wanting any of these potential side effects! Getting in shape and gaining muscle mass is absolutely possible without these drugs. It may take a bit longer, but the results will stay, and the health risks will be eliminated.
- Steroids are illegal without a doctor's prescription.
- Steroids bought anywhere but a pharmacy may not be the real thing. There have been stories of students taking supposed steroids that turned out to be mixed with other substances like unsterile chemicals, or some such undesirable ingredient. In addition, many of these drugs need to be injected, and your buddy from the gym probably is not exactly trained in this kind of procedure.

The bottom line is that steroids are bad news all around. Many people who get involved with them become psychologically attached to the results and struggle with them for long periods. Keep any potential vice out of your life, and focus your time and energy toward a natural physique. Save your money, too. If you think supplements are expensive, steroids are much more so (and they may not even be real).

IT IS YOUR LIFE, YOUR BODY, AND YOUR FUTURE

College is an ideal time to get in the habit of balancing exercise with other responsibilities so that you can look and feel great for the rest of your life. And with all the benefits, how can you go wrong?

So get started!

Eating for Energy and Health

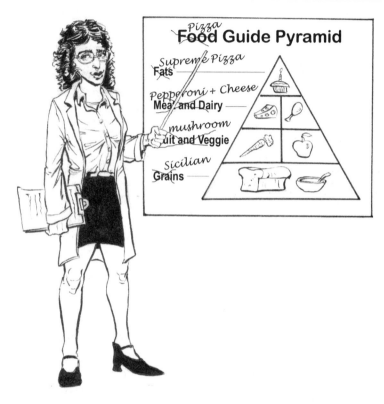

Pizza
Food Guide Pyramid

Supreme Pizza
Fats

Pepperoni + Cheese
Meat and Dairy

mushroom
Fruit and Veggie

Sicilian
Grains

*"To insure good health: Eat lightly, breathe deeply,
live moderately, cultivate cheerfulness, and
maintain an interest in life."*
—William Londen

THE COLLEGE DINING EXPERIENCE

To make sure you are ahead of the pack at college, you have to eat right. Knowing what to eat on campus (if your school has on-campus food service) can be hard to figure out, to say the least. It tends to go something like this.

You walk into the on-campus eatery and survey the array of choices. First, you look at the grill. This place is a bona fide grease pit with cheese steaks, burgers, and other horrible tasting, horrible-for-you fine dining. There is one healthy item—the veggie burger that has been cooked in animal fat to give it some flavor. Ugh!

Next, you move to the taco line. Here you find the same ground-beef-like substance they spoon-fed you in the high school cafeteria. Didn't they get the message then? IT IS GROSS!

Anyway, none of this looks appetizing, so you decide to settle for a slice of the less-than-great good ol' pizza and one of those decent-tasting brownie things.

Sound familiar? If you are in college, it does. And if you are not in college yet, it will.

Though the situation is improving, eating decent healthy food is a real struggle for many college students, especially if they are trying to stay in shape. The steady diet of Miller Time does not help the situation either. For the exercising, health-conscious student, it is definitely a challenge, especially with all the fad diets, rumors, and misinformation.

When I got to college, I thought: "How in the world am I going to piece together some sort of decent dietary habits with this kind of stuff everywhere??!"

Well, it was not easy, but I managed, and other students have too. In this chapter, I'll give you some hints to help you put together your own healthy eating habits, including eating healthy with common college cafeteria food. But first, let's review some common questions on eating well.

Eating Q & A

Q: *Isn't starving yourself the only way to lose weight and get lean?*

A: No way! Starving yourself makes your body burn more muscle than fat (which further slows your metabolism). It can even slow your metabolism permanently, and this means more stored fat when you get back to eating normally. So do not starve. The way to burn fat and keep it off is through regular exercise and eating right.

Q: *For guys to gain muscle mass and strength, they practically have to eat a whole side of beef every day, right?*

A: False. Although protein is an extremely important part of the diet, it is not necessary to eat 12 chicken sandwiches a day to build and keep muscle. People who do regular weight training need more protein than the average person, but they also need more food in general. Eating balanced meals is plenty to see results from your exercise regimen.

THE IMPORTANCE OF HEALTHY EATING

Because you are focused on college success, healthy eating habits are a necessity. To repeat: For the best performance and overall success as a college student, it will be important to learn about and implement healthy eating. This is not to say that pizza is never allowed or that ice cream can never be eaten again (oh no!). Rather, this is about taking a look at the general eating habits you have now, and if need be, working to make them healthier.

If you owned a Porsche, would you put 87-octane gasoline in it? I would hope not. After working very hard and spending a huge amount of money to buy one of these cars, why go cheap on the food for your car? Well, you just would not! As a college student, you are the cream of the crop. Though many people go to college these days, many do not, or cannot. So, consider your body your Porsche. (And when you think about it, if something goes hugely wrong with you, it is much more expensive to fix than a Porsche!)

Your body is capable of very high performance, but then again, it depends on how you treat yourself. Stuffing yourself with Doritos, French fries, mayonnaise-dripping bacon cheeseburgers, and any choice of the 31 flavors at Baskin Robbins will certainly drag down that performance. Any of the previously mentioned foods are commonly seen in college, and it is even all right to have them—sometimes! Yet the difference between chowing down now and then on a meal like that just described and doing it every day is huge. Many times, people who clean up their eating habits will have a meal like what I have described and feel sick afterward. After you experience the refreshed feeling of healthy eating, your craving for huge, unhealthy meals will decrease.

The GIGO Principle

GIGO stands for Garbage In, Garbage Out. If you mostly eat unhealthy foods, expect to feel unhealthy.

Developing the Habit

First to address is the misconception that eating healthy requires missing out. Nothing is further from the truth. Just as with studying, exercising, or anything else in college (and life), healthy eating requires developing a habit (which can be tough at the start). But, just as habits can be your enemies (smoking, drinking excessively, drugs, etc.), they can be your friends also by making your life easier once you have put in the initial work.

If you or someone you know tried cigarettes as a young kid, you will know what I am talking about. It took a lot of effort to smoke back then. Think about all the trouble there was: getting your hands on cigarettes at a young age, making it out of the house to take a few puffs, and then the McGyver-esque process of getting the smell off yourself. Now that was a lot of work and determination! Eventually, over time though, this type of situation forms

"People ask me, 'Wouldn't you rather eat pastries and other stuff?' No, I don't see it as being a sacrifice, there are just certain goals you have, and certain things you do to get there. I enjoy eating healthy, so I do it. If you call that discipline, OK!"

—Graduate, Economics Major

into a habit, which is easier and considered an everyday affair—hence, the habit is formed.

To change your eating habits and eat a more balanced diet may seem tough at first. You have to be concerned with everything you eat, instead of just grabbing what looked good before. You have to work to find the healthier items at restaurants and dining halls when you eat out. You feel deprived at first, wondering what the big deal is with eating a piece of that chocolate cake, and so on. This is mostly temporary, though. Once you get used to eating more balanced and clean meals, it will seem like the regular way of life.

The lesson? Buckle down and get yourself through the hard part. It will get easier as time goes on.

The System

Hopefully you have noticed something in this book—that excellence requires planning and goal setting. Eating is no different from any of the other challenges.

When committing to an eating change, most people have the best intentions. They figure that they will fight the urge to eat badly every meal, every day, and figure it out as they go. Wrong! Instead of flying by the seat of your pants, plan! Planning is a big part of this book because it is a big part of college and a big part of success. When you commit to a goal and plan for it, you set yourself up for victory, not for some wishy-washy finish. The system is the plan for your eating—it means identifying your sticking points and solving problems *before* they arise. After you read this section, fill out Worksheet 12-1 to make your own system.

Falling off the wagon does not usually happen out of nowhere. It is always that change in schedule where you forgot to bring your apple or that trip out of town where you grab a McDonald's meal on the road. Then, after one of these initial screw-ups, you become discouraged and figure that your entire plan is shot. And out the window it goes, back to the old lifestyle. Working with the system will allow you to see the problems in advance so that you are prepared for them.

The system is simple. If you see a potential problem with having no food after English Literature at 2 P.M. and Macroeconomics at 5 P.M. and see yourself gorging after class because you are absolutely starving, pack something. Whether it is a PBJ, a health food bar, or some fruit, just be ready! If you are heading out of town, do the same. Be ready to pack your own stuff (you will save money this way, too) and have some backup restaurant ideas just in case. Plan on ordering the grilled anything without the fries and adding a side of veggies instead.

Everyone has different trip-ups when it comes to sticking with their plans, just try to see yours coming so that you can defeat it. For example, my friends and I were continually hungry throughout the day. In case we could not find something healthy to eat (or were out of money!), we kept health food bars in our book bags. They definitely came in handy more than once!

Another big sticking point for healthy eating are those tired, long days. Arriving back home at 8 P.M. is not very conducive to fixing a huge healthy meal. Simple: Keep some backup food.

There will be some days or nights when fixing a whole meal is the last thing you will want to do. After all, you have laundry, cleaning, and everything else as your responsibility. If you can spare the cash in your budget, it might be a good idea to have some lean frozen dinners in the freezer. Lean Cuisine, Healthy Choice, and Smart Ones are all examples of decent frozen dinners that are a quick fix. Though they are more expensive than other foods, if you can find them on sale and stock up a bit, they can be a great deal. Once again, these should not be staples. They have high sodium content as well as other processed food additives, so be sure to drink plenty of water along with these meals.

Go ahead and fill out the system worksheet, working on your personal trip-ups and easy remedies to deal with them. You cannot be perfect, but you can be prepared!

Cook Every Day?

If you only like to cook food every few days, it can simplify your life. Try fixing a healthy lasagna in a huge dish that will last for a number of days. All you have to do is toss it in the microwave, and there's a meal!

Online Grocery Shopping

If you live in a larger city, look into online grocery shopping. Because many companies are just trying to stay afloat, the delivery fees are reasonable (especially if you are purchasing a week's worth of food because it is usually a flat fee). If you are extremely busy during midterms or finals, you can study and have your shopping done for you. It is convenient, fast, and efficient. You can't beat that!

WORKSHEET 12-1

The Eating System

The System is all about identifying the obstacles that throw you off track. Take a minute to write down the problems you have with eating healthy—what arises to throw you off? Then, design remedies to deal with these issues.

Three obstacles in way of eating healthy:

1.

2.

3.

Remedies to the three obstacles:

1.

2.

3.

It is important to find solutions to these problems. Plan what you will do so that nothing will get in the way next time!

It Is Possible and Easier Than You Think

In college you design your own schedule for the most part. For many students, you will have more free time than at any other time in your life! So you get to make your own decisions.

Although individual circumstances differ, this is the freest stretch (time- and decision-wise) of your life. Take advantage of having the ability to make and buy the food YOU want; designing class schedules the way YOU see fit; and living the way YOU want to live! College is all about freedom, and that can play directly to your advantage in the goal to eat healthier.

Do not worry, though. To feel energetic and enthusiastic does not require eating like a tropical bird. It just requires balance. Later in this chapter, there is a list of some very healthy foods to eat in college.

SO, WHAT IS EATING RIGHT?

To eat right, the most important factors are balance and portion control. Take a glance at the following two meals:

Meal 1:

- Large bowl of pasta and red sauce/no meat
- Large serving of mashed potatoes with gravy
- Large bowl of vanilla ice cream
- Large Coke

Meal 2:

- Small bowl of wheat pasta with grilled chicken breast and red sauce
- Medium serving of salad with some tomatoes, cheese, and onion and olive oil and vinegar dressing
- ½ sweet potato
- Tall glass of iced tea with low calorie sweetener

Portion Size and Balance

In case you cannot tell which meal is healthier, here is a hint. Meal 1 is full of mostly carbohydrates and fat. There is little fiber and not much fruit or vegetable. Neither carbs nor fat are bad for you, but they need to be combined and rationed a little bit better.

Meal 2 has carbs with the pasta (but a little bit less); protein with the grilled chicken (low fat protein at that!); vegetables with the salad, tomatoes, and onions, and some fat (the cheese, olive oil dressing, and chicken all have some fat).

Further than just the makeup are the portion sizes in each meal. If you notice, everything in Meal 1 is large. Having a large serving of salad, other vegetables, iced tea, and water is fine; supersizing everything else is not.

It is common sense. Look at the French. They seem to cook with a disproportionately large amount of butter, cream, and other fats. If you notice though, their portions are kept small. Foix gras (duck liver), a French delicacy, is an enormously fattening food, but it is usually eaten in small portions. And study after study has proven that many Europeans are far from overweight. In other words, Europeans do not have anywhere near the weight problems we Americans do.

I am not suggesting using a lot of butter or eating foix gras at every meal. What I am suggesting is that lessons can be learned from different kinds of cooking and thinking. Learning to combine balance with decent-sized portions will bring your healthy eating right to where it needs to be.

Balancing your meals has other benefits, too. If you are trying to lose weight, it will keep down the cravings often felt by those on crash diets. If you are not trying to lose weight, balance is equally important; the right portion size will keep you from packing on the pounds through your years on campus. If you are lucky enough not to have to worry about weight gain now, it can happen just a few years down the road. Many people struggle with weight gain for a long time, and one reason is setting those bad habits early on. The faster you correct those habits and turn them into good habits, the easier it will be to feel great.

To eat healthy, you do not need to weigh everything to the ounce and broil it in the oven. Just make sure that each meal has a little bit of everything. At the end of the chapter are some types of foods that can be pieced together to assemble a great and healthy meal.

Keeping Hydrated

Water makes up over half of our body weight, so as you might guess, water is very important to keep in balance. Many college students living off soda, coffee, and beer are perpetually dehydrated. Although any of the previous beverages can be all right in moderation, they can have negative effects when used frequently (and alcohol can have a far more damaging effect than just dehydration when excessively used). The effects of being dehydrated can go as follows:

- Losing 2 percent of your body weight in fluids can translate into a 10 to 20 percent drop in physical performance, not to mention the washed out feeling.

- Losing 3 to 5 percent of your body weight in fluids can translate into an even larger loss of athletic performance, as well as impaired judgment and decision-making skills.[23]

As you can see, not only can dehydration have a deleterious effect on your physical abilities but on your mental faculties as well. Staying well hydrated will not only keep your performance up, but you will feel refreshed if you make most of your beverages water. Because you are all active college students and exercising, try to drink 8 to 10 glasses of fluids per day (soda and beer do not count!). In addition, drink more before, after, and during exercise.[24]

And just in case you are thinking how inconvenient it is to drink that amount, take it easy. Just keep a large water bottle in your book bag and you will be sure to easily fit that amount in throughout the day. In addition, because college is very flexible, you can duck out of class whenever it is necessary to use the restroom.

Why Are You Eating?

As I mentioned earlier, you do not want to starve yourself to lose weight. But sometimes our bodies' signals get confused, and we think we are hungry when we really are not. Here are some things to try at those times:

- Eat when you are hungry, not bored.
- Eat smaller, more frequent meals.
- If you are hungry, drink some water and wait a few minutes. If your hunger passes, you were not hungry, just thirsty.
- Eat slowly.

The Hints

Almost every college out there has an all-you-can-eat food hall on campus. That sounds attractive, sure. But 13.5 percent of all 18- to 29-year-olds are obese, so it is obvious that lots of people are eating all they can eat.[25] These places can turn into a nightmare if you are trying to stay in shape. But if you learn some self-control, they usually have some pretty decent food. This leads right into the first hint.

Hint 1

Do not eat all you can eat. I know you are trying to get your money's worth, but shoving 3,000 calories of glorified processed foods down your throat will work directly against your getting-into-shape goals.

Hint 2

Eat balanced. The super low-fat, super low-carb, super high-fat, super no meat, super blah blah blah . . .

Stop now. The only way to get the nutrients your body needs is to eat normal, healthy foods from all the categories. You need carbs for energy. If you think working out is hard now, try it on an extremely low-carb diet. It is like going to the gym on one hour's sleep!

Low-fat diets can be just as hard on your stamina. Folks who eat virtually no fat have problems not only with stamina but also with getting full. Also, eating no fat usually means that you are pumping yourself full of sugar and too much starch. Think about it: If they remove the fat, it has to be replaced with something— again, not a good dietary habit.

If you are a vegetarian, you will need to take a bit of extra care with your diet to make it balanced. Although eating too much protein can potentially have adverse health effects, you need some meat or other sources of complete proteins to supply vital amino acids and minerals. You can still get complete proteins if you make the right choices.

Do not skimp on the protein or fats or go too nuts with them. Either can do you a dietary disservice.

Vegetarian Choices for Protein

Dairy	Nondairy
• Eggs	• Soy products
• Milk	• Beans
• Cheese	• Seeds
	• Nuts
	• Brown rice

Hint 3

Watch what you drink! Drinking a bunch of juice, soda, and other sweetened drinks can easily add hundreds of needless calories every day. These are chock-full of sugar, with little or no nutritional value. If you are a soda addict, switch to diet. That one trick alone can save you a few pounds every year. If you have to have juice, have some. Juice—that is 100 percent juice—is good for you in moderate amounts. Just make sure to drink it in moderation.

Hint 4

Earlier is better than later. Try not to eat much after 9 P.M. Your metabolism starts to slow down late in the evening, which means there is a greater chance of calories being stored (as fat). If you are starving, by all means have a healthy snack; just make eating at this time the exception and not the rule.

Hint 5

Keep track of what is going into your mouth, using the College Eats worksheet (see Worksheet 12-2). Sometimes just seeing what you have eaten during the day will show you some of your problem areas.

WORKSHEET 12-2

College Eats: The Tracker

It's simple. Just fill in the time, what foods and how much, and how you felt when you ate them. Were you starving, bored, sort of hungry, and so forth? Also, you do not have to eat four snacks; there is room in case you do, though.

Meal	Time	What and How Much	How You Felt
Breakfast			
Lunch			
Dinner			
Snack #1			
Snack #2			
Snack #3			
Snack #4			

STUDENT PROFILE—Mike T. on Eating

I do not go on fad diets. I eat everything: fat, carbs, and protein. I eat plenty of vegetables, fruits, lean poultry, fish, eggs, dairy on occasion, and limit intake of sweets. I cook meals in advance for the week. It is easier to have stuff there to eat during the week, but also keeps me more disciplined to eat healthier. If the healthy food is available, you will eat it as opposed to the kind of snacking when junk food is everywhere. If you are hungry and the only thing to eat is a candy bar, that is what you will eat.

Following these hints can have a tremendous impact on your efforts to improve the way you feel, and keep your energy up. In my experience, what you eat can either double your results in the gym, or halve them. It is like building a house. To make the most out of the builder's skills and handiwork, the materials have to be good. It does not matter how great the carpenter is. If the material is second-rate, the house will be, too. Food and activity are building materials for your body. Eat the right things and improve your building skills in the gym to make it easier to develop your personal best body and mind.

"I Can't Afford Good Food." Yes You Can!

One of the most common misconceptions about eating healthy is that it has to cost a fortune. To eat healthy and not spend your inheritance follow this advice:

- Avoid specialty grocery stores. Health food stores and organic grocery stores tend to have higher prices than the good old A&P supermarket. Unless you have an issue with regular food, use the local supermarket, and you will stretch your food dollar further.

- Keep an eye out for sales. As discussed in the money section, keeping an eye out for sales is essential. As a college student, you will surely get plenty of junk mail. Be sure to glance through those grocery store inserts to see the good deals that week. You can potentially save a ton of money this way. It is common to find some foods for half-price.

- Learn to freeze. Maybe you can go to Sam's Club or another wholesale place to buy your food. If so, great, but you may have too much. If your roommates are not into splitting grocery bills and buying in bulk, learn how to freeze. If you buy a large amount of an item on sale at the grocery store, it may go bad rather quickly. Items such as meats can easily be divided up and frozen until a more convenient time. To freeze items, do the following:

  —Get some Ziploc bags (the kind that says "Freezer Bags" on the label).

  —Be sure to get most of the air out. Air causes freezer burn. The food will be safe, but might not taste as good.

  —A label never hurts. Use a Magic Marker or Sharpie pen to mark what is in there, and the month and year it went into the freezer so that you will know for later.

It is simple to defrost the items. Toss the food in the microwave and use the defrost feature. If you do not have a microwave, you can take the package out the night before and leave it in the refrigerator overnight. It should be thawed by the next day.

Some of the Cheapest Foods Are Healthy

Eggs, canned tuna or chicken for sandwiches, and canned soups all can usually be found for very reasonable prices. The most expensive food is convenience food. Food prices tend to increase with convenience.

Finding Good Deals

Try the discount meat rack. The meat usually has two to three days left before it needs to be cooked. You can find some great deals there for perfectly good food.

Cookbooks

The Healthy College Cookbook: Quick, Easy, Cheap
By Nimetz, Stanley, and Starr
Storey Books, Copyright 1999
ISBN# 1580171265

The College Cookbook: An Alternative to the Meal Plan, Reissue Ed.
By Harrington and Oxley
Storey Books, Copyright 1988
ISBN# 0882664972

The College Student's Cookbook, Spiral Ed.
By Lambert and Lee
Blue Mountain Arts, Copyright 2001
ISBN# 0883965917

College Cuisine, Spiral Ed.
By Peltosaari
Tikka Books, Copyright 1998
ISBN# 1896106013

The College Student's Guide to Eating Well on Campus
By Selkowitz
Tulip Hill Press, Copyright 2000
ISBN# 0970013906

- Raw, uncooked foods are the cheapest.
- Uncooked, but seasoned and packaged conveniently yourself are the next cheapest.
- Cooked and frozen (frozen dinners) are pretty reasonable but try to find them on sale, and stock up.
- Prepared and hot (a restaurant meal) is the most expensive.

If you are buying a lot of food that needs to be cooked and seasoned, there are some simple ways to do it. Of course, buying a few spices can add much flavor. An easy and pretty healthy way is using soups to complement the food (they can make it stretch further, too). Many soup cans have ideas or recipes to make on the label. Some simple recipes can turn out tasting great and saving you a few bucks. Adding cooked chicken meat and a few vegetables to a can of chicken gumbo soup can make a great, filling meal. Even though most prepared soups have a very high sodium content, drinking plenty of water can balance out the increase for most healthy people. And you can look for soups labeled as "reduced sodium," too.

Filling Your Pantry

To eat the right foods, you need them available. To keep on the right track for healthy eating, stock your pantry with the foods suggested in Table 12-1.

Table 12-1. The Shopping List
Carbohydrates
Brown rice, sweet potatoes, whole wheat pasta, whole grain breads, whole grain crackers, unsweetened whole grain cereals (like Cheerios), green vegetables (frozen are fine) as well as bagged salads, fruit, and beans
Proteins
Fish, chicken, lean beef (flank steak and lean ground beef—5 percent fat)
Dairy
Eggs, low fat milk, low fat cheese, and low fat cottage cheese
Spices
Oregano, Basil, Bay leaves, Chives, Garlic salt, Chili powder
Sauces and Soups
Chicken Noodle, Tomato, Chicken Gumbo, Spaghetti Sauce
Other
Olive Oil—when using it for cooking, use a mister, that way you will use a little less.

College Foods (and Drinks) to Watch Out For

Alcohol: Drinking your weight in beer will push you in the opposite direction from staying smart and fit—and besides, if you are falling over with one eye open, how appealing do you think you look?

Pizza: Lots of fat and carbs, plus it is usually eaten late at night.

Soda: Tons and tons of empty calories.

Fast Food: You do not want to know the nutritional content. Just stay away from it—by "it," I mean the burgers and fries. If you need to stop and eat at one of these restaurants, try one of the salads or grilled chicken sandwiches (and skip the mayonnaise). The burgers and fries should be an absolute last resort. If you are not going to die of starvation in the coming hours, do not even consider it—and if you are dying, think long and hard!

Some others:

- Chips
- Candy
- Junky snack foods like those honey-bun and minicake-type things
- Almost anything out of a machine

Little Foods That Make a Big Difference

Mayonnaise: Either stay away from it or get the low fat kind. Full fat (regular) mayo can turn a perfectly healthy sandwich into a fully functional fat bomb. Or, adjust your taste buds to being happy with a lot less, like a teaspoon or two.

Salad dressing: So you have some raw vegetables, and they would taste a lot better soaked in ranch dressing. Same as the mayo—either stay away, get used to less, or get the low fat version. These types of food can wreak havoc on nutrition.

Cheese: Some cheese is good, as we saw, but getting cheese on everything is a no-no.

Some others:

- Butter and most margarines
- Cream cheese
- Whole milk
- Peanut butter (more than a couple of tablespoons a day)

EATING DISORDERS

Remember, healthy eating should be a part of your life, not no eating. When college students think of eating disorders, they usually think of women. But increasingly men are becoming more

> **Eating and Workouts**
> Eat a balanced meal soon after your workouts. It will help you build your muscles and cut down on a raging appetite later.

Symptoms of Anorexia[26]

- Fear of gaining weight
- Always thinking of oneself as fat
- Weighing less than 85 percent of a normal, healthy body weight
- Absence of a monthly menstrual period
- Following a strict diet
- Excessive exercising
- Refusal to eat in front of others
- Denial of having an eating disorder

Symptoms of Bulimia[27]

- Fear of gaining weight
- Episodes of binging on food in a short period of time
- Feeling of a lack of control over eating habits
- Feeling of guilt associated with overeating and eliminating the food through induced vomiting, fasting, excessive exercising, or misuse of laxatives or diuretics
- Increased social isolation
- Surprising rate of tooth decay

Signs of Compulsive Overeating[31]

- Binge eating
- Depression
- Feeling of a lack of control over eating habits
- Increased social isolation and embarrassment
- Obsession with dieting
- Obsession with weight
- Little if any eating in front of others
- Self esteem tied to weight

susceptible to the pressures of having that mythical perfect body. There is a difference between taking care of your body and obsessing over it to the point of harm. Eating disorders stem from psychological issues that in turn distort perceptions of one's own body. You can think of this as a psychological circus mirror. Eating disorders are serious threats to health that can even prove to be fatal.

Anorexia and Bulimia

If you suspect that you or someone you know has anorexia or bulimia, look over these symptoms. If any or all are present, you may need help. As mentioned before, the university has plenty of resources, from the student health center to the student counseling center. There are also hotlines to discuss eating disorders or to find help.

Compulsive Overeating

Some people suffer from compulsive overeating, which, like other eating disorders, can be very detrimental to both physical and psychological health. Similar to other eating disorders, the cycle of compulsive overeating runs on feelings of depression, guilt, anxiety, and body-image distortion.

If you or someone you know has some or all of these symptoms, do not hesitate to get help. These diseases are extremely serious, and you could be saving a life.

Help and Information for Eating Disorders
- Rader Programs—800-841-1515
- Eating Disorders Awareness and Prevention—800-931-2237
- American Anorexia/Bulimia Association—212-575-6200

BUILD YOUR HOUSE STRONG ENOUGH TO LAST THE REST OF YOUR LIFE

Keeping your nutrition under control is an enormous challenge in college, but it is important. Eating poorly for the next four years almost guarantees health problems later on and makes it difficult for you to achieve your academic and weight and fitness goals, too. But if you follow these hints, you will make a noticeable difference in your energy and appearance, and set yourself up for a lifetime of good health.

Planning Ahead: There Is Life After College!

CHAPTER 13

"I do not believe in principle, but I do in interest."
—James Russell Lowell

FOLLOW YOUR GUT

So, we know that a big part of this college thing is helping to make life better, for later. That is what this chapter is about, making yourself interesting for the after-college goals.

Take a moment to ponder this: What do I want to do later in life?

Simple question, but hard to answer. I don't know about you, but over a few years' space, I had a few different ideas of what I wanted to do—from CIA agent (yeah, you know you have thought about it!), to doctor, to lawyer, and the list goes on and on.

And if you think I am the only one who has changed his mind, keep thinking.

- Some of us have had ideas of careers we want to tackle—well thought-out, solid choices—and changed them around a little bit.

- Others have never settled on anything and are clueless where to start in figuring this out.

- Most of us are probably somewhere in the middle. We thought about it a little, played around with a few ideas, but our adult career was so far in the future, we did not think it was all that important to think about right now.

Well, guess what? Your career is now just a few short years away!

As we discussed previously, chasing money will never do the trick. It will not lead to a great time in college or a great time afterward. One individual I met while researching for this book was a history major at a liberal arts college. After graduation, he began working in finance and now works for a venture capital firm on the West Coast (not an easy job to get, even for a finance major!).

The point is, be yourself and follow your gut. You will end up enjoying your studies more, and will show your true passion pursuing whatever you would like in the future. Keep the two separate. A major and a career do not necessarily mean the same thing.

One thing is for sure—if you choose a career for the wrong reasons, you will have a lifetime to regret the decision. But college majors tend to be a bit more flexible.

Figuring out your path is best done by listening to your real interests—sometimes only a gut feeling. That sounds easy, but that kind of listening is not always the easiest thing to do. Many people would listen to their interests, but they are more interested in making money, not what they like to do. After all, money is important. Many students are in college for one reason: to get a degree to get a great job to make great money. Too many of those people find out a little too late that chasing a terrific career that they will hate not only makes them less productive, it is also pure misery!

Money Will Come!

When asked what surprised him most about studying millionaires, Tom Stanley, author of *The Millionaire Next Door*, said, "I discovered that building wealth was about . . . choosing the right business for you. 'It's not the shape and size of the shovel, it's where you dig.'"[17]

Of course, there is another side to the equation. Although you should enjoy what you do after college, you will need to pay the bills! And if you are waiting for the perfect career, you might be disappointed—there isn't one. Focus on something you like, but think twice about holding back because an opportunity is not perfect.

> "Differing interests may require differing strong points: The importance of almost-perfect grades depends on what you are going into. In medicine and law, grades are paramount. In business, internships are paramount. Think ahead a little bit."
>
> —Graduate, Philosophy Major

> "To help narrow your job search, find where you want to work, and more importantly, why you want to work there."
>
> —Graduate, Marketing Major

Success Through Any Path

Have you ever tried to choose your career by looking at lists of the most successful (read, highest-paying) jobs? It may surprise you that you can be successful through any major or career path you choose, extremely successful. If your interest is sports and you dream of working in the big leagues, there is sportswriting (journalism major). Or what about sportscasting? Hey, Dick Vitale had to start somewhere! Or, there is athletic training—all pro sports teams need athletic trainers! Actually, sports teams use medical and health professionals of all types. Or maybe you do not want to set your sights on the pros. Perhaps working for a business degree to open a gym would interest you.

What is important is that as long as you work hard toward your interests and goals, there is no limit on success. Success can be realized through any field or path you decide to take.

JOBS: WHAT IS SO SPECIAL ABOUT YOU?

What do great jobs, terrific grad schools, and interesting opportunities all require in common? Leadership and initiative. All post-college prospects want not only book-smart individuals but also people who can lead and have the confidence and know-how to put plans into action.

Questions they will ask: Who are you? What have you done? Anything impressive? How about your extracurricular activities? Anything special?

Where Do You Stand?

Take a minute to fill out the Résumé Worksheet (see Worksheet 13-1). When applying for jobs down the line, consulting this worksheet will make life a lot easier—all your information will be in one spot! Big ones, small ones—doesn't matter. Write them all down.

To make résumé writing easier, start keeping track of your accomplishments now. Not only will it motivate you to see everything on paper, it will be handy in the future.

Now, ask yourself the following two questions: Are you impressed? Would you want to meet or hire yourself?

Being in a sweet position after college graduation is not the plight of most graduates. Unfortunately, most undergrads worry about their résumé a little too late and pay dearly for it.

But you are not most undergrads. Now that you have read this far, you are a strategic thinker, always planning and thinking about the next move. So in appreciation, I am going to help you set yourself up for a great plate of options when you graduate.

> "A skill may help your marketability. In the science field, if you are not sure what you want to do at school, do research. With the skills I learned in that lab combined with a bachelor's degree, I can go into the real world and get a job leveraging my experience."
>
> —Senior, Microbiology Major

WORKSHEET 13-1

Résumé Worksheet

Keep track of your accomplishments to make résumé writing a cinch.

Work 1

Organization: _____

Dates: _____

Job title: _____

Responsibilities: _____

_____

Work 2

Organization: _____

Dates: _____

Job title: _____

Responsibilities: _____

_____

Work 3

Organization: _____

Dates: _____

Job title: _____

Responsibilities: _____

_____

Volunteer 1

Organization: _____

Dates: _____

Job title: _____

Responsibilities: _____

_____

Volunteer 2

Organization: _____

Dates: _____

Job title: _____

Responsibilities: _____

_____

Volunteer 3

Organization: _____

Dates: _____

Job title: _____

Responsibilities: _____

_____

Internship 1

Organization: _____

Dates: _____

Job title: _____

Responsibilities: _____

_____

Internship 2

Organization: _____

Dates: _____

Job title: _____

Responsibilities: _____

_____

Extracurricular 1

Organization: _____

Dates: _____

Job title: _____

Responsibilities: _____

_____

Extracurricular 2

Organization: _____

Dates: _____

Job title: _____

Responsibilities: _____

_____

Extracurricular 3

Organization: _____

Dates: _____

Job title: _____

Responsibilities: _____

_____

Honors/Awards

1.

2.

3.

Other

1.

2.

References

1.

2.

3.

4.

5.

Whether it is graduate school, a corporate job, or some kind of entrepreneurial idea, having a bulletproof and impressive résumé is a must. Let's get started learning about some options to build your résumé if you are not totally satisfied with your Résumé Worksheet profile.

Let's start building the Rolls Royce of résumés, but first, we need to get a better idea of what those jobs and graduate schools look for!

THE ADVISOR SAYS:

Look on your campus for résumé help. Many colleges have free help available.

> **Places to Find Résumé Templates**
> - Most word processors have résumé templates.
> - Monster.com has many sample résumés.
> - College career counseling centers have résumés and workshops.

Their Perspective

We have all seen those serial-killer movies where the detective gets in the head of the killer to nab the criminal. Well, what we are doing here is not too different—except that your new boss or the law school admissions director is your prey.

Look at that list you just made, and think about it: Whatever you see on paper is what people who might interview you for a job or graduate schools glancing at your application are going to see. Stand in their shoes for a moment. If you were any of those people, what would you want?

Applicant A: Can drink a beer with no hands; always arrives promptly at tailgate parties; voted best local customer at the pub; graduated with 2.2 cumulative average.

OR

Applicant B: Graduated with 3.7 cumulative GPA; two-year treasurer for student government; organized Turkey Day Food Drive; avid runner and second place for age group in New Year's 5K Run.

You would be surprised how many folks have a personal record closer to Applicant A's. But unless you want to make it big as a comedy writer someday, you will want to think of ways to make your own résumé look a bit more like Applicant B's. You do not have to lie or misrepresent yourself. Just learn how to, as the old song says, "accentuate the positive" in your list of accomplishments.

In spicing up the résumé, we will start with schoolwork, then internships, volunteering, and your personal stuff.

Jobs and GPA

So how do people get great jobs? They stand out! GPA is the most obvious way to give yourself a boost. So where do grades fit in? Do they really matter, really make a difference?

If you think grades cannot help, you are kidding yourself. Good grades are terrific tools for breaking down some barriers and screening techniques. For example, some internships require a 3.0 GPA to even apply! This does not mean that without great grades you are out of luck; only that good grades can really give you a boost.

Something no one pointed out to me when I got to college was the fact that GPAs are here to stay. Trying to ditch a bad GPA is like trying to shake the feds after you rob the Federal Reserve Bank—they just do not disappear.

Unlike me, you will know what I am about to tell you going in to college. And knowing this going in puts things in perspective. Knowing that you have a good college GPA will

- line up great opportunities for you.
- help keep your sanity when trying to find a real post-college job.
- put you one step ahead of the game.

A stellar academic record will never hinder you in your search, and it may help you a great deal. But if you just do not have the grades, do not panic. There are other ways to stand out.

And this, friends, is why academics is such a large part of this book—because they really matter and can really help!

Internships

Ah, the bread and butter of a job application. Internships are "the most bankable credential you can put on a résumé."[18] They are a must for going into the business world and can be an extremely large help for any major looking to apply to graduate school.

STUDENT PROFILE—Randy S. on Internships

I wanted to get out and try some real world stuff and get outside the box a little bit. I had been interning at my school's radio station, but decided to take an internship at the flagship for the Kansas City Royals, News Radio 980 KMBZ. For the first half of the internship, I just sat around and basically did nothing and started getting frustrated and should have stuck with what I had. Then, I got the opportunity to go out to a Royals game with an all access pass, which excited me. During a three-game series I had the pass and got to mingle a little bit with pro athletes and I learned how to be around them. Because it was something that I wanted to do, it was awesome; I was able to sit with the broadcasters in the booth during the game. I don't know if it improved my skills necessarily, but it really motivated me. After that first game, I said, "Ok, I definitely want to do this!"

➤ *Name two of your passions and write one opportunity, for each that may let you work with those passions.*

> "I definitely think internships are important for landing that offer. Many times the companies you intern for will give you offers at the end of the summer, which is a big perk."
>
> —Graduate, Accounting Major

The bottom line is that real-world experience can translate into a real-world job. It is as simple as that. Employers want experience these days, and the better the job, the more experience you need.

How can you get experience, though? After all, everyone seems to require it to get hired, but to get experience, you have to get hired!

Tricky situation, but lucky for you, internships are a great way to nab some real-world experience without having been a CEO.

Landing a top internship can be a large selling point for getting a great job. Here is why: If you managed to land a great internship, you most likely impressed someone along the line and are genuinely interested in the job. Employers are not dummies; they already know this, and if this knowledge applies to you, you get extra points toward getting that job you want.

> "Internships are valuable for what they show about you. Not necessarily what you know. It shows the places that you have put a large amount of energy and time toward their industry and they are more likely to hire you. More than I didn't just think of this and throw the application in."
>
> —Graduate, Chemistry Major

The Differences

So, with what company should you intern? Internships vary greatly in size, prestige, number of copies you must make, and so on.

Well, you get the picture. Some are paid, some unpaid; some give housing, others hand you a cardboard box. There are even rumors of some interns having to dig through the coffee room trash can for half-eaten doughnuts to stay alive. Okay, so maybe you will only have to go and pick up the coffee and doughnuts. The point is, you need to pick an internship that fits with your goals and needs.

If prestige is your goal, get a big name internship on your résumé. Nothing like having "White House Intern," "Intern at the *Washington Post*," or "Intern at Merck Pharmaceuticals" on your résumé. Big names can mean big opportunities in the job market.

At the same time, landing internships at smaller companies is not always a bad deal. The project experience and hands-on learning can sometimes be much better at a smaller company—rather than restock the copier at a prestigious Wall Street firm, you are working with, say, an experienced auditor, learning how to run a jazzy new spreadsheet program your college cannot afford yet.

Applying for an Internship

The first rule of thumb is to start early! Deciding which internship is right for you can be a drawn-out process. And then you have to apply. As one example, the State Department application process takes nine months, and many applications require essay writing and letters of recommendation.[19] That is a lot to put together in a last-ditch effort.

To find internships, a great place to start is your college's career center. They usually have information on opportunities locally and beyond. If you would like to start looking on your own, you may want to look at a book such as *Peterson's Internships*. Not only do they provide a listing of internships, but they also give contact information and parameters for the positions.

As far as applying, you will have to send a résumé including everything from the schools you have attended to degrees you have earned, along with your impressive list of extracurriculars and work experience. Make sure that all your materials are in order and formatted correctly before you send them—yet another benefit to keeping track of your accomplishments on the résumé worksheet. If you cannot properly complete an application, chances are that you will probably be passed over for the position.

Deciding which internship is right for you is your choice. To help you decide, some internship workshops suggest having a list of items you would like to accomplish through the internship. Not only will this make you look prepared, you will be prepared. Base your internship decision on what you want to do in your career and how important a prestigious internship is to your choice.

Start Working the Network

That network of contact that you have built through college will come in handy right around this time. Make phone calls and connections, it can help land you the position. But, in the meantime, keep working on your paper-self.

Jobs Are Not Always There

The economy can be good or bad when you graduate from college, and the industry you are interested in could be doing phenomenally well or just plain tanking! Be prepared for anything, no matter how stellar you appear on paper.

STUDENT PROFILE—Randy S. on Jobs After College

Do not assume that there is a job for you right away. I did radio, laid carpets, and worked at the baseball stadium doing promotion, just to get experience. I didn't make much money, but gained great experience and boosted my résumé by sacrificing a little bit of pay. If you want to do a certain kind of work, find a little something in that field to add to your résumé. If you have a passion, you have to do work at least related to that field. It can be discouraging getting out of school and trying to find a good job, so build your résumé early.

> ➤ *Have you taken Randy's advice and begun building your résumé yet? If so, name your next step in building your résumé? If not, name one person/place you could call this week to start.*

> "Networking is very important, it's as important as anything else in finding a job."
> —Graduate, Marketing Major

Maybe you have considered graduate school from the start. If not, you may be now!

GRADUATE AND PROFESSIONAL SCHOOL

Heading to graduate or professional school is a goal for some students.[1] Plenty of hugely successful people have gone to graduate school, and plenty have not. There are many reasons for deciding to attend. Some students have a keen eye for their future profession, and attending graduate school can help them with a boost toward the top, or just the accreditation to work in that profession.

Others like the idea of further study, without much regard to what will happen afterward. Still others have no clue what they would like to do, or where they would like to end up, and graduate school is another way to avoid living in the real world quite so soon (after all, how many places can you live off loans and study your passion?).

> "Take a look at the money situation because you can get a great price for a graduate education with state schools."
> —Graduate, Biology Major

The Options

Depending on the type of graduate school and the particular professional program, gaining acceptance can range from falling off of a log to a prerequisite of establishing peace in the Middle East. If you are unsure about future plans or lack a very definite path (which many of us students do), it can be a very wise choice to attend. In no way is it necessary or required to attain an advanced degree to be successful in life; on the other hand, it will not hurt. In any case, it is a good idea to have a contingency plan.

> "Always have a backup plan. Things don't always pan out perfectly, so it's always good to have something to fall back on. Find out your interests, gather the necessary info, do what you need to do, and see what happens."
> —Senior, Creative Writing Major

Business

Gaining acceptance to an MBA program can be done straight out of college, but top programs require a few years of work experience.

Most programs require applicants to take and submit scores from the GMAT. The GMAT tests basic verbal, math, and writing skills that have been ingrained (or not) over years of education. For more information on the GMAT, go to the Graduate Management Admission Council's homepage at http://www.mba.com.

Law

Law schools are also challenging to gain acceptance to, especially top programs. Good grades are important, as well as exposure to the profession (through volunteering or shadowing, more on those later) and a submission of your LSAT scores. The LSAT tests reading and reasoning skills, not subject-specific information. For more information on applying to law school, try the Law School Admission Council's Web site at http://www.lsac.org.

Medicine

Acceptance to medical school is generally very rigorous. Good grades are a must, as well as volunteering, clinical exposure to a hospital/physician, and a good showing on the MCAT. Unlike the GMAT and LSAT, the MCAT has a large amount of subject-specific information to be tested on. To obtain more information on the whole process, try the Association of American Medical Colleges' Web site at http://www.aamc.org.

Graduate Programs

Beside the big three, you can go on to higher education in a number of areas. Just to name a few:

- Public Affairs
- Education
- Journalism
- Engineering
- Sciences
- Social Sciences and Humanities
- Arts

THE ADVISOR SAYS: *For graduate school, have a faculty mentor who knows about the research interests you have. You need to look at your research interests and schools that have faculty in that area. Develop a relationship with a professor who teaches in your area of interest. Such help is necessary for applying to programs.*

Gaining acceptance to these programs may require taking a Graduate Record Examination (GRE). The GRE has different tests: the general test and subject tests. The general test examines a person's ability in reading, writing, and mathematical skills without subject-specific questions. The subject tests (of which there are eight choices) test a person's knowledge in a subject-specific manner. For example, applying to a graduate program in chemistry would require you to sit for the Chemistry GRE. If you are required to take the GRE (many programs require it), try the Graduate Record Examinations homepage at http://www.gre.org for more information.

Help for Admission

Because getting into graduate school can be very difficult (especially getting accepted to your dream school), use all the help you can get your hands on:

- On-campus groups
- University advisors
- Professors
- Other sources:
  - Business: http://www.Vault.com
  - Law: http://www.FindLaw.com
  - Medicine: http://www.StudentDoctor.net

On-campus groups may be clubs or societies that apply to your professional aspirations. Remember in Chapter 9 the Pre-Law Society, Pre-Med club, and others? Here is where they can be put to great use! Many campuses have groups for the big three such as a pre-law society, pre-med society, and a business college council. These clubs can help answer questions about the admissions process, find volunteering and shadowing opportunities, and give you access to individuals in the community who work in the particular profession.

Advisors, just like for major advice, can help with graduate school admissions, too. Find out who the expert(s) is/are at your school for the particular type of graduate program in which you would like to enroll. Make an appointment with these individuals, and ask for their advice. They can assist in class selection, and application and admissions information. Use them as a resource.

Note: Some students have reported their advisors to be very negative, even encouraging them to try for another option in their postgraduate training, telling them they will never be accepted. Sometimes they are right, but many times they are wrong. Stay focused on your dreams and never give up!

Professors

Professors can be instrumental in helping with graduate school planning and admissions. If you are considering doing your graduate work at your current institution, meet and talk to the professors in that department. They may be able to help you piece together the best possible application, as well as throw in a good word come application time. In addition, you might be able to help with a research project or lab with a professor, enhancing your application and chances of acceptance. Chances are that you will need one or more letters of recommendation (see Chapter 6 for more info). Approach the professors you know the best and follow the pointers.

Although tough, gaining admission to graduate school is very possible. If you set your goals and follow through on them daily, I have no doubt that you will achieve the end result. It can be a nerve-racking process. But if you put in the time and effort, it will eventually pay off.

Other Sources

The better the program, the more doors it will open, so put your best effort into applying. Because most graduate programs require a standardized test—whether the GMAT, LSAT, MCAT, or GRE—it is to your advantage to perform well. In recent years, the popularity of testing help centers has risen significantly. Kaplan and the Princeton Review are two such companies that help students refine their skills to achieve the best possible scores. Though expensive, if you can gain access to the extra cash, these programs are worth considering.

In addition, many schools require essays as a part of their admissions application. There are multiple editing services to help proofread your paper if you do not have friends or family that are quite capable (no offense to them, I hope). Take a look in the Appendix for some services.

Getting Your Ducks Lined Up

The earlier you begin preparing for graduate school, the easier it will be. Yes, I said before that applying can be a nerve-racking process. And you will probably have to apply to several (sometimes many) graduate programs to have the best chance of acceptance. Being prepared both mentally and financially (between applying and travel/interview expenses, the process can become quite expensive) will position you for the best outcome. Also, because of the many requirements and hoops to jump through, the more time you have to complete these requirements, the more comfortable you will be. The more comfortable you are, the more it will reduce the bad stress. And, keeping that bad stress to a minimum, as we know, will make your life at school more fun and productive.

The Benefits

Earning a graduate degree can be extremely beneficial.

To Learn

In many types of programs you have the opportunity to push the edge of current knowledge or attain the ability to help many people lead better lives. The satisfaction of helping others (in any way that you choose) is certainly a fringe benefit of any graduate degree that you attain.

To Cash In!

Getting a master's, doctorate, or professional degree can also pay off (literally) in the long run. A recent census study showed an average difference of $10,000 to $35,000 per year between any of these three degrees and a bachelor's degree.[20]

Of course, these are averages, so they are not statistics to live and die by. But there are some valuable indications in them. They tell us that, in general, the higher your degree, the more money you will earn on average, and the more options you will have. With a postgraduate degree—master's, doctorate, or anything else—more opportunities will reveal themselves. Keep this in the back of your head if you are considering whether postgraduate training is right for you.

INTERVIEWS

Know: Résumé, Self, and Organization

No matter whether you apply for an internship, graduate school, or a job, chances are that you will face an interview. For many students, this is their first serious job interview. To prepare for your interview, do the following:

- Know your résumé.
- Know yourself (and stick to it).
- Know the company, organization, or school.

Knowing Your Résumé is Extremely Important

This is the blueprint for the start of many interviews, and the place many questions can come from. If you do not know much about what is written on your résumé, it is not a good sign. So try to

Keep it Simple! Every accomplishment since pre-school should not be on your résumé. Things like high school merits? Unless it was something truly amazing, like a 1600 SAT, national student leader to meet the president, and so on, it should not go on there. (No one at J.P. Morgan cares if you were president of the Key Club in 10th grade.)

Programs where you spent little time and/or contributed little effort should also be left out. This is important. If you put "Committed volunteer for Habitat for Humanity," and you worked there once two years ago for one day, you may have a tough time discussing the place. It may be your interviewer's favorite charity, or he might even volunteer there every week! Uncovering dishonesty on a résumé is a sure bet to canceling any hope at all. So put your serious accomplishments down, and keep it simple!

The story of George O'Leary, a career football coach and assistant coach, can teach you a lesson about lying. O'Leary, in his seven seasons at Georgia Tech, helped the Yellow Jackets garner a record of 52-33. Both his players and his peers respected him for his work in football.

In 2001, O'Leary was chosen to fill the vacancy as head football coach at the University of Notre Dame—a very sought-after and prestigious position. Soon after arriving at Notre Dame (and before any games were played), it was revealed that O'Leary had lied on his résumé. He claimed to possess a master's degree in education from New York University and to have lettered in football at New Hampshire. Neither of these claims was true. O'Leary admitted that many years ago he had falsified his résumé and had failed to remove the lies ever after. Due to the uncovering of his dishonesty, he resigned as head football coach of Notre Dame. Not only did he lose his job, his integrity and reputation were irreparably tarnished as well.[21]

As you can see from Coach O'Leary's situation, lies are not always uncovered right away. You may lie and get away with it for a while, but this action can come back to harm you. In addition, some universities will take away a diploma for lying, and graduate schools will most likely ask you to leave if you lie on an application. It is not worth that extra credential to ruin your integrity, your degree chances, and job/internship/graduate school opportunities.

Know Yourself

The worst thing you can do at an interview is try to be someone you are not. It can sure be tempting to try and fit with the culture or assume the type of candidate you have heard they prefer. But even if it pays off in the near future, in the long run, look out. At an interview, you are interviewing the company just as much as they are interviewing you. No matter how great an opportunity it is, if the fit is not right, better to walk away. If you are a slaphappy, funny, and talkative person, forget taking the internship at the stuffy, quiet and ultratraditional firm or school. Know yourself, stick to it in the interview, and interview them as well.

Know the Company, Organization, or School

You may be surprised how many students apply for a job, internship, or graduate school and know hardly anything about the program. Too many of us toss out large numbers of applications without knowing much about the places. Come interview time, this can spell disaster. Most likely, an interviewer is proud to work or teach for his/her organization. Strutting in without knowing the slightest bit about them can easily be taken as an insult. On the other hand, walking in with a well-versed knowledge of the company or school can shine light on your application. Do not sound fake, but when necessary, sprinkle your knowledge into your answers and questions alike. Your interviewer will likely be very impressed with your knowledge, and you might just get an offer out of it.

There are great resources at the college library and on the Internet where you can find out about any company or organization you are interested in. Even better, talk to others who have interviewed for the place for which you are aiming. If it is a firm, talk to employees; if it is a school, talk to students. Nobody can give you perspective like those who are in the mix already.

A TWIST FOR YOUR RÉSUMÉ

If you are still looking to give your résumé that extra umph!, look no further. There are still options left.

Volunteering

So maybe you have done an internship, or maybe you are waiting to do one. You might be asking yourself, "What can I do between now and then to beef up my application? How can I get some experience before I get to my place of work?"

Well, I have the perfect answer—Volunteer!

Volunteering has become much more prominent nowadays, and rightly so. Volunteers not only help those in need—and "need" is a broad term—but also succeed in helping themselves. Volunteering is a great way to give your résumé a boost and give yourself a good feeling along the way.

The Payoff

Volunteering will add a nice touch to any résumé, and might help in your quest after college. There is more of a payoff, though. Donating your energy to a good cause is always a fulfilling thing to do. Time is the scarcest resource we posses, which also makes it the most valuable. Taking your time and giving it to those in need is a special gesture, one that will help you with much more than your résumé.

The Options

Opportunities to volunteer are never-ending. Unlike an internship, which you have to search out, submit a terrific application for, and sweat bullets for days after the interview hoping you are the one, volunteering is much more open. With volunteering, all you have to do is find an area that interests you, identify some service organizations that perform that type of work, and voilà!, you are ready to go. Although many volunteer programs require applications, the chance of your landing the position is pretty high.

Where to Look

You might be wondering, "Where do I look?" To save time, narrow your search. Ask yourself what type of work you want to do or what type of work certain graduate schools or jobs require.

As a premed student, I knew that medical schools and future employers look very favorably on an applicant's volunteer work at a hospital or medical clinic. Knowing this, I found the local VA hospital, filled out an application, completed orientation, and have been happily volunteering there for close to two years now.

Through my experience at the VA, not only do I have a candid view of the medical world, but I have also met some fascinating people, heard interesting stories, and counted my own blessings. Along the way, I have met a few doctors who have shared a wealth of knowledge with me about the profession, information that will be valuable to me later on.

Medical school is not the only type of graduate school that smiles on volunteering efforts, though. A student looking to attend law school might work for the public defender's office. A business or accounting student might find résumé-enhancing opportunities working in the finance department of a nonprofit, or in helping people with credit problems at a nonprofit debt-help organization.

These are just a few ideas. You can find more information by visiting your school's Office of Volunteering or Career Counseling Center. To find a listing of some great volunteer opportunities elsewhere, look in *A Student's Guide to Volunteering* by Theresa Digeronimo. This book gives specific information about volunteering in particular fields, as well as listing a boatload of volunteering options.

References like this one are great if you are undecided. If you are not sure what type of work you want to do, get hold of the book and thumb through it. There is an organization for just about everything. If you have an interest, this book can help you give your time for it somehow.

Make it Fun

If you are in a club or greek organization, you may already have fun opportunities to which to give your time. Students without membership (or the chance to get it) with greek organizations may need to be more creative. The first step to making volunteering enjoyable is to get friends involved.

Dragging your roommate along or asking some friends to go with you will certainly help. If you are having trouble getting them to go based on the noble talk, try the old "it'll help your résumé" ploy! Sometimes bringing some selfish benefits to the table will motivate people to try something, and then they find out they really like it.

One example: Having friends help you paint a Habitat for Humanity house can be a blast. A number of years ago, a large group of students (author included) worked one day at a Habitat job site. It was terrific. We were basically hanging out together the entire day while helping to build some needy families' homes.

The point is, volunteering does not have to be boring; it can be extremely fun and exciting. Use a little of that creative power we have been talking about throughout this book and put it to use here. Community service–oriented projects are a win-win situation. The opportunities are endless and enjoyable, and everyone comes out on top.

Not Everyone Has Time

If you are married, work full-time, or have other obligations that make volunteering close to impossible, do not sweat it! Volunteering is a chance to give your time, but if you do not have time to give, do not be hard on yourself. At the same time, do not go too easy either. It goes back to something I said before—it is simple for almost everyone to conjure up excuses for why they have no time. Make sure that if you are saying this, it is true, and not a maneuver to squirm out of volunteering.

Looking for a Supersized Volunteering Opportunity?

The Peace Corps is a great organization with noble goals. Many people, because of other commitments, will not have the chance to volunteer for this organization. But if you can take the time (a couple of years perhaps), you will come out on the other side as a better person. The PC helps individuals all over the world in developing countries to make their life better. There are opportunities for volunteers in science, health care, education, business, and others. Volunteers give of themselves to help an important initiative, like educating natives about the threat of and ways to prevent HIV/AIDS.

Helping these countries to stop and prevent diseases like this one is only one aspect. If you enjoy both helping people in need and studying business, there is a place for you as well. Aiding in the economic development of these nations is a further goal of the organization.

Although the Peace Corps is a more serious commitment than helping sort clothes every Saturday at the local Salvation Army, it is well worth it. Many people who have tried the Peace Corps think of it as a high point in their lives. If you are looking for something serious and different, it can be a real option. Check out their Web site at www.peacecorps.org.

Organizing Your Own Charity Project

So maybe you have checked out the book I recommended and other books and asked around, but you cannot find an organization you are interested in. Or maybe you have a plan to help an existing charity, but you want to maintain some control over your own plan. What a great opportunity to display your leadership skills, initiative, and maturity—characteristics that any employer or graduate school would die for!

As only one example, you can organize your own fundraising drive—a great way to demonstrate your abilities and leadership qualities, help the community or a certain group of people, and help them in your own special way.

One summer I volunteered as a counselor at a camp for children with chronic illnesses. The camp depended on volunteers to keep its doors open because it was free for the kids to attend. During my short weeklong tenure, I realized how important this camp was and how much of a release and good time it was for the kids attending.

Daydreaming one day, I was thinking how much I would like to ride my bike across the country like my uncle once did, and what an adventure it would be. And then it hit me—what if a friend and I did a bike ride, starting from the camp in Florida, up to another one of the camps in North Carolina to raise money for the kids?

Here the idea was born. From there, it was a few months of preparation to cross all the t's and dot all the i's, and soon we were off to North Carolina. Not only would we raise money for a good cause and organize a charity fundraiser, we did it while doing something we wanted to—take a long bike adventure.

To organize your own charity, you have to be creative and willing to put in time, effort, and a little sweat. Organizing is not a cakewalk, but it can be done. Piecing together a volunteer initiative shows leadership, organizational skills, caring, and networking ability—not to mention meeting the big names you might run across while putting it all together. Besides that, you get to help a group of folks who might not be as fortunate as you or I. Also, it gives you experience putting together a project that many folks never get the opportunity to do. And because it is your idea, you get to do what you want.

THE ADVISOR SAYS: *The options for organizing your own project are endless. One student saw her peers throwing out perfectly good furniture at the end of finals. She noticed the wasted materials that less fortunate people could use. So, she salvaged the furniture and gave it to a number of poor migrant farm families.*

Cool Stuff That YOU Want to Do!

"So," you ask, "do high-level internships, impeccable community service records, and Ivy League schools only count when it comes to a job or graduate school?"

No, no, and no. One of the biggest mistakes people make when crafting their futures is the notion that *you* count. But what you are interested in and the fun things you want to do do count!

One day, I was flipping through a Harvard Business School pamphlet I came across, looking for the school's selection requirements. While skimming, I stumbled on some snapshots of students there, with descriptions of their accomplishments. One guy in particular caught my eye. Under his name and age, it listed a couple of things he had done, one of which was a backpacking trip across South America!

When I saw that, my eyes lit up. His backpacking trip was impressive. Think about it: He (presumably) had to survive in the wilderness for a couple of months; be in harm's way with snakes, exotic animals, and other scary creatures; and have the mental and physical ability to eke it out.

Somehow, it had always slipped past me that cool stuff counts. Sure, it was probably something he wanted to do—a vacation, maybe. But even though this was probably an adventure to this guy, it told much about him and his character. And hey, it helped him get into Harvard!

And that got me thinking.

Live a Little Bit!

Do something fun—anything fun—over your time at school. It can be

- studying abroad.
- living at the beach or lake.
- working on a cruise ship.
- backpacking.
- mountain climbing.
- camping.
- a bike trip.
- attending concerts.
- cross country road trip.

No matter what you choose, do something exciting! College happens during some of the most enjoyable years of your life. It is important to take it seriously, but it is more important to laugh at yourself (and with others) once in a while! So have some fun. Do

> "Two guys who did a cheesy campus radio sports show received press passes to the Super Bowl! There are definitely 'real' opportunities out there."
> —Graduate, Graphic Design Major

> "If you work over the summer, save as much as possible. This will make the school year less stressful in terms of cash flow."
> — Sophomore, Undecided Major

something a little bit crazy! Adventures, unbelievable trips, and quality time with friends are what life is made of. Even the most successful and dedicated college student can find time for this.

You do not always have to come up with something yourself. The college you attend may have opportunities that will allow you to do great things.

The Summer

College students find all kinds of ways to spend their summers off. In the later years of school (junior or senior), a popular choice is a paid internship. If you are not the intern type or have not decided on a specific field in which to focus, have a blast. As mentioned previously, working on a cruise ship is a viable option as is living at the beach or lake. College is the last free time in some students' lives, so put it to good use. Whether you want to take one of those backpacking trips or travel across the country, try something fun.

And just because you have to work does not mean that all the fun is over. There are plenty of fun summer jobs—remember the cruise ship? Make the most of your college life (summer included), you will not regret it.

One student who lived at the beach during one summer of college had a great time, saved some money, and came away with great memories. Beyond this, the experience came up in a job interview and helped show him to be a well-rounded, great candidate for the job. There is more to you than grades and awards. You count, so make the most out of yourself.

Even if you happen to be a nontraditional student, this point still holds. If you work full-time, take a week's vacation to go to the beach or hit the slopes at the end of a crazy semester. Perhaps spending time with your family is your favorite pastime. If so, then get to it.

College is far too important a time (whoever you are, and however old you are) to constantly study and be removed from fun. If there is anything you should take away from this book, it is that recreation and fun helps! Not only does it help you mentally deal with the stresses of life, it also makes you a better rounded, more interesting, and more successful student. Instead of viewing fun times as a drag away from the important things, use interesting, exciting, and fun experiences to propel you further toward success. Let loose! If you do, it might just open your eyes in college, and beyond.

Study Abroad

> "A semester studying abroad in France was the single best thing I have done so far in college."
> —Senior, French Major

A semester studying abroad can be a whole lot more than just a great time. It is the chance to travel and experience different cultures and customs, all under the guise of education. Not to say

STUDENT PROFILE—Stephanie K. on Studying Abroad

It was terrifying. I did not know the language well, and finally just put aside my fears, put my pride on the line, and put myself out there. I learned an important lesson living in another country—that I could handle anything. Just let me get my bearings and I'll take off. I basically learned a whole new language, and at the same time learned a great deal about new cultures. It helped me see the world from a different perspective.

➤ *How do you believe or not believe a study-abroad program could help your education?*

there is no work involved, but when else can you travel to a continent to hang out, observe the culture, do a tad bit of work, and stay on track with your graduation plans, too? College is the last time in your life, at least for a while, that you will have the chance to just dump everything and head to Europe and have it count for something. In addition, some schools have programs that combine a semester abroad with an internship so that you can really fatten your résumé while learning and seeing other parts of the world. Students have found that many graduate schools and employers look favorably on these experiences, too, which makes them that much more valuable.

If you are looking for more information on studying abroad, look no further than the USC Center for Global Education http://www.usc.edu (search: Study Abroad).

Keep in mind that anyone looking to go overseas has quite a large number of considerations to prepare for and think about. This Web site provides checklists for the things you need to do, such as

- emergency planning.
- information for parents (if they are helping you out).
- finding a program.
- financing the trip.
- safety.
- information on foreign laws.
- arriving back home.
- making the most of your experience abroad.

For even more info on making your study abroad experience a great one, check out the Institute for the International Education of Students at http://www.iie.org.

"Studying abroad was a great chance to experience people of different cultures that you would not meet otherwise."
—Graduate, Economics Major

"Study abroad is great; the only drawback is that it can cost a lot of money."
—Senior, International Affairs Major

"Take the chance now and get away, that's what college is for. You do not want to flip out at forty, buy a Corvette, and leave your family because you never let loose a little!"
—Senior, Business Major

Fun Things Count Too!

So when you are getting ready to write your résumé or go on that once-in-a-lifetime job interview, do not just think about clubs you belong to or even awards you have won, but also think about any cool stuff you have done that might be interesting or even impressive on an application.

What is most interesting about cool stuff that you want to do is that you catch a little more notice on your application than Jane or Joe 4.0, or even Volunteer-and-intern (wo)man.

The main thing to remember: Do your best to be a well-rounded and hard-working person (not just student). Show your true colors and character on your application in whatever way possible, because you never know what might impress those looking at you!

Additional Resources

CHAPTER 2

Communication Skills

How to Win Friends and Influence People
By Dale Carnegie
Pocket Books, Copyright 1990
ISBN# 0671723650

*Conversationally Speaking: Tested New Ways to Increase Your
Personal and Social Effectiveness*
By Alan Garner
McGraw Hill, Copyright 1997
ISBN# 1565656296

CHAPTERS 6 and 7

Studying and Related Items

Studying and Test-Taking Made Incredibly Easy!
By Springhouse Corporation
Lippincott, Williams, & Wilkins, Copyright 1999
ISBN# 1582550190

Studying Smart: Time Management for College Students
By Diana Scharf-Hunt and Pam Hait
Perennial, Copyright 1990
ISBN# 0064637336

http://www.How-To-Study.com. This site has tips on study skills:
note-taking, listening, and reading skills.

Research Papers

http://webster.commnet.edu/mla/index.shtml. This site, part of
Capitol Community College, has a thorough breakdown of writing
a research paper.

Writing Research Papers: A Complete Guide (10th ed.)
By James D. Lester
Longman Publishing Group, Copyright 2001
ISBN# 0321082079

MLA Handbook for Writers of Research Papers (6th ed.)
By Joseph Gibaldi
Modern Language Association, Copyright 2003
ISBN# 0873529863

Other

http://www.Accepted.com. This site has great information on letters of recommendation.

http://webhome.idirect.com/ ~ kehamilt/spklearn.html. This Web site provides ideas for presenting to the three different types of learners. You can also use the ideas to help yourself study.

CHAPTER 8

Loans

http://www.StudentAid.ed.gov. This Web site is a one-stop resource for student loans. Look at their publication, *The Student Guide,* for a detailed look into loans for schooling.

http://www.FAFSA.ed.gov. This is the Free Application for Federal Student Aid. You may fill out the application online.

Personal Finance

The Wall Street Journal Guide to Understanding Personal Finance (3rd ed.)
By Kenneth M. Morris
Fireside Books, Copyright 2000
ISBN# 0743216962

CHAPTER 9

Depression

http://www.DBSAlliance.org. This site provides in-depth information on depression as well as contact information to help lines and local groups and resources.

Wellness/Home Remedies

Doctor's Book of Home Remedies: Simple, Doctor-Approved Self-Care Solutions for 146 Common Health Conditions (Rev. ed.)
By Editors of *Prevention* Magazine
Rodale Books, Copyright 2002
ISBN# 1579546110

Sexually Transmitted Diseases

http://www.nlm.nih.gov. Very informative site on STDs.

Other

http://www.WebMD.com. Great site for any health-related questions.

CHAPTER 10

Alcohol

http://www.CollegeDrinkingPrevention.gov. This site has loads of information and resources on college drinking.

http://www.AlcoholicsAnonymous.org. There is plenty of information to get help for a drinking problem on this site.

Drugs

http://www.NarcoticsAnonymous.org. There is plenty of information to get help for drug addiction on this site.

CHAPTERS 11 and 12

Encyclopedia of Exercises

The New Encyclopedia of Modern Bodybuilding: The Bible of Bodybuilding, Fully Updated and Revised
By Arnold Schwarzenegger and Bill Dobbins
Simon & Schuster, Copyright 1999
ISBN# 0684857219

Fitness and Nutrition Resources

http://www.FitnessOnLine.com. This site has new training advice and information for everyone as well as useful items such as a monthly newsletter.

http://www.nlm.nih.gov. For news and information on health topics, including exercise and nutrition, check out this site.

http://www.Health2Fit.com. This site has some useful nutritional information and work-out tips.

Eating Disorders

http://www.Something-Fishy.org. This organization's purpose is to help individuals with eating disorders. There are resources including information on disorders, physicians, treatment centers, online support, and hotlines.

CHAPTER 13

Internship Information

Peterson's Internships 2003 (23rd ed.)
By Peterson's/Thomson Corporation
Thomson Corporation, Copyright 2002
ISBN# 076890904X

The Best 106 Internships (8th ed.)
By Mark Oldman and Samer Hamadeh
Random House, Inc., Copyright 2000
ISBN# 037575637X

http://www.Vault.com. This site has terrific internship, career, and education information for different industries including:

- Accounting
- Advertising and Public Relations
- Consulting
- Entertainment
- Fashion
- Government
- Health/Biotechnology/Pharmaceuticals
- Investment Banking
- Investment Management
- Law
- Media and Marketing
- Nonprofit
- Real Estate
- Technology

- Television
- Venture Capital

Graduate and Professional School Information

http://www.USNews.com. USNews.com has information on graduate school rankings and statistics. Users need to pay to access much of this information. Bookstores also carry the magazines with program rankings.

http://www.Petersons.com. The Peterson's site has information on graduate programs including facts and statistics about the particular programs.

http://www.PrincetonReview.com. Has information on prep classes for the SAT, GRE, GMAT, LSAT, and MCAT (and others) as well as information on particular programs.

http://www.Kaplan.com. Kaplan's site also has information on prep classes and study guides.

Graduate and Professional School Admissions Help

http://www.AdmissionsConsultants.com. AdmissionsConsultants.com is a business that, for a fee, helps students present the best application to any type of graduate or professional school.

http://www.Accepted.com. Accepted.com is a business that, for a fee, helps students present the best application to any type of graduate school, professional school, or job.

http://www.EssayEdge.com. EssayEdge.com provides services similar to the previous two companies.

Graduate School Information

The Grad School Handbook: An Insider's Guide to Getting In and Succeeding
By Richard Jerrard and Margot Jerrard
Perigee Books, Copyright 1998
ISBN# 0399524169

MBA Program and Admissions Information

ABC of Getting the MBA Admissions Edge (Update and reprinted ed.)
By Matt Symonds and Alan Mendonca

MBAsite, Copyright 2001
ISBN# 0971482209

Law School Program and Admissions Information

How to Get into the Top Law Schools
By Richard Montauk
Prentice Hall Art, Copyright 2001
ISBN# 0735201013

Medical School Program and Admissions Information

Get into Medical School: A Strategic Approach
By Maria Lofftus and Thomas C. Taylor
Kaplan, Copyright 2003
ISBN# 0743240960

Résumé and Interview Resources

http://www.CollegeGrad.com. This site has information for recent or soon-to-be college grads regarding every aspect of finding a job.

Best Answers to the 201 Most Frequently Asked Interview Questions
By Matthew J. Deluca
McGraw-Hill Trade, Copyright 1996
ISBN# 007016357X

Volunteering

http://www.VolunteerMatch.org. This site enables users to search for volunteering opportunities in their area.

http://www.Volunteer.gov. Users may search for volunteer opportunities by keyword, state, or partner organization.

Study Abroad

Study Abroad 2004 (11th ed.)
By Peterson's/Thomson Organization
Peterson's, Copyright 2003
ISBN# 0768912733

College Information Resources

CAREER SCHOOL INFORMATION

http://www.CareerSchools.org. CareerSchools.org is the hub for professional, trade, and vocational schools. Their Web site has resources for students to find career schools in the United States, Canada, and online to earn degrees/certifications in many areas including (but not limited to):

- Culinary arts
- Information technology
- Graphic design
- Web design
- Animation
- Fashion design
- Interior design
- Business
- Education
- Nursing
- Health care
- MBA programs
- Master's degrees
- Counseling

CareerSchools.org also has Career Resource links that can help students find career coaching, search classified ads for employment, take personality tests, and get job interview help.

http://www.ACCSCT.org. The Accrediting Commission of Career Schools and Colleges of Technology (ACCSCT) is one organization that accredits career schools to maintain a standard for education in these fields. To check accreditation on an existing school or search for a new institution, the ACCSCT's School Directory can help. In addition to searching for schools, a message board is available for questions as well as links to other accreditation organizations for other types of career and trade schools. Web sites for pertinent state and federal education departments are also listed.

http://www.Search4CareerColleges.com. Search4CareerColleges.com has resources for

- finding career schools.
- assisting with career information.
- finding financial aid, grants, and scholarships.

TWO-YEAR COLLEGE INFORMATION

http://www.AACC.NCHE.edu. The American Association of Community Colleges (AACC) provides a Community College Finder that connects users to community colleges around the country and elsewhere. More information about the individual school may be found on its Web site.

FOUR-YEAR COLLEGE INFORMATION

http://www.Students.gov. Students.gov has loads of information on education and careers. You can find resources for

- Returning students.
- Vocational students.
- Traditional students.

    There is information on
- Financial aid including military and ROTC scholarships.
- Distance education.
- Studying abroad.
- Internships.
- Fellowships.
- Graduate school.
- Students jobs.
- Diversity.
- Health.

http://www.CollegeView.com. CollegeView.com has resources including

- College searches.
- Financial aid.
- Career information.

http://www.CollegeBoard.com. CollegeBoard.com has vast resources on everything for college, including

- SAT preparation.
- College planning.
- College searches.
- Applying.
- Financial aid.

NONTRADITIONAL/RETURNING COLLEGE STUDENTS INFORMATION

http://www.Back2College.com. Back2College.com is an excellent resource for students returning to college. The site has articles written on a range of subjects about returning to school and coping with different circumstances. There is also information on financial aid, career planning, and academics.

http://www.FurtherYourEducation.com. FurtherYourEducation. com is a Web site designed to help adult, transfer, distance, and military students. Features include profiles of students as well as links for financial aid and career exploration.

Additional Worksheets

Planning Worksheet

Fill out this sheet to plan your day, either in the morning or the night before.

Date: _____

7 AM	5 PM
7:30	5:30
8	6
8:30	6:30
9	7
9:30	7:30
10	8
10:30	8:30
11	9
11:30	9:30
12 PM	10
12:30	10:30
1	11
1:30	11:30
2	12 AM
2:30	12:30
3	1
3:30	1:30
4	2
4:30	2:30

Planning Worksheet

Fill out this sheet to plan your day, either in the morning or the night before.

Date: _____

7 AM	5 PM
7:30	5:30
8	6
8:30	6:30
9	7
9:30	7:30
10	8
10:30	8:30
11	9
11:30	9:30
12 PM	10
12:30	10:30
1	11
1:30	11:30
2	12 AM
2:30	12:30
3	1
3:30	1:30
4	2
4:30	2:30

Planning Worksheet

Fill out this sheet to plan your day, either in the morning or the night before.

Date: _____

7 AM	5 PM
7:30	5:30
8	6
8:30	6:30
9	7
9:30	7:30
10	8
10:30	8:30
11	9
11:30	9:30
12 PM	10
12:30	10:30
1	11
1:30	11:30
2	12 AM
2:30	12:30
3	1
3:30	1:30
4	2
4:30	2:30

Planning Worksheet

Fill out this sheet to plan your day, either in the morning or the night before.

Date: _____

7 AM	5 PM
7:30	5:30
8	6
8:30	6:30
9	7
9:30	7:30
10	8
10:30	8:30
11	9
11:30	9:30
12 PM	10
12:30	10:30
1	11
1:30	11:30
2	12 AM
2:30	12:30
3	1
3:30	1:30
4	2
4:30	2:30

Time Tracker

For two days, write down where you spend time. This will allow you to find what you are doing right and what you are doing wrong.

Date: _____

7 AM
7:30
8
8:30
9
9:30
10
10:30
11
11:30
12 PM
12:30
1
1:30
2
2:30
3
3:30
4
4:30
5
5:30
6
6:30
7
7:30
8
8:30
9
9:30
10 PM–1 AM

Date: _____

7 AM
7:30
8
8:30
9
9:30
10
10:30
11
11:30
12 PM
12:30
1
1:30
2
2:30
3
3:30
4
4:30
5
5:30
6
6:30
7
7:30
8
8:30
9
9:30
10 PM–1 AM

After two days of recording your activity:

Q: *Did you find any time-consuming activities that you could trim? If so, which activities and how will you be more efficient?*

Q: *Did you find any ways you could use spaces of time more wisely (like studying in between classes instead of getting on the Internet)? If so, when and how will you be more efficient?*

Time Tracker

For two days, write down where you spend time. This will allow you to find what you are doing right and what you are doing wrong.

Date: _____   Date: _____

7 AM	7 AM
7:30	7:30
8	8
8:30	8:30
9	9
9:30	9:30
10	10
10:30	10:30
11	11
11:30	11:30
12 PM	12 PM
12:30	12:30
1	1
1:30	1:30
2	2
2:30	2:30
3	3
3:30	3:30
4	4
4:30	4:30
5	5
5:30	5:30
6	6
6:30	6:30
7	7
7:30	7:30
8	8
8:30	8:30
9	9
9:30	9:30
10 PM–1 AM	10 PM–1 AM

After two days of recording your activity:

Q: *Did you find any time-consuming activities that you could trim? If so, which activities and how will you be more efficient?*

Q: *Did you find any ways you could use spaces of time more wisely (like studying in between classes instead of getting on the Internet)? If so, when and how will you be more efficient?*

Time Tracker

For two days, write down where you spend time. This will allow you to find what you are doing right and what you are doing wrong.

Date: _____   Date: _____

7 AM	7 AM
7:30	7:30
8	8
8:30	8:30
9	9
9:30	9:30
10	10
10:30	10:30
11	11
11:30	11:30
12 PM	12 PM
12:30	12:30
1	1
1:30	1:30
2	2
2:30	2:30
3	3
3:30	3:30
4	4
4:30	4:30
5	5
5:30	5:30
6	6
6:30	6:30
7	7
7:30	7:30
8	8
8:30	8:30
9	9
9:30	9:30
10 PM–1 AM	10 PM–1 AM

After two days of recording your activity:

Q: *Did you find any time-consuming activities that you could trim? If so, which activities and how will you be more efficient?*

Q: *Did you find any ways you could use spaces of time more wisely (like studying in between classes instead of getting on the Internet)? If so, when and how will you be more efficient?*

Time Tracker

For two days, write down where you spend time. This will allow you to find what you are doing right and what you are doing wrong.

Date: _____   Date: _____

7 AM	7 AM
7:30	7:30
8	8
8:30	8:30
9	9
9:30	9:30
10	10
10:30	10:30
11	11
11:30	11:30
12 PM	12 PM
12:30	12:30
1	1
1:30	1:30
2	2
2:30	2:30
3	3
3:30	3:30
4	4
4:30	4:30
5	5
5:30	5:30
6	6
6:30	6:30
7	7
7:30	7:30
8	8
8:30	8:30
9	9
9:30	9:30
10 PM–1 AM	10 PM–1 AM

After two days of recording your activity:

Q: *Did you find any time-consuming activities that you could trim? If so, which activities and how will you be more efficient?*

Q: *Did you find any ways you could use spaces of time more wisely (like studying in between classes instead of getting on the Internet)? If so, when and how will you be more efficient?*

References

1. Lewin, T. (2003, August 7). First test for freshmen: Picking roommates. New York Times, sec. A, p. 1, col. 5.

2. Horn L., et al. Changes in financial aid awards between 1992–93 and 1999–2000. In *What students pay for college: Changes in net price of college attendance between 1992–93 and 1999–2000* [online]. Cited 8 January 2004. Available from World Wide Web: < http://nces.ed.gov/das/epubs/2002174/netprice1.asp >.

3. American college students get an "F" in personal finance. In *Intuit press releases* [online]. Mountain View, CA: Intuit, Inc., 1998 [cited 15 January 2004]. Available from World Wide Web: < http://www.intuit.com/about_intuit/press_releases/1998/05-13b.html >.

4. Security tips: Web & email. In *Secure with Visa* [online]. Visa U.S.A., 2004 [cited 5 February 2004]. Available from World Wide Web: < http://www.usa.visa.com/personal/secure_with_visa/online_security.html?it = h2_/index.html >.

5. Choosing a field. In *Career center* [online]. Hobson's College View.com., 2004 [cited 12 October 2003]. Available from World Wide Web: < http://www.collegeview.com/career/career_planning/choose_career/techprep.html >.

6. Welch, J., & Byrne, J. A. (2001). *Jack: Straight from the gut*. By Jack Welch with John A. Byrne. New York: Warner Business Books.

7. Signs of stress. In *Health guide A–Z* [online]. WebMD, 2003 [cited 6 February 2003]. Available from World Wide Web: < http://my.webmd.com/hw/health_guide_atoz/ta4684.asp?navbar = hw153409 >.

8. What are the symptoms of depression? In *Health guide A–Z* [online]. WebMD, 2002 [cited 6 February 2004]. Available from World Wide Web: < http://my.webmd.com/hw/depression/hw30711.asp?lastselectedguid = {5FE84E90-BC77-4056-A91C-9531713CA348 >.

9. Today's greek community. In *Press releases* [online]. North American Interfraternity Conference [cited 23 October 2003]. Available from World Wide Web: < http://www.nicindy.org/index.html >.

10. Table 246. In Chapter 3, Postsecondary education [online]. *Digest of education statistics*, 2002 [cited 28 December 2003]. Available from World Wide Web: < http://nces.ed.gov/programs/digest/d02/tables/dt246.asp >.

11. 1999 statistics on alcohol and other drug use on American campuses. [online]. Core Institute, 1998 [cited 22 July 2003]. Available from World Wide Web: < http://www.siu.edu/departments/coreinst/public_html/1999.htm >.

12. About CAS. [online]. Harvard College Alcohol Study, 2001 [cited 2 February 2004]. Available from World Wide Web: < http://www.hsph.harvard.edu/cas/About/index.html >.

13. MDMA (Ecstasy). In *NIDA info facts* [online]. From National Institute on Drug Abuse [cited 2 June 2004]. Available from World Wide Web: < http://www.nida.nih.gov/Infofax/ecstasy.html >.

14. Dave Matthews Biography. [online]. www.BandBiographies.com [cited 3 February 2004]. Available from World Wide Web: < http://www.bandbiographies.com/dave_matthews/biography.htm >.

15. Adult ADHD, What's the treatment? In *Diseases and condition* [online]. WebMD [cited 21 January 2002]. Available from World Wide Web: < http://my.webmd.com/content/article/ 63/2 >.

16. Tice, D. M., and Baumeister, R. F. (1997). Longitudinal study of procrastination, performance, stress, and health: The costs and benefits of dawdling. *Psychological science, 8*, 454–458.

17. Horton, J. Interview with Tom Stanley, author of *The Millionaire Next Door*. In *AMI newsletter* [online]. Auction Marketing, July 11, 2001 [cited 17 March, 2003]. Available from World Wide Web: < http://www.auctionmarketing.org/ShowArticle.asp?TxtId = 238 >.

18. Oldman, M., & Hamadeh, S. (2000). *The best 106 internships* (8th ed.). New York: Random House/Princeton Review Publishing.

19. *Internships 2003* (23rd ed.). (2002). New Jersey: Peterson's/Thomson Learning, Inc.

20. Annual demographic survey. In *A joint project between the Bureau of Labor Statistics and The Bureau of the Census* [online]. Bureau of the Census, March 2002 [cited 20 January 2004]. Available from the World Wide Web: < http://ferret.bls.census.gov/macro/032002/perinc/new03_001.htm >.

21. O'Leary out at Notre Dame after one week. [online]. *Sports Illustrated*, December 14, 2001 [cited 7 January 2004]. Available from the World Wide Web: < http://sportsillustrated.cnn.com/football/college/news/2001/12/14/oleary_notredame/ >.

22. American Council on Exercise. (2003) Body fat chart. *ACE personal trainer manual* (3rd ed.). < http://www.acefitness.org >.

23. Merry, J. Avoiding dehydration. In *TriSport epping* [online]. [cited 25 January 2004]. Available from World Wide Web: < http://www.trisportepping.co.uk/trainadv/dehyd.html >.

24. Dehydration prevention. In *Health guide A–Z* [online]. WebMD, 2001 [cited 7 February 2004]. Available from World Wide Web: < http://my.webmd.com/hw/health_guide_atoz/aa124381.asp >.

25. Obesity trends for 2000. In *Nutrition and physical activity* [online]. National Center for Chronic Disease Prevention and Health promotion, April 22, 2003 [cited 12 July 2003]. Available from World Wide Web: < http://www.cdc.gov/nccdphp/dnpa/obesity/trend/prev_char.htm >.

26. Anorexia nervosa topic overview. In *Health guide A–Z* [online]. WebMD, December 13, 2001 [cited 10 February 2004]. Available from World Wide Web: < http://my.webmd.com/hw/health_guide_atoz/hw46497-Bib.asp#ty6310 >.

27. Bulimia nervosa symptoms. In *Health guide A–Z* [online]. WebMD, December 13, 2001 [cited 10 February 2004]. Available from World Wide Web: < http://my.webmd.com/hw/health_guide_atoz/aa32973.asp >.

28. Wyler, L. Variations on "effortless perfection." In *The Chronicle online: The independent daily at Duke university* [online]. December 12, 2003 [cited 14 January 2004]. Available from World Wide Web: < http://www.chronicle.duke.edu/vnews/display.v/ART/2003/12/12/3fd6007bdd90b >.

29. "Ten tips for recommenders". In *Grad school: Letters of rec* [online]. From Accepted.com [cited 12 May 2004]. Available from World Wide Web: < http://www.accepted.com/grad/lettersrec.aspx >.

30. Developing an outline. In *Owl online writing lab* [online]. From Purdue University Online Writing Lab [cited 23 May 2004]. Available from World Wide Web: < http://owl.english.purdue.edu/handouts/general/gl_outlin.html >.

31. Thompson, C. Compulsive overeating. In *Eating disorders* [online]. From Mirror-Mirror.org [cited 16 June 2004]. Available from World Wide Web: < http://www.mirror-mirror.org/compulsive.htm >.

32. Hamilton, K. E. Presenting to different types of learners. In *Handouts* [online]. From Speaking with Confidence—GHUM 1025 [cited 25 May 2004]. Available from World Wide Web: < http://webhome.idirect.com/ ~ kehamilt/spklearn.html >.

33. Types of federal student aid. In *The student guide* [online]. From The U.S. Department of Education [cited 18 June 2004]. Available from World Wide Web: < http://studentaid.ed.gov/students/publications/student_guide/2004_2005/english/index.htm >.

Index

Ron Fry's

HOW TO STUDY PROGRAM

Ron Fry's best-selling How to Study series is now completely updated and revised to help students meet the increasing demands of the school environment.

What makes the How to Study books so successful? According to Ron Fry, it's the concepts of time management and organization around which all six books in the series are built. "The keys," says Fry, "are to make the most of the time you have and enjoy what you're doing. It's easier than you think."

About the Author

Ron Fry is a nationally known spokesperson for the improvement of public education and an advocate for parents and students playing an active role in strengthening personal education programs. Aside from being the author of the vastly popular How to Study Series, Fry has edited or written more than 30 different titles — dynamic resources for optimum student success.

"Helpful for students of all ages from high school and up." – Small Press Book Review
"These are must-read guides every family should have in its library." – Library Journal

How to Study Series

• HOW TO STUDY, SIXTH EDITION
1-4018-8911-5, 2005
224 pp., 5 1/4" x 8 1/4", softcover,

• "ACE" ANY TEST, FIFTH EDITION
1-4018-8912-3, 2005
128 pp., 5 1/4" x 8 1/4", softcover

• GET ORGANIZED, THIRD EDITION
1-4018-8913-1, 2005
128 pp., 5 1/4" x 8 1/4", softcover

• IMPROVE YOUR MEMORY, FIFTH EDITION
1-4018-8914-X, 2005
128 pp., 5 1/4" x 8 1/4", softcover

• IMPROVE YOUR WRITING, FIFTH EDITION
1-4018-8916-6, 2005
128 pp., 5 1/4" x 8 1/4", softcover

• IMPROVE YOUR READING, FIFTH EDITION
1-4018-8915-8, 2005
128 pp., 5 1/4" x 8 1/4", softcover

Ordering Information

To Place an Order please call: (800) 347-7707 *or fax:* (859) 647-5963
Mailing address: Thomson Distribution Center, Attn: Order Fulfillment
10650 Toebben Drive, Independence, KY 41051

SOURCE CODE: CCCSNAH064

Each of the books in The Pathway to Excellence Series will address key issues such as career transition, excelling in the workplace and improving on business writing skills.

WRITING EXCELLENCE
Lee Clark Johns
224 pp, 6" x 9", softcover
1-4018-8203-X

CAREER EXCELLENCE
Peter M. Hess
224 pp., 6" x 9", softcover
1-4018-8201-3

PERSONAL EXCELLENCE
Robert K. Throop & Marion B. Castellucci
224 pp., 6" x 9", softcover
1-4018-8200-5

Writing Excellence presents strategies to help make business writing more reader-friendly. It helps to identify the audience and purpose for writing, and presents a logical organizational plan. It emphasizes the importance of a main idea with a good balance of clearly stated key points and supporting evidence, words that are appropriate and clear to your reader, sentences that are clear and grammatically correct, and a predictable format that allows your reader to find information easily.

Lee Clark Johns
Owner of Strategic Communication, Inc., a consulting and training company, has been teaching business and technical writing for 25 years. She has worked with everyone from corporate executives, to bankers, to attorneys, to customer service representatives.

Career Excellence is a comprehensive guide for those preparing to change careers. Unlike any other book of its kind, this guide takes the reader from the initial stages of making a career change, to landing the job to success in the workplace. It advises on how to excel on the job by making decisions based on inner drive. It includes tips on how to excel with new colleagues, how to impress the boss while maintaining integrity, how to build alliances, and how to continue to make decisions with honesty and consistency.

Peter M. Hess
Founder of Young Adult Professional Associates, Inc. (YAPA). He prides himself on providing a single organization offering career success through resources, services, education, networking, and cutting-edge technology.

Personal Excellence shows you how utilize your values and beliefs and how they can be better understood to bring you personal success. Begins by developing effective, measurable goals that will lead you to personal success. You will learn the steps that can be taken to create an action plan for completing your goals and also know when to adjust your goals to meet the ever-changing landscape. You will gain techniques that will help you effectively reach your goals and measure their impact.

Robert K. Throop
Former Corporate Director of Education for ATE Enterprises. With over 35 years of experience in education, spanning from elementary to graduate school levels, he is presently the Chief Academic Officer for ITT Educational Services Inc.

Marion B. Castellucci
Earned a B.A. from Barnard College. She has over 25 years experience as a writer and editor of educational publishing.

To place an order please call: (800) 347-7707 or fax: (859) 647-5963
Mailing Address: Thomson Distribution Center, Attn: Order Fulfillment, 10650 Toebben Dr., Independence, KY 41051

The Five O'Clock Club Job-Search Series
for Professionals, Managers and Executives

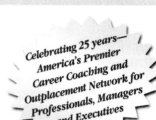

Celebrating 25 years—
America's Premier
Career Coaching and
Outplacement Network for
Professionals, Managers
and Executives

We'll take you through your entire career. 1. Start by understanding yourself and what you want in **Targeting a Great Career**. 2. *Package Yourself with a Targeted Résumé* done The Five O'Clock Club Way. 3. Then **Shortcut Your Job Search** by following our techniques for getting meetings. 4. Turn those interviews into offers with **Mastering the Job Interview** and **Winning the Money Game**. 5. Finally, do well in your new job with *Navigating Your Career*.

- Figure out what to do with your life and your career
- Develop a résumé that separates you from your competitors
- Shortcut your search by using the Internet and other techniques properly
- Learn how to turn those job interviews into job offers
- Use our Four-Step Salary Negotiation Method to get what you deserve

Launching the Right Career
Now, students, recent grads, and those who want a career instead of a job can use the same techniques used by thousands of professionals, managers and executives. Get that internship, develop a resume that gets you interviews, and learn how to interview well.

Targeting a Great Career
ISBN: 1-4180-1504-0

Packaging Yourself: The Targeted Résumé
ISBN: 1-4180-1503-2

Shortcut Your Job Search: The Best Way to Get Meetings
ISBN: 1-4180-1502-4

Mastering the Job Interview and Winning the Money Game
ISBN: 1-4180-1500-8

Navigating Your Career: Develop Your Plan, Manage Your Boss, Get Another Job Inside
ISBN: 1-4180-1501-6

Launching the Right Career
ISBN: 1-4180-1505-9

258 pp., 7 3/8" x 9 1/4", softcover, 2006

The Five O'Clock Club's Book Series has enabled thousands of professionals, managers, and executives to correct their job-search mistakes. Most who attend regularly and read our books–even those unemployed up to two years—have a new job within only ten weekly sessions.

Most people conduct a passive job search. Their approach is ordinary, non-directed, fragmented, and ineffective.

The Five O'Clock Club was started in 1978 as a research-based organization. The methodology was tested and refined on professionals, managers, and executives (and those aspiring to be)–from all occupations and economic levels.

Ever since the beginning, The Five O'Clock Club has tracked trends at every meeting at every at every location. Over time, our advice has changed as the job market has changed. What worked in the past is not always sufficient for today's job market. Today's Five O'Clock Club Book Series contains all the relevant old strategies–and so much more. The Five O'Clock Clubbers who do best read and re-read the books, marking them up and taking notes. Do the same and you will do better in your search.

About the Author:
Kate Wendleton is a nationally syndicated careers columnist and recognized authority on career development, having appeared on *The Today Show*, CNN, CNBC, *Larry King Live*, National Public Radio, CBS, and in the *New York Times, Chicago Tribune, Wall Street Journal, Fortune, Business Week,* and other national media. She has been a career coach since 1978 when she founded The Five O' Clock Club and developed its methodology to help job hunters and career changers at all levels. A former CFO of two small companies, Kate has twenty years of business experience, as well as an MBA.

www.delmarlearning.com

To place an order please call: (800) 347-7707 or fax: (859) 647-5963
Mailing Address: Thomson Distribution Center, Attn: Order Fulfillment, 10650 Toebben Dr., Independence, KY 41051